THE HUMAN SHORE

The Human Shore

SEACOASTS IN HISTORY

JOHN R. GILLIS

The University of Chicago Press   Chicago and London

The University of Chicago Press, Chicago 60637
The University of Chicago Press, Ltd., London
© 2012 by John R. Gillis
All rights reserved. Published 2012.
Paperback edition 2015
Printed in the United States of America

24 23 22 21 20 19 18 17 16 15   2 3 4 5 6

ISBN-13: 978-0-226-92223-2 (cloth)
ISBN-13: 978-0-226-32429-6 (paper)
ISBN-13: 978-0-226-92225-6 (e-book)
DOI: 10.7208/chicago/9780226922256.001.0001

Library of Congress Cataloging-in-Publication Data

Gillis, John R.
    The human shore : seacoasts in history / John R. Gillis.
        pages. cm.
    Includes bibliographical references and index.
    ISBN 978-0-226-92223-2 (cloth : alk. paper) —
    ISBN 0-226-92223-5 (cloth : alk. paper) —
    ISBN 978-0-226-92225-6 (e-book) —
    ISBN 0-226-92225-1 (e-book)   1. Coasts. 2. Seashore. I. Title.
    GB451.2.G555 2013
    909'.0946—dc23
                                        2012023404

To the memory of Rachel Carson, who brought us all back to the sea

CONTENTS

ILLUSTRATIONS

INTRODUCTION

> Coasts. There are all manner of coasts. Every person born in this world has a coast, an edge, a boundary, a transitional zone between themselves and the world.   JOHN A. MURRAY[1]

Around the world there is an unprecedented surge to the sea. Half of all the globe's peoples now live within one hundred miles of an ocean. In the United States, coastal populations have increased about 30 percent in thirty years. Today, what has been termed the coastal zone, constituting only 15 percent of the US land area, is inhabited by 53 percent of the US population. In similar ways, Australia, South America, Asia, and Europe have been turned inside out. Only Africa has not been hollowed out, and even there coastal populations, particularly urban ones, are exploding. We are all now creatures of the edge, mentally as well as physically. Having experienced one of the greatest physical migrations in human history, we are in the midst of a cultural reorientation of vast significance.[2]

In my own lifetime, coasts have changed more than any other feature of the landscape. Not only has the colonization of the coast by interior peoples drastically altered marine environments, but it has utterly transformed the nature of coastal communities. The coasts themselves have taken on an entirely new cultural meaning, not only for those who live there but also for inlanders, who are increasingly oriented toward the sea. Today we are all, in some way or another, coastal. Not only do we live on coasts but we think with them. They are a part of our mythical as well as physical geography.

My own life recapitulates in a small way this epic return to the sea. I was born in New Jersey and taken to its shore as a small child. But most of my childhood and youth was spent in the American interior, and it was not until I was married and the father of two boys that I took up seasonal residence on a small island off the Maine coast. Though I did not realize it at the time, I was participating in what, in retrospect, now appears to have been a historical shift of great significance. Today I am member of that demographic called bicoastals, living in the Bay Area for most of the year and Maine in the summer.

It has taken me a half-century to become fully aware of what this has meant to me and to society more generally. Even now, I am still discovering the different ways it is possible to be coastal. Every summer I am made painfully aware of just how different my relationship to the sea is from that of my Maine neighbors who make their livings from the ocean. I have come to appreciate the difference between living *on* coasts and living *with* them, and have learned to make a sharp distinction between people located on coasts and coastal people whose historical relationships with the coastal environment goes beyond mere residence. Mainers like to remind those of us "from away" just how different we are from those native to their shores. I now accept their judgment.[3]

In Rachel Carson's classic *The Sea around Us*, the ocean is the beginning of all life. In time some creatures learned to live on land, and a few, like the whale and the seal, found their way back to the sea. "Eventually man, too, found his way back to the sea," not to return to it physically but rather to "re-enter it mentally and imaginatively." This is precisely what Carson did so brilliantly as a scientist and supremely gifted writer. She brought millions of readers to the edge of the sea, reintroducing them to the precious environment that lies on both sides of the tide line. And this is also what I aspire to do as a historian, except that my task is to cross the time line that separates coastal present from coastal past.[4]

Writing about coasts and coastal people has been a marvelous journey of the mind, full of surprises and discoveries. Many of them have come from our small island within sight of Acadia National Park, where I find it easier to cross the line of tide and time than anywhere else. Its cemetery records two hundred years of island life and death. We occupy a nineteenth-century sea captain's house that once belonged to one of Maine's best-known writers, Ruth Moore, who knew the lay of both land and sea as well as anyone. Her poems capture the enduring features of the coast but also the massive changes that have come to it over the centuries.[5]

The first summer people were Indians.
For some five thousand years
They built up shore-line shell heaps before
They lost to the pioneers.

Theirs was a time of history
And written records show

That their hold on the offshore islands began
Less than four hundred years ago.

Now comes the era of real estate,
Of the hundred thousand dollar lots,
Of the condominiums, side by side,
Along the shoreline [sic] choicest spots.

What follows the time of developers
No human voice can tell
But the silent offshore islands know,
And they handle their mysteries well.

On Moore's coast, the past is ever present. Native Americans have never really gone away. Descendants of those who left shell heaps dating from the time of Christ return annually to clam and shoot deer. They are joined by the heirs of the first European settlers, who still fish and build boats in ways that would be familiar to any ancient mariner. On this coast, even summer people from the suburbs know how to hunt, gather, and garden in ways not much different from those of Stone Age peoples.

Evidence of such continuities is everywhere on Maine's shores, but the connective tissue is largely invisible. I had been living there for almost a half-century before realizing how little I knew about their natural and human history. In part it was my own training as a historian that had blinkered me, for we have been taught to treat coasts as places where history begins and ends, of interest only as thresholds. Historians learn to privilege land over water, interior over coastal peoples. And we are not alone in our limitations. Despite Carson's pioneering exploration of the edges of the sea, environmentalists have been slow to take up her challenge to occupy it "mentally and imaginatively," to incorporate coasts into their historical perspective. They show deep concern for the fate of coastal flora and fauna but seem indifferent to the human element of coastal ecology, namely *Homo littoralis*, whose history is inseparable from that of the shore itself. We all suffer from a crippling amnesia, forgetting that coasts are very special places, known as *ecotones*, where two ecosystems overlap, the primal habitat of *Homo sapiens* and the locus of much of subsequent human history.[6]

There was once a time when coasts were home to a significant part of humanity, when, like any home, they were the locus of a sense of belonging, the center of a world rather than a periphery. Now, when coasts are considered edges of something else, of continents or islands, we live not *in* but only *on* them. Humanity's current relationship to the shore is that of the stranger, for after millennia of coastal existence, it has forgotten how to live *with* coasts and oceans. Not that inhabiting shores was ever easy. Rising sea levels, overfishing, and pollution all happened in the past, and coastal peoples have always had to cope with natural and man-made disasters. By trial and error, they became adept at dealing physically and culturally with this challenging environment. But never before has the scale or frequency of threats been as great as now, complicated by the fact that so many who live on shores have no idea of how to live there in a sustainable way. There is not only an urgent need to understand the dynamics of climate change but also an imperative to draw on the adaptive strategies preserved in the historical record from times when coasts were a here rather than a there, places to dwell rather than just visit.[7]

James Hamilton-Paterson, author of *Seven-Tenths: The Sea and Its Thresholds*, who knows the seas and coasts as well as anyone, thinks "we have lost our place and no longer know how to return." I am not quite so pessimistic; otherwise I would never have begun a journey that has traversed hundreds of thousands of years and taken me to the shores not just of North America and Europe but also of Africa, Australia, New Zealand, Japan, and Tasmania. Carson warned us that "the edge of the sea remains an elusive and indefinable boundary." Not only are the physical properties of coasts constantly changing, but there are as many ways of being coastal as there have been coastal peoples. We need to recover some sense of all the ways that humans have lived *with* coasts, a story that spans at least 200,000 years. There are important lessons to be learned from our coastal ancestors, whether they be prehistoric hunter-gatherers, ancient mariners of the Indian Ocean and Mediterranean Sea, Dutch polder builders, or Long Island baymen.[8]

I did not anticipate when I set out on this journey into deep time and far space that I would end up writing an alternative account of global history. It came as something of a shock to discover that it was not the interior but the shore that was the original Eden and that *Homo sapiens* are best described as an edge species that has consistently thrived in the coastal ecotone where the ecosystems of land and sea meet. From the Stone Age to our own era of globalization, coastal peoples have been in the vanguard. It turns out that change has been consistently generated on edges rather than from interiors, and therefore we need to turn our

FIGURE 1. Cliffside sign at Sea Ranch, California. Photo by author.

landlocked histories inside out. This represents a challenge not only to the conventions of terracentric history, but also to the deep-sea preoccupations of conventional maritime studies. In what follows, I assay six major periods of coastal history beginning with the moment when mankind first came back to the sea from the interior of Africa, emphasizing the continuities but also the changes that have taken place around the world.

The sign in figure 1 greets visitors wandering down to the cliffs of California's Sea Ranch, a magnificent stretch of coast north of San Francisco. It stopped me in my tracks one fiercely bright April afternoon in 2007, and I could not get it out of my mind for weeks thereafter. In time I would come to see that NEVER TURN YOUR BACK ON THE OCEAN was as much an invitation as a warning. It launched a quest to understand our complex relationship with the sea that took me around the world and into depths of time that few historians have ever visited.

In the process of writing this book, I was to learn that the shore was the original home of *Homo sapiens*. Our relationship to it has changed markedly over the last 200,000 years, but we have been inseparable from it from the very beginning and still are today. Coasts have played a vital role in making us human, and we, in turn, have made coasts what they are. I call this study *The Human Shore* to underline this interdependency. This is a story of coevolution, of cocreation. In this era of ecological crisis, it is vital that we be again at home in the place where land and water meet. We must learn to live with our shores, not just on them. Our survival and theirs depends on it.

1 · AN ALTERNATIVE TO EDEN

> The seashore is an edge ... and it defies the usual idea of borders by
> being unfixed, fluctuant, and infinitely permeable.
> REBECCA SOLNIT[1]

Western civilization is landlocked, mentally if not physically. While it
has a long history of aquatic accomplishments, these do not constitute its
primary identity. In the Western world we imagine human history as beginning and ending on terra firma. Our understandings of our origins,
both religious and scientific, are decidedly terrestrial, and we have had
great difficulty in finding a place for water in either our histories or our
geographies. We remember Lucy, whose three-million-year-old remains
were found in 1974 in the bone-dry Olduvai Gorge, but forget that when
she was alive the gorge was a lake and she was most likely a shore dweller.
Only recently has underwater archaeology challenged assumptions based
on terrestrial excavations, showing the extent to which humankind has
been semiaquatic, foraging not just in freshwater but also, perhaps more
important, at the edge of the sea.

"The inability to regard place as anything but terrestrial, the eternal assumption that societies are boundaried, centered, contained, and enduring structures, is a distortion of retrospect," writes Eric Leed: it is "a view
of history filtered through the results of history." Sustained by religious as
well as secular traditions, terracentricity has assumed the status of myth
in Western culture. The oldest of the Greek gods was Gaia, Mother Earth:
"Mother of us all, the oldest of all, hard, splendid like a rock." The peoples
we have come to know as the ancient Hebrews had just begun to settle
down to an semiagrarian existence when they seized upon the idea of
Eden. This terracentricity was passed on to Christianity, and, reinforced
by Greek and Roman understandings of earth and water, became foundational to Western civilization. As long as the mass of humankind was
tied to the land, it made sense, but now that this is no longer true, it must
be called into question.[2]

In the Western tradition, the sea has always been an alien environment. Other societies have felt much more at home with its waters,

although, as far as I know, no people entirely deny their terrestrial connections. Even the Moken and other so-called sea gypsies of Southeast Asia do not live entirely at sea. Fijians believe their island was brought into being by Rokomautu, who dove into the sea to bring soil to surface. The earth-diver story is common among people who live by or from the sea. The Haida people of the Queen Charlotte Islands of the Canadian Northwest tell a story of Raven, flying above the sea, who sees a small island and turns it into earth. Later, as Raven explores this new world, he hears a sound coming from a small clamshell and discovers five tiny humans, who became what the Haida people refer to as the "earth surface people."[3]

For coastal and island peoples, it has been the edge of the sea that has been their perpetual Eden, for them not the margin but the center of their world. Unlike the Hebrews, for whom history was a long series of exiles, the coastal-dwelling Haida have no memory of coming from somewhere else. In the stories they tell themselves, the shores of the Pacific Northwest had always been their home. They live in a capacious environment of abundance, in an unchanging present, which produces no yearning for a lost past nor dreams of a redemptive future. It was not until Christian Europeans arrived and told them that all humankind had dispersed from a single landlocked place called the Garden of Eden, making them one of the Lost Tribes of Israel, that they even considered the possibility that they were strangers in their own land or that the sea constituted a danger. And even then they refused this tragic view of history as implausible, at odds with their sense of always having been the people of the *xhaaydla*, their term for the coast, belonging wholly neither to land or to sea, a different kind of place living on a different kind of time, somewhere not normally found on the surveyor's map or the historian's page.[4]

For the most part, coasts are still an unmarked category in both history and geography. Even today we barely acknowledge the 95 percent of human history that took place before the rise of agricultural civilizations. In this postindustrial era, our image of paradise is still the Garden of Eden and our model human the gardener. The book of Genesis would have us believe that our beginnings were wholly landlocked, but it was written at the time that the Hebrews were settling down to an agrarian existence. The story of Eden served admirably as the foundational myth for agricultural society, but it bears no relationship to the history and geography of humankind, including that of the Jews, that took place before it was written some 8,000 years ago. The story of modern humankind, *Homo sapiens*, that which I am concerned with here, begins 164,000 years ago. For most of our existence we have been foragers, and much of human evolution has taken place not in landlocked locations but where land and water meet. Not only does the idea of Eden misrepresent our past, but, now, when for the first time more humans live in cities than on the land, it is wholly misleading about our future.

We need to rediscover *xhaaydla* and find a narrative that is less terra-centric, one that recognizes humanity's long relationship with the sea as an *edge species*, occupying the ecotones where land and water meet. We need to know ourselves as aquatic foragers, as gamekeepers as well as gardeners. Gardeners attempt to control nature, gamekeepers accept it and adapt to its conditions. As we shall see, on coasts gardening was often combined with hunting and gathering. And now that the limits of human beings' control over nature are becoming so evident, it is all the more urgent that we recover that element of adaptability that was present when humans had a working relationship with the sea as well as with the land. In short, we require a new narrative, one with, as Steve Mentz suggests, "fewer gardens, and more shipwrecks," one more in tune with the fluctuant nature of coasts in this age of massive climate change.[5]

Myth of the Garden

It is said that the Hebrews were "the first people to conceive of themselves as living a life whose meaning was defined apart from nature." Their god was a gardener who provided Adam and Eve with a ready-made abundance that precluded any need to work and promised everlasting life. In the beginning, there was no wild nature. Wilderness was the product of the disobedience of Adam and Eve, which destroyed the original paradise and condemned humankind to toil and mortality. This was the origins story the Hebrews shared with other agrarian civilizations of the ancient Middle East, one that would have been utterly incomprehensible to hunter-gatherer peoples, whose gods were gamekeepers rather than gardeners, and who were at home in what Jews and Christians came to regard as wilderness.

The biblical creation myth begins with the declaration that "the earth then was welter and waste and darkness over the deep and God's breath hovering over the waters." One of his first acts was to tame the unruly waters. He created the heavens, saying, " 'Let the waters under the heavens be gathered in one place so that the dry land will appear,' and so it was. And God called the dry land Earth and the gathering of waters He called Seas, and God saw that it was good." Earth produced grass and trees, while the waters were filled with fish and the air with birds. "And God created the great sea monsters and every living creature that crawls . . ." Only then did he create man and woman "in our image, by our likeness, to hold sway over the fish of the sea and the fowl of the heavens," commanding them to "be fruitful and multiply and fill the earth and conquer it." [6]

Land is the central player in biblical geography. As Alain Corbin has noted, there is "no sea in the Garden of Eden." After the fall, the sea appears as an alien environment, a perpetual threat to humankind. It was from soil that God created man, giving him the name Adam, which comes from the Hebrew word *adama*, for earth. In this story, man gives birth to woman. Nowhere in Genesis is there any notion of Mother Earth, for land is itself a paternal rather than a maternal force. It is a creation of God the Father, who uses it to make Adam and from Adam's rib to create Eve. Thus in this rendering of creation the biological norm is reversed. Earth is birthed by a patriarchical god.[7]

God the gardener created a world of limitless plentitude, promising an everlasting life without toil, disease, or death. Adam and Even might have lived forever in peaceful coexistence with other creatures had they not disobeyed God's will. Their punishment for eating the forbidden fruit of the tree of knowledge was not only the forfeiture of everlasting life but the transformation of the earth itself into a wilderness of "thorn and thistle," where daily bread could be won only through painful toil.

At the moment of the fall, the whole earth ceased to be paradise and the Garden of Eden was removed to the east, where it would remain inaccessible until the end of time. Everlasting life gave way to the everlasting ordeal of production and reproduction, for God burdened Eve and all the women who followed her with the pain of birth. Her firstborn, Cain, the first farmer, and Abel, the first shepherd, were also cursed. Cain was angered when God slighted his offering of the fruits of the soil in favor of his brother's animal tribute. He killed Abel, and this led to a second exile to the even more barren lands of Nod east of Eden, where he began a family that was ultimately to become the people of Israel, who mixed sedentary farming with pastoral pursuits. Their fate was henceforth tightly bound to the vicissitudes of agriculture. Indeed, the story of expulsion from the Garden of Eden and the subsequent famine-related exiles narrated in the Old Testament were clearly related to the ecological disasters that we now know punctuated the history of agriculture in the ancient Middle East. The story of paradise lost was a product of the neolithic revolution and was the way that the Jews rationalized their own tragic history, their enslavement to the tragedies of landed existence.

The descendants of Adam wandered in lands repeatedly visited by both drought and flood. The commandment to "go forth and multiply" proved to be a further burden, because, in contrast to hunter-gatherers whose mobility keeps fertility relatively low, settled agricultural production favored large families, leading to overpopulation of the arid, fragile environments of the Middle East. It was farmers, not hunter-gatherers, who were forced to take up nomadic, diasporic strategies of survival. As the anthropologist Hugh Brody puts it: "Genesis is the creation story in which aggressive, restless agriculture is explained, is rendered an inevitability." Foraging cultures also encounter periodic suffering at the hands of nature, but the story they tell is marked not by catastrophic events but by cycles of challenge and response in which continuity outweighs change. The Haida were also visited by floods, but their stories tell of how canoes repeatedly came to their rescue.[8]

Genesis provided the ancient Hebrews, and later, equally restless Christians, with an explanation of their expansionist history and an excuse for the conquest of lands once shared with neighboring hunter-gatherers. Contrary to conventional wisdom, it was not foragers but agriculturists who were most burdened by scarcity. The neolithic agricultural revolution had not lightened the toil of subsistence but intensified it. Hunter-gatherers remained the healthiest, least stressed part of humanity. They had no need to tell themselves tragic stories of loss and recovery, for as far as they were concerned, the world had never ceased to be an Eden.[9]

When the Hebrew God's chosen people again displeased him, water would come into play as an instrument of divine publishment. He would send a great deluge, taking care that this act be witnessed by Noah and his family as a lesson to future generations. As torrents gushed from below the earth and rains began to fall, dry land disappeared for 150 days. Here water again plays a destructive role, with land being the ultimate giver of life. Once again it is the male who is the creator. Noah is a second Adam, only this time he will not be born into a paradise. When the waters receded and the ark came to rest on solid ground, Noah and his sons would find themselves occupying an even more inhospitable world. The once smooth earth was now a ruin, internally divided by high mountains and raging rivers, surrounded on all sides by seas that threatened to invade land along every coast. As the Old Testament story unfolds, the sea becomes an ever more dangerous force.[10]

Agrarian peoples were not the only ones to fear the sea. To the coastal Greeks and Romans the sea was a void, something to cross as quickly as possible to return home to humans' only true home: land. Christianity, following on Judaic traditions, would also endow the ocean with negativity. It is not Noah the seafarer but Noah the farmer who is the central character in the story of the Flood. Once back on dry land, he becomes the world's first vintner, but his own product leads him to disgrace himself and his children. Once again, the land fails the Hebrews and they are again forced into exile, "and from them the nations branched out on the earth after the Flood." Noah's progeny are dispersed to the African, Asian, and European parts of a great earth island that was subsequently called Orbis Terrarum, surrounded by an impassable river known as Oceanus. Somewhere deep inland, far to the east, the Garden of Eden still existed, but it was now walled off, inaccessible to humankind until the end of time.[11]

What makes the Old and New Testaments together such a compelling narrative is not only its plausible account of the failings of an agrarian civilization but also the hope for future redemption that it engenders. In the Old Testament, the Jews are assured their Promised Land. In the New Testament, Christ is the new Adam, but his death is not the end of the story: there will be a new beginning in which the promised land encompasses the whole earth and is extended to all humanity. Once all peoples are converted to Christianity, the world will again become a paradise. As foretold in the book of Revelation, upon the second coming of Christ, earth will again become a garden, and, significantly, there will be "no more sea."

Until the eighteenth century, the biblical version of geography and history portrayed the postdeluvian earth as a ruin, subject to an endless series of divinely initiated disasters meant to punish its wayward inhabitants. The plant and animal world was equally cursed and degenerate. Only gradually was this declension narrative replaced by a more optimistic view of change. Beginning in the sixteenth century, the discovery that Earth was not an island surrounded by an impassable river but a series of islands and continents connected rather than divided by water caused the sea to lose its satanic properties. But it would take another two centuries before islands came to be perceived as stepping stones to progress, and coasts, which had previously been seen as barriers, became passages, assets rather than liabilities. By the eighteenth century, the new earth sciences began to question the biblical chronology that had set the beginnings of the world at a mere six thousand years earlier. Evidence of changes occurring over millions of years not only demanded a new story of origins but suggested alternative endings that did not involve apocalyptic divine intervention but steady evolutionary progress.[12]

Yet both Europe and North America clung to their agrarian mythology well into the nineteenth century. The sea remained, as it had been in Genesis, a void to be traversed rather than investigated, a nonplace alien to humankind. It constituted its own realm, existing beyond human control. The catch of the sea was regarded as a "gift" to humans, over which they had little control. And nothing could stop the sea from taking human life. As a placeless, timeless space, the ocean was outside both human geography and history. Oceanography was the last-born of the earth sciences, and geographers paid little attention to the seven-tenths of the planet's surface covered by water. Historians also ignored the waters that joined the world together: as far as they were concerned, time began and ended at the edge of the land. The story of nations continued to be told in terms of loss and recovery of land, so that even as Europe and North America became more industrialized and urbanized, anthropology and archaeology, as well as history, remained landlocked, concentrating on interiors at the expense of edges.[13]

The Shore as the True Home of Humankind

Until the late eighteenth century, the Bible remained the foundational text for both history and geography in Western societies. In the seventeenth century the date of human beginnings was firmly set at 4004 BC by James Ussher, archbishop of Armagh, in a place that was assumed to be somewhere in the deserts of the Middle East but was inaccessible. Given this legacy, it is not surprising that when secular archaeology developed in the nineteenth century it was fixated on the same region. Until quite recently, prehistorians assumed that everything had its origins in the ancient Middle East and Mediterranean before being gradually diffused from there to the rest of the world. Until radiocarbon dating was invented by the Chicago chemist Willard F. Libby in 1949, all chronologies were keyed to Middle Eastern archaeological finds. "By looking east for a date, it was also natural to look east for an *origin*," Francis Pryor has noted.[14]

It is still common to distinguish between prehistory and history, as if there were some fundamental difference between humans who lived before and after the agricultural revolution. "Little of significance happened until 20,000 BC—people simply continued living as hunter-gatherers, just as their ancestors had been doing for millions of years," writes one leading scholar, Steven Mithen. As far as he is concerned, nothing important happened before the onset of farming. This is simply not true, but even scholars who have studied hunter-gatherers intensively are in the habit of placing them in the category of "the primitive." A short distance from where I live in Berkeley, Shell Mound Street marks the location of what was once a huge shell midden created by the Ohlone people. The famous Berkeley anthropologist Alfred Kroeber convinced his patron, Phoebe Hearst, to fund an investigation of the site, already partially leveled by the Emeryville racecourse and crowned with a popular dance pavilion. Kroeber's colleague Max Uhle was chosen to lead the dig, whose results were published in 1907. Uhle's study is a model of archaeological precision. He estimated the midden to have gone back about a thousand years and to have been abandoned only relatively recently. From his worksite, Uhle could readily see local people gathering shellfish at low tide. But he imagined them to belong to the same "primitive" stage of life to which he assigned the original inhabitants, the Ohlone people. "In all parts of the world, even today, people may be seen on the shore at low water gathering for food the shells uncovered by the retreating tide," and "these people always belong to the lower classes of society, and lead in this manner a primitive as well as simple life."[15]

The distance between the shell mound and the tide line was only a few yards, but the temporal distance that Uhle imposed between himself and these latter-day hunter-gatherers was immense. Anthropologists of his generation, trained to think of agriculture as the highest stage of civilization before the advent of their own urban-industrial age, insisted that life at the shore must have been a "last resort" of people who would never have chosen this as a way of life had they still had access to land. The possibility that the place where land and water meet could be a true Eden did not even occur to Uhle, for he, like all those who clung to Western civilization's creation myth, remained mentally landlocked.

As "primitives," hunter-gatherers were automatically exiled from the present to a remote past, seen as archaic survivors, living on borrowed time in a modern world where they had no place and no future. The evolutionary scheme favored by Uhle's generation assumed preference for the land over water and posited that marine hunter-gatherers had not changed from the moment humankind first came to the shore. Despite evidence of variation over time and space, they were judged incapable of change. According to the evolutionists' concept of progressive develop-

FIGURE 2. A 1907 photo of the massive shell mound at Emeryville, California, then topped by a dance pavilion. Courtesy of Wikipedia.

ment, they had been left behind first by the great hunters of large animals and later by the agriculturalists. According to this story, it was only when the supply of megafauna was exhausted that Man the Hunter turned to fishing. The male of the species never stooped (literally or figuratively) to gathering, work that Uhle's generation associated with women and lesser peoples. The notion that movement toward the coast was nothing but a step backward still haunts contemporary anthropology.[16]

This fable clearly reflected the gender and class biases of the first generation of gentleman social scientists, who, while only recently removed from agrarian society, had little contact with actual foragers. Viewing prehistory through the condescending eyes of agriculturists, they got several things wrong. First of all, the domestication of plants and animals began well before the so-called Agricultural Revolution, and most likely it began in places where land and water met—lakes, rivers, and seashores—rather than on dry lands. Surpluses gained through hunting and fishing probably provided a cushion that allowed experimentation with plant and animal domestication. As Carl Sauer was one of the first to point out, fisher-farmers led the way in human development. They were not the laggards but the pioneers among early humans. His contention that domestication began on the shores of Southeast Asia has been only partially confirmed, but his early resistance to the evolutionists' land-locked creation myth deserves our consideration. It was the emergence of a purely agricultural society, prone to periodic visitations of disease and famine, that may have been, at least from an environmental point of view, the first of many missteps humankind has made.[17]

As long as archaeology and anthropology continued to think of research as "fieldwork," the sea would remain outside their interests. Coasts and coastal peoples were initially of little interest to prehistorians, who focused on the land-cruising Man the Hunter, consigning fishing and shell gathering to the category of humanity's "last resort," things done when animals became extinct or scarce. As far as professional archaeologists were concerned, everything of importance began inland. The evolution from great apes to the first humans was traditionally seen as taking place on the African savannah, where, having left the safety of life lived in trees, bipedalism first developed and humans became separated from apes.[18]

But this did not fully explain other evolutionary changes leading to the emergence of distinctive human species. There was no accounting for humans' hairlessness or swimming ability until an Englishman, Alister Hardy, came up with the novel idea that it was not the savannah but the sea that occasioned the divergence of apes and humans. He suggested that wading and then swimming in water encouraged not only humans' upright position but also their hairlessness and their swimming and diving abilities. Hardy did not publish his speculations until 1960, when he announced that apes may have been forced into water by the disappearance of forests and the flooding of their former homelands. He speculated that they had lived for several million years on the shores of rivers and lakes, where they ultimately became *Homo habilis*, capable of exploiting stone tools to open shellfish.[19]

The idea that water was a resource for rather than a barrier to early humans was slow to catch on in anthropological circles, but was taken up by the Berkeley geographer Carl Sauer in 1962. He surmised that the shore was not the last resort of humankind but the starting point of modern *Homo sapiens*. When Sauer called the seashore the "primitive home of man," he did not mean to associate it with primitivism or stasis. On the contrary, for Sauer "our evolution turned aside from the common primate course by going to the sea. No other setting is as attractive for the beginnings of humanity. The sea, in particular the tidal shore, presented the best opportunity to eat, settle, increase, and learn."[20]

Sauer was a midwesterner whose curiosity was awakened by huge shell mounds he found in Baja California in the 1920s. As a member of the Berkeley faculty, he was surely aware through his close friend Alfred Kroeber of Max Uhle's findings only a few miles from the campus. Sauer was one of the great academic trespassers, who never met a boundary he did not wish to cross. He had long been interested in human origins and dispersal, and when invited to give the Isaiah Bowman Lecture by the American Geographical Society in 1952, he was ready to throw down a gauntlet to the archaeology and anthropology establishment, to challenge the notion of unilinear human evolution. "There is no general law of progress that all mankind follows; there have been no stages of culture, through which all people tend to pass."[21]

Sauer relocated Eden from the interior to the shore: "It may be, as it has been thought, that our kind had its origins and earliest home in an interior land. However, the discovery of the sea, whenever it happened, afforded a living beyond that at any inland location." It was at the shore that humans parted not only with primates but also with less developed hominids. There *Homo sapiens* developed the attributes of civilized life, including enduring family units, rules of kinship, and a matrifocal sense of home. The human learning curve accelerated, making possible generational continuity and the foundations of a complex, ongoing social and cultural order. Ultimately, access to water would enhance communication over ever longer distances, ultimately resulting in dispersal of advanced human cultures from Africa coastwise along the eastern shores of the Indian Ocean, then to Australia, to Eurasia, and ultimately around the northern rim of the Pacific to the Americas.[22]

Here was a clear challenge to the Genesis story, positing not only a new Eden but a new Adam and a new Eve, evolved from contact with the sea rather than inland. Relocating Eden from interior to shore undermined the glorification of Man the Hunter that was so popular in Sauer's day. It also upended the prevailing gender and class bias by assigning to women a central role in human development. Sauer placed women at the core of the domestic unit, but his women were by no means mere housewives. At the shore "the sexes are of equal ability, endurance, and performance in the water, and they could participate equally in the work of collecting and in water sports." Sauer reflected the postwar California enthusiasm for all things coastal at a moment when the state was refashioning itself as the Coast of Dreams. His own life recapitulated what he perceived to be the future of humankind. As he turned his back on his midwestern agrarian roots, he wrote that "when all the lands will be filled with people and machines, perhaps the last need and observance of man still will be, as it was at the his beginning, to come down to experience the sea."[23]

It took almost forty years for Sauer's speculations to be confirmed by prehistorians, but the landlocked creation myth was already under assault from another quarter, which in the 1950s and 1960s had a much greater popular audience than either anthropology or archaeology. Rachel Carson, who grew up in Pennsylvania and did not come down to the sea as an apprentice marine biologist until 1929, did not publish her *The Sea around Us* until 1951. Yet it was an instant success and remained on the *New York Times* bestseller list for twenty eight weeks, its impact due as much the author's mythopoetic style as to the scientific information it conveyed. Carson inverted the relationship between land and sea, declaring that "as life itself began in the sea, so each of us began his individual life in a miniature ocean within his mother's womb, and in the stages of his embryonic development repeats the steps by which his race evolved, from gill-breathing inhabitants of a water world to creatures able to live on land." Like Sauer, Carson foresaw humanity making its way "back to the sea," where, if it could not literally return to the ocean physically, it would "re-enter it mentally and imaginatively."[24]

Archaeology Finally Gets Its Feet Wet

Carson and Sauer were not alone in their mental journey. In postwar America and Europe, millions of their contemporaries were making their own personal rediscovery of the coasts in one of the great human movements that continues with ever greater acceleration today. These new Adams and Eves were seeking their own version of Eden, but their longings were not those of agrarian peoples. As creatures of an industrial era, perhaps even a postindustrial era, they were seeking a new kind of paradise. In the process of going back to the sea, a journey through time as well as space, they were bound to unearth the forgotten history of humankind's involvement with the marine environment.

Despite the plausibility of this alternative story of human development, the notion of aquatic origins has until recently remained marginal. For most historians, time still begins and ends on land. In a similar manner, geographers continue to treat waters as external to their subject. This landlocked perspective retains a strong gender bias. In prehistory the focus has been almost exclusively on Man the Hunter. It has also been taken for granted, despite evidence of female participation, that fishing was an exclusively male activity.[25] We can now see that the distortion of retrospect was operating here as elsewhere. Man the Hunter was largely an invention of Victorian gentleman anthropologists and bears a striking resemblance to the modern big-game hunter, who also travels far from home in search of his prey. University-educated gentlemen, operating on the contemporary assumptions of separate spheres, paid little attention to the activities of aquatic women, assigning them to the lowly status of gatherers and vastly underestimating the importance of gathering itself to the course of human development.[26]

Life has always been dependent on water, and we can be certain that hominids were using the shores of lakes and rivers long before they began to leave the interiors of Africa as early as 1.5 million years ago. Hominids began to separate from apes six or seven million years ago, and several different species—*Homo habilis, Homo erectus*, Neanderthals, among others—emerged prior to the arrival of the modern human, *Homo sapiens*, roughly 200,000 years ago. Neanderthals migrated to Eurasia but eventually died out. *Homo erectus* was the first to migrate to Southwest Asia and then through Southeast Asia to China, but there they stopped and eventually gave way to the more advanced *Homo sapiens*, who left Africa much later but were better equipped to ultimately occupy the entire world.[27]

Homo sapiens, from whom we are the direct descendants, seem to have migrated from the interior of Africa to its eastern shores at least 160,000 years ago. They migrated out of Africa 50,000 years ago, after having developed a set of cognitive abilities that made them superior to the other hominids, including the Neanderthals, with whom they coexisted in Europe for a considerable period of time before the latter became extinct. Decisive *Homo sapiens* dominance was the product not so much of any one anatomical feature but its brain development, crucial to language acquisition and symbolic behavior, those things that distinguish *Homo sapiens* not only from apes but also from other humanoids.[28]

Ecologists tell us that "the human species, from the beginning, was an animal of the edge," flourishing where ecosystems overlap, places known as *ecotones*. Ever since our species came down from the trees and turned its back on the forest to roam the savannahs of Africa, it has found ecotones most attractive. At first it was the edges of the forest and later the shores of rivers and lakes, where we find evidence of the earliest gatherers of shellfish and aquatic plants. This may have gone on for hundreds of thousands of years, but the real turning point was reached at the edge of the sea, for saltwater environments are known to be more productive than freshwater ones.[29]

There is good reason to think it was there that we became fully human, developing the large brain-to-body ratio that, along with dolphins and some other marine mammals, became our distinguishing trait. The British neurochemist Michael Crawford attributes this to the availability of shell and fish food containing fatty acids (especially DHA) necessary to large brain development. Earlier herbivore and carnivore humans lacked access to these, and it was only when humankind reached the sea that the brain could evolve to its present human dimensions. This was the launching pad for all subsequent social and cultural change. No other moment, not even the foundation of agricultural societies roughly 155,000 years later, seems to have produced such a fundamental transformation.[30]

It was when gardening was combined with gamekeeping that humankind learned to live *with* nature in ways that were sustainable over very long periods. Seen in this perspective, the journey to the shore was not the last but the first resort of humankind. For too long it has been believed that humans gave up hunting only when those animals became extinct. Now it seems safe to say that people settled on the coasts not for what the interiors lacked but because of the abundance that the seashore provided. It was there that they developed the first sedentary communities and learned to communicate and trade with one another—in other words, to attain a civilized existence. There they also developed horticulture, the forerunner to agriculture itself. It was also on the shore that the journey out of African began. Without the sea, human development would have been inconceivable.[31]

True Eden: Pinnacle Point

Over the centuries, the search for biblical Eden has left no stone unturned, no place unexplored. In the United States alone, hundreds of places bear the name. It is a favorite with real estate developers and travel agents. On Mossel Bay, at the very southernmost tip of South Africa, the sprawling Pinnacle Point Beach and Golf Resort stands high above an often frenzied sea. When its promoters nominated it "a new Garden of Eden," they could not have known that the caves in the cliffs just below the ninth tee would come to lay the strongest claim to date for being the true origins of humankind.[32]

FIGURE 3. View from cave at Pinnacle Point, South Africa. Courtesy of Curtis Marean and Mossel Bay Archaeology Project.

The discovery of a new Eden is the accomplishment of a team of archaeologists headed by Curtis Marean of Arizona State University. Marean had a hunch that in periods of peak glaciation, when the interior of Africa was cold, dry, and inhospitable, humans had moved by necessity to the coast, where the weather was warmer and food sources more abundant. Excavations in a cave that has since become famous as PP13B proved to be a revelation. In almost ten years of careful digging, his team discovered not only evidence of habitation but proof of material and cultural development that has revolutionized our understanding of *Homo sapiens*'s origins. Thanks to the work of Marean and others, the evolutionary clock was reset and origins pushed back from 125,000 years to 164,000 years ago. There was evidence that the inhabitants of PP13B exploited both sides of the tide line, relying heavily on shellfish that they harvested at low tides when marine life below the caves, including washed-up whales and seals, was exposed and easy to gather. There was evidence that they were already adept at shaping stone knives, but of even greater significance was proof of symbolic behavior documented in the presence of traces of ochre, thought to be the first evidence of body painting ever discovered. The inhabitants of the Eden at Pinnacle Point may have arrived as nomads, but their coastal diet enabled a sedentary existence, much as Sauer had imagined it.[33]

Here was evidence that in a period of potentially devastating climate change humans proved, perhaps for the first time, to be not only adaptable but extremely creative. The coastal environment was their salvation, but to take advantage of its resources they needed to learn to avoid its dangers. The caves above the waterline provided shelter, but in order to harvest the feast below the tide line they needed to time their descent very carefully to take advantage of low water. Marean has speculated that this may have involved mastery of the lunar calendar, a mental leap no less significant than the calculation of the solar cycles.[34]

The Eden at Pinnacle Point seems to have been occupied for a considerable period of time, though humans moved inland again when the climate became more tolerable. But ultimately a new round of climate change brought humans back to the sea, and in this case to the Red Sea, about 125,000 years ago. We are certain that *Homo sapiens* were present in the area we now know as Palestine soon after this, but they disappeared from this region before making a second and more significant exit from Africa around 50,000 years ago. And now, with the aid of genetic markers to map ancestry, we can follow the descendants of a tiny band who exited Africa to populate the entire globe in a little over forty thousand years. While other hominids had exited Africa much earlier by taking northern and eastern routes, the most significant group of *Homo sapiens* left by way of the Red Sea's southernmost point, Bab al-Mandab, now known as the Gate of Grief.[35]

The first *Homo sapiens* to cross these waters did not come to grief because in this era of increased glaciation the sea levels had dropped 230 feet lower than they are now, narrowing the strait between Africa and Arabia still further. Once the group began to move, they clung to the coasts, what Spencer Wells calls the "prehistoric superhighway." In this period, the shores were much broader, by as much as two hundred kilometers, than they are today, providing an immensely rich surf-and-turf diet. *Homo sapiens* moved quickly along coastal India, branching north

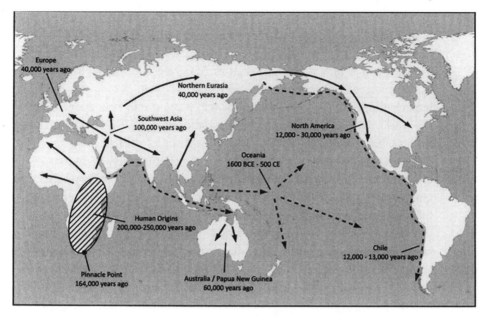

FIGURE 4. Map of World Migration from 100,000 BCE. Drawn by Adam Davis.

and south, ousting hominid and Neanderthal rivals who had proceeded them. *Homo erectus* had never been able to cross water, so *Homo sapiens* had Australia all to themselves when they arrived there. When they moved north into interior India and Asia, they did so from the shores they had already settled. It can be truly said the coast was the "staging post for the settlement of the rest of the world."[36]

This was a species capable of mastering the most daunting environments, including the Arctic. By twenty thousand years ago, they had reached the eastern edge of Siberia and were extending their hunting-gathering range to Beringia, then a land bridge between Asia and North America. Recent research encourages us to think of the peopling of the Americas as an extension of coasting rather than a overland process. Knut Fladmark and others surmise that the migrants moved swiftly along the shores, taking advantage of the riches on both sides of the tide line. At the time, sea levels were 350–400 feet lower than they are now, making the North American continent larger by a factor of the size of the present state of Texas. One must imagine that what is sometimes called "Kelp Highway," a biomass of richness and diversity comparable to a tropical forest stretching from Japan across the southern shores of Beringia down to Baja California, and resuming along the Andean coasts down to the tip of South America. As Charles Darwin noted in 1834, these vast aquatic forests sustained not only sea mammals, fish, and birds but peoples like the Fuegians.[37]

Migration routes from Asia to the New World remain controversial, but it now seems reasonably clear that coastal migration played at least as important a role in the Americas as it did throughout the rest of the world. To date, all efforts to find evidence of trans-Pacific or trans-Atlantic boat passage have failed; and while it is possible that boats were used to transit along the coast, it is very unlikely that these early coasters were deep-sea sailors. However, the speed with which they traveled alongshore is quite astonishing. The Monte Verde site in Chile predates by at least a thousand years the earliest documented inland settlement, the so-called Clovis site. Monte Verde was a long-term settlement, located on a river only a little more than thirty miles from the sea, which seems to have had trade relations with other coastal communities. Evidence of shellfish and seaweed consumption there strongly suggest the presence of marine hunter-gatherers rather than the inland big-game hunters who for so long have been the heroes of conventional continent-centered migration theories.[38]

Why does the story of the human edge species remain so obscure? An obvious reason lies in the absence of the kind of evidence that is so abundant at inland sites. For the last 150,000 years sea levels have undergone major fluctuations, repeatedly wiping out the record of human habitation along the shore. In the last period of glaciation, which peaked 20,000 years ago, sea levels were, as noted above, 350 to 400 feet lower than they are now. Humans occupied many places that have long since disappeared, either washed away by the rising tides or drowned so deep beneath the waves that only now, with the aid of the new technologies of wet archaeology, have we been able to explore them. In our time, each year brings new finds just offshore that reveal the hidden history of our edge species, its prowess in turning coasts into travel and trade routes unmatched by anything that occurred inland. Until quite recently, archaeologists were convinced that North America was entered by way of an ice-free interior corridor. Now it can be shown that terrestrial routes through the Cordilleran and Laurentide ice fields would have been immensely more difficult than following the great Kelp Highway along the coasts. There is simply no other explanation of how humans reached the southern reaches of the continent within so short a time after entering North America.[39]

Initially, coastal migrants seem to have used the shores lightly, moving along when they had exhausted a place, rarely settling for long periods of time. But about ten thousand years ago, coastal routes became coastal roots, as settlements became more permanent. This was about the time that settled agriculture was also beginning. While it was once thought that the development of the coast was dependent on that of the interior, it seems that it may have been the other way around, with horticulture getting its start on the shores. Hunter-gatherers had long been adept at cultivation, and in many ecotones where land and water overlapped, fishers and farmers were indistinguishable from one another. The proteins available from fish and shellfish had always to be supplemented by calories provided by animal flesh and edible plants, but these could be as easily found on the seashore as in the interior. And it is now certain that human development did not follow a simple sequence from hunting-gathering to agriculture. Agriculture can no longer be seen as some sudden great leap forward, but rather as an extension of techniques learned at the water's edge.[40]

Fishing and farming, gamekeeping and gardening, had developed in tandem from the very beginning, each complementing the other. Nineteenth-century notions of distinct "stages" of development must now be abandoned for a more continuous, overlapping history that recognizes that land and water are interdependent parts of the same ecology. It was not until the nineteenth century, when both agriculture and fishing became commercial enterprises, that separation occurred, first in the capitalist developed world and only later in other parts of the globe. For most of our existence, however, land and sea constituted a single ecotone, sometimes occupying only a narrow coastal strip, but increasingly, through the expansion of transportation and trade, becoming an immense zone extending far inland as well as well offshore, sometimes stretching across bodies of water to connect quite distant lands.

The Evolution of Our Edge Species

For many prehistorians, the invention of agriculture remains the great turning point. They insist on drawing a sharp line between foragers and farmers, ignoring the overlap between gamekeepers and gardeners. The idea that hunter-gatherers had no ability to cultivate automatically placed them on a lower rung of the human species, one labeled "primitive." The notion of the primitive, another distortion of retrospect invented by

Victorians eager to distance themselves from their ancestors, has stuck despite all evidence of hunter-gatherer resourcefulness. We know, for example, that hunter-gatherers of the northwestern coasts of America developed an aquaculture by planting clams in artificially protected places along the shore. But even Franz Boas, who knew their ways better than any scholar of his generation, ignored evidence of their clam gardens.[41]

Scientific archaeology has always had to contend with the perceived alienness of the sea. Until the late eighteenth century, shores were places to be avoided, their inhabitants thought to be lesser creatures than inlanders. Places where water and land met and mixed were "fraught with misunderstanding and fear." It was not until the 1850s that Europeans began seriously investigating the well-preserved Stone Age bodies that were turning up in newly drained peat bogs, bodies that revealed the extent to which people had occupied lakes and coastal regions before they did interiors, living in what appeared to be stilted houses or on mounds that were called crannogs in Ireland, terps in the Netherlands and Northern Germany.[42]

At about the same time, a Philadelphian named Clarence H. Moore was pioneering the study of the shell mounds and pile dwellers of Florida's southwest coasts, revealing a parallel world on this side of the Atlantic. Frank Cushing's 1890s excavation of Key Marco revealed an unexpectedly high level of culture hidden in what was then a mangrove swamp. Still, there was resistance to seeing wetlanders as anything but agrarians living at the edge of the water. "Prehistoric man was a man and not an amphibian," Oskar Paret concluded in the 1950s. However, another half-century of energetic wetlands archaeology has brought their inhabitants to the fore of worldwide interest. On the Cheshire coast of England, low tides had long exposed a dense concentration of tree stumps and roots that locals called Noah's Forest. Scientists had paid no heed until Clement Reid published his small book *Submerged Forests* in 1913, speculating that this might be the edge of a lost world lying beneath the North Sea between Britain and Denmark. Reid's hunch was given further credence when a harpoon made of antler bone was dredged from the Dogger Bank by fishermen in 1931. Further sonic exploration after the Second World War confirmed the existence of a territory the size of Britain itself that had existed between twenty thousand and five thousand years ago, a place that was in all probability home to hunter-gatherers until post–Ice Age inundation forced them to move to what are now the coasts of Britain and the European continent. In 1998 this was christened Doggerland, joining the submerged area between Siberia and Alaska, Beringia, and undersea

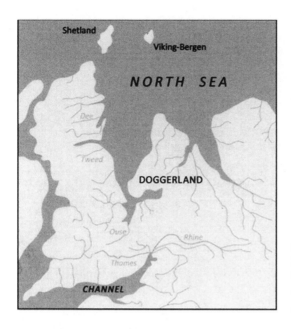

FIGURE 5. Drawing of Doggerland, a land bridge between Britain and Europe, ca. 3000 BCE. Drawn by Adam Davis.

areas of the South China Seas, known as Sundaland, as the principal lost lands of the Mesolithic era.[43]

Initially considered "land bridges" rather than lands as such, these were gradually understood to actually be homelands of permanent populations who had colonized them for the abundance of resources—plants and animals—found there. Mobile and adaptable, the populations of Doggerland, Beringia, and Sundaland "lived rich and social lives in an environment that may have teemed with opportunities." While most of the evidence remains submerged, discoveries along the coastal shelves of both Europe and America have thrown new light on creative and adaptable hunter-gathers, placing them on parity with better-known inlanders, whose archaeology had always been much more highly developed. Now an alternative creation story is emerging as submerged coasts begin to give up their secrets to sophisticated sonar and diving equipment.[44]

One of the most spectacular finds of recent archaeology is England's Star Carr House, discovered near Scarborough in North Yorkshire. It is the oldest known dwelling in Britain, inhabited some 10,500 years ago at a time when Britain was still connected to the Continent by Doggerland. At the time of its occupation it was located on a lake, which was also the site of a large wooden platform, the oldest known carpentry project in Europe. A boat paddle and an antler headdress have been found, indicating that Star Carr was also a ritual center. Until its discovery in 2008,

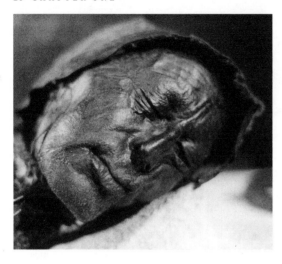

FIGURE 6. *Tollundmannen*,
bog man found in Denmark.
Courtesy of Wikimedia
Commons.

it was thought that only nomadic hunters had inhabited the area. Now it
is clear that this was a sedentary society with a highly developed cultural
life. And there is a good chance that even earlier settlements will be found
as wet archaeology progresses.[45]

Stone Age Coastal Affluence

In the legends told by the Haida peoples of the Canadian Northwest there
are hints of a time when it was possible to walk between what are now
offshore islands. Eventually, however, sea levels would rise and the edge
between land and sea would take on the shape that it has remained until
our own time. With the retreat of the glaciers in both the Northern and
Southern Hemispheres, estuaries and major rivers assumed their present
positions, allowing anadromous fish to assume their present migratory
patterns. The development of stable mudflats and wetlands facilitated the
growth of shellfish populations, fixed the migratory paths of birds, and
produced permanent breeding grounds for seals, walruses, and other seagoing mammals.[46]

It was in this narrow ecotone between land and sea that hunter-
gatherers flourished and developed the first coastal societies that exhibit
common characteristics all around the world. Certain things distinguished coastals from inlanders from the very beginning. For one thing,
they were highly mobile. Movement was the normal mode of existence;
both survival and further development depended on it. Once they had

exited from Africa, coastal people filled up the planet with a speed that no other species ever accomplished. This mobility had many advantages, for example a higher level of health than that of sedentary populations, which were likely to pollute their environments. Similarly, when people husband rather than hunt animals, they make themselves vulnerable to the diseases that other species carry. While it is not clear that foragers lived longer lives, it is probably the case that, with their lands less densely settled, they were freer from epidemics.

And foragers maintained relatively low population levels. While they endured 95 percent of all the time humans have occupied this planet, they constituted only 12 percent of all the people who have ever lived. We know that contemporary foragers use various means of birth control, and ancient foragers may also have done so. Perhaps more important to their low birth rates were the high levels of mobility that encouraged forager mothers to breast-feed for longer periods, thus spacing births farther apart and limiting the total number of offspring. In any case, we can be reasonably sure that they lived in very small groups, more like extended families, which moved about and exploited resources over territories combining different ecosystems that they had come to know so intimately.[47]

It is likely that marine foragers also knew how to get out of the way of certain kinds of natural disasters. Long experience with shore conditions taught our edge species to live above existing sea levels, usually well back from the high tide line, thus avoiding storms and tsunamis. The legends of the coastal peoples of the Canadian Northwest make reference to periodic inundations but also tell of successful escapes by canoe. People who occupy edges between ecosystems often show a greater resiliency, a greater adaptability to the effects of wind and fire as well as water. There is evidence that they knew how to use water to protect themselves from their enemies, animal and human. In Ireland and Scotland, occupation of small artificial islands called crannogs served this function. And it was not just the poor who sheltered there. Crannogs were occupied by kings and priests, who knew how to exploit the supernatural powers associated with the liminal places where land and water met.[48]

The attractions of ecotones were not just material, however. It seems that places where land and water mix have long been a symbolic resource and stimulus to cultural development. There were not only myriad spirits and deities to be encountered but also access to other worlds, where dead ancestors resided. The transformative powers of water, reflected still in modern rites of baptism, were universally recognized. Shores were often the site of rites of passage. The remarkable wooden trackways that have been recently discovered in European coastal wetlands are now seen as having more symbolic than practical value. Like the modern piers and boardwalks that they resemble, they gave prehistoric people access to the watery worlds, not for pleasure in this case but to communicate with the dead. The many votive offerings and burials that have been found in such places as England's Witham Valley leave little doubt about the cultural generativity of places where land and water meet. Wetlands were among the first terrains to be encultured, transformed through ritual performances from undifferentiated nature into memorable sacred places. From the earliest times, ecotones produced not only a good but a meaningful life.[49]

What is certain is that our edge species enjoyed an abundance of resources, cultural as well as material, that other peoples did not. Those northern Europeans who occupied the raised lands called terps on the shores of the North Sea grazed sheep and cattle and were able to trade for grain with inlanders. It has been said that "terp life was probably a good life, for the density of settlement was more than twice that known from the sandy inland soils." They were the ultimate omnivores, crossing the tide line to satisfy their desire for protein, moving inland to obtain necessary carbohydrates, trading over long distances for both luxuries and necessities that were not within such easy reach. It would be wrong to think that once foragers settled the shore, they turned their backs on the land. On the contrary, evidence suggests that they made seasonal journeys inland to hunt and gather. The indigenous people of the northwest coast of Canada wove clothing of mountain goat hair; the Chumash of southern California's Channel Islands were connected by trade to communities hundreds of miles inland. Later, when encouraged by European fur traders, both eastern and western New World coastal peoples extended the range and seasons of their hunting activities, in effect expanding the size of their ecotones.[50]

Long before they became adept at offshore fishing, hunter-gatherers were skillful coasters who traveled alongshore in search of resources. This contributed mightily to their spread around the world but also led to the establishment of onshore bases from which they went out daily or seasonally, returning with surpluses that sustained communities year round and provided leftovers for trading with other coastal or inland communities. They were also pioneers in exchange and long-distance communications long before the emergence of a specialized merchant class. Operating without a monetary system, they were adept at sustaining long-distance exchange. Used to dealing with strangers, North American coastal peoples were, like their counterparts around the globe, not just ready but eager to incorporate Europeans into their trading networks when these strangers blundered into their world centuries later.[51]

Early coastal peoples traveled light. The development of rafts and boats appears to have been one of humankind's earliest technological accomplishments. It would not be until the nineteenth century that land transportation offered any advantage over water, so the kind of rapid movement we know took place along the coasts was nowhere matched by inland transit. Indeed, the rate of change along the coasts was much greater than anything imaginable in the interiors. The rates of innovation that occurred alongshore from 100,000 BCE seem to have outstripped anything that had happened earlier, due in part to higher levels of cultural diversity, which proved an incentive to exchange of ideas. As we now know from current studies of ecological edges, these are also likely to be cultural edges, where the rates of interchange are the greatest and change most frequent.[52]

Archaeologists date the beginning of human ingenuity with the making of stone blades roughly 200,000 years ago. Grindstones and point making followed rather quickly, but the next great breakthrough was shell fishing starting about 140,000 years ago, followed very quickly by long-distance exchange. The first sea crossings by Homo sapiens to Australia have been dated to 40,000 years ago, but it now turns out that another kind of hominid, Homo erectus, was voyaging in the Mediterranean as early as 130,000 years ago. Recent finds on the southern shores of Crete indicate that people of the North African Acheulean culture made it to that island with their stone tools, which have been preserved in the uplifted cliffs at Plakias. Elsewhere, the invention of bone hooks and harpoons has been dated to about 100,000 years ago, and offshore fishing presumably followed in due course.[53]

Above all, what the edge species had in its favor it was adaptability and flexibility. This was perhaps enhanced by the small scale of marine forager groups, most of them not much larger than an extended family and not subject to any internal hierarchy or external authority. There is little evidence of class divisions before the invention of inland agriculture. Relations between men and women, and between age groups, seem to have been very flexible, with matrilineage being at least as common as patrilineage. Where communities practiced shell fishing, both the very old and the young were able to make substantial contributions to the common good. Along land edges, mastery of the environment demanded a higher level of cooperation than that necessary among agrarian populations.[54]

From what we now know from recent archaeology, the coastal foragers enjoyed what Marshall Sahlins famously called "stone age affluence," advantaged by access to a range of resources greater than those of any other geography. While coastal and lakeside wetlands are perhaps the most biodiverse and productive of all the earth's places, they vary widely in fertility. Peat bogs yield a source of fuel but are infertile. And not all shores are as rich in seafood as those temperate coasts blessed by upwelling or rapid currents, which provide the most favorable environment for all forms of marine life. It is clear that coastal waters were far more productive than the deep oceans; and the richest place of all were the temperate intertidal zones and estuaries, which produced as much as ten times the biomass of coasts in general. Of particular importance in the early millennia were the shellfish that appeared at each low tide. River mouths were ideal locations because there the fishers did not have to seek out their prey, but set their weirs and nets for the anadromous fish that came to them on a regular basis once the shoreline had stabilized between 6000 and 4000 BCE. This process is visible in both the Old and New Worlds, where developments in the higher latitudes of the Northern Hemisphere were strikingly similar around the world. In both North America and northwest Eurasia the end of the Ice Age was transformational, creating an environment that had a decisive effect not just on the coasts themselves but on the continental interiors. In these parts of the world, it is not an exaggeration to say that for the next several millennia new life came by both land and sea.[55]

Everywhere, coasts offered greater biodiversity. Northern shores were habitats not only of shellfish but also of a variety of plants (sea kales, sea cabbages, seaweed) rich in nutrients such as iodine, which, in addition to fish oils, made for better diet and health among humans. Beaches where seals and walruses gave birth were further gifts from the sea, but best of all were the wetlands that attracted not only fish but amphibians, land animals, and the migrating birds whose rookeries provided yet another bonus. Having adapted to the diversity and seasonality of the ecotone where land and sea met, coastal populations were less vulnerable than those that depended on a narrower range of resources. We are told that inland populations also moved in search of their food, but the peoples of the coast had the luxury of being able to settle in one place, moving out by water to bring back supplies to their home site.[56]

To be sure, the early edge species' levels of consumption were quite low by our standards; and their life spans were less than half of ours. Until they began to settle at the end of the Ice Age, they moved too frequently to be able to accumulate anything like the amount of goods that constitute our measure of affluence. On the other hand, they were not subject to the kinds of catastrophe that so frequently mark the history of agrarian peoples. They may not have known the meaning of leisure, but they almost certainly worked less. It has been estimated that forager adults were able to provide for themselves with between six and seven hours effort per day, while farmers required about nine hours. In today's industrial societies, work time still hovers around eight hours, and is certainly far more stressful and monotonous.[57]

The First Coastal Cultures

Fifteen thousand years ago there already existed what James Dixon describes as a "continuous marine coastal-intertidal ecosystem extending between northeastern Asia and northwestern North America and further south to the southern hemisphere." There was a Pacific Rim long before there was an Atlantic Rim, a good reason not only to rethink our Eurocentric notion that history proceeds east to west but also to question its terracentricity. In some of the most forbidding environments of the rugged northwestern coast of America, the availability of a rich ecotone had given what Canadians call the First Nations "time to develop the greatest artistic culture in the New World." Archaeologists once imagined civilization expanding from interiors outward. Now it is possible to see multiple points of origin, with places once thought marginal assuming a central role in human development.[58]

In the higher latitudes of the Old World as well as the New, "the quality and abundance of the maritime diet encouraged a rapid increase in population and led to a more sedentary life style." Now a settled way of life was possible, not just in places like the Middle East where agriculture was to develop, but all along the coasts themselves. Around seven thousand years ago a new phase in the history of our edge species begins. It was no longer a multitude of transient bands but now a set of settled societies, often in touch with one another, exchanging goods but also ideas and languages. At this point we can begin to speak of seaboard civilizations, each shaped by its particular coast but sharing certain common characteristics. The old modes of extensive exploitation of resources gave way to an intensification of hunting and gathering on both sides of the tide line. Offshore fishing, which had been practiced for at least a hundred thousand years as a supplement to inshore trapping and shell fishing, now began to emerge as a major activity. There is evidence of increased technical innovation, new forms of fishing nets and lures and new kinds of boats, more seaworthy than those available earlier.[59]

The nutritional return on hunting is normally higher than that of agriculture, but fishing's return is higher still. With access to even greater abundance from the sea, restraints on population growth relaxed and many coastal communities became not only larger but considerably more complex. The experience of the Chumash, who established themselves on the islands around 7500 BCE in what is known to us as the Santa Barbara Channel, has been documented in considerable detail. A people who had gravitated from the interior to the coast, they now found that the islands offered much better access to fish, both local and migratory. They experienced a burst of creativity in fishing gear and boats, which by 1500 BCE included plank canoes. The level of cooperation demanded by fishing encouraged the development of hierarchies, usually male-dominated, that have been associated with fishing ever since. Shell fishing and other related inshore activities did not lose their material importance, but when they became the domain of women, children, and the elderly, their status was considerably diminished. Fishing encouraged life rooted in one place, and with it new understandings of territory, leading ultimately to a sense of proprietorship over resource-rich parts of the coast. While rarely expressed in terms of ownership as such, a notion of sea tenancy appeared, leading to rivalries, even war, over contested waters. But fishing also encouraged specialization and the development of trade in fish with mainland communities, which provided food in exchange.[60]

This was true in northern Europe as well. Agriculture originated in the interior regions of the Middle East, but it arrived in the Mediterranean by sea, first planted on the islands of the Aegean before moving onto the Greek mainland and ultimately transported along Atlantic coastal routes established by maritime foragers to arrive in northern Europe after 7000 BCE. As Barry Cunliffe has put it, "it was the sea that set the pace." Farming took root first in estuaries along the Iberian coast, moving only gradually inland along the rivers. In what is the Netherlands today, habitation of the wetlands did not begin until about five thousand years ago. The people there were semiagrarian, centered on husbandry of pigs and cattle.

FIGURE 7. Mural representing a Chumash fishing village. Master artist Robert Thomas. Photograph by David J. McLaughlin. Courtesy of California Mission Resource Center.

Their world has been described as "one of water, variegated water, broken by sinuous lines of the raised banks that followed rivers and creeks." Interiors showed the influence of their coastal neighbors. The circulation of seashells well inland suggests to Barry Cunliffe the hold that the sea had on early European farming populations, who traced their origins back to it.[61]

Skara Brae

Just to the north of Scotland lie the Orkney Islands, a place so exposed to the ferocious winds off the North Sea that they have never been able to support forests. Even today, it is an unlikely place to find civilization, yet evidence has been found there of a thriving culture that predates Stonehenge and the pyramids of Egypt. The landscapes of the Orkneys are filled with Stone Age chamber graves, rings of standing stones, and the oldest known European house, Knap of Howar, on the island of Papa Westray. But the most impressive remains of all is Skara Brae, an intact Stone Age village, which provides us with our best glimpse of a fully developed Atlantic community five thousand years old. Since 1999 it has

FIGURE 8. Unearthed Stone Age village of Skara Brae, Orkney, Scotland. Photo by author.

been, deservedly, a World Heritage Site, a rare instance of recognition of the contribution of the littoral to human development.

The village of Skara Brae was built in two phases, beginning in 3100 BCE, abandoned about 2500 BCE. The tight cluster of ten stone houses visible today is now on the very edge of the Bay of Skaill on the west coast of Orkney's largest isle, known as the Mainland. When the village was first built, it was well back from the sea, surrounded by meadows, with access to a freshwater lake. Its Stone Age inhabitants, who had probably come across the Pentland Firth from the Scottish mainland, perhaps on rafts, bringing with them cattle, pigs, and sheep, knew how to grow barley and wheat but also preserved their ancestors' skills in hunting, fishing, and gathering. At first they probably moved from place to place, stopping long enough to build up large middens of discarded bones, shells, and refuse. Later, their well-constructed stone houses would be sunk into these mounds, which provided them with protection from wind and weather and offer us invaluable information about their diet and way of life. We know that the meat of their domestic animals was supplemented with varieties of shellfish, cod, and saithe, as well as an occasional beached whale and other sea mammals.

Skara Brae hosted a community of not more than fifty persons, who appear to have lived in small family groups, relatively equal in status to one another. No house was larger than any another. Each was equipped with stone furniture, which included box beds, dressers, a central hearth, and stone tanks used to soften limpets employed as fish bait. It appears that their semisubterranean dwellings were equipped with drains to remove human waste. They had pottery, stone tools (including the famous Skaill knives), and stone or bone jewelry. This was a people with sufficient leisure to develop a sophisticated cultural life. Carvings suggest a high level of symbolic activity, short of writing. And the existence of red ochre similar to that found at Pinnacle Point points to a similar taste for body painting. The evidence of chamber tombs throughout Orkney suggests efforts to communicate with ancestors and, through them, with the spirit world. Many chambered tombs are constructed on top of middens and bear a striking resemblance to the houses of the living. The place where land and sea met was from the beginning a sacred place, where life and death were joined as nowhere else.[62]

Skara Brae's remarkable state of preservation is due to the fact that for more than four thousand years it was abandoned and filled with sand, perhaps as the result of one of the gigantic storms that are frequent in the area. It was uncovered only in 1850, when another megawind revealed parts of it to the local landowner, who happened to be an amateur archaeologist. A good deal of damage was done before the site came under the care of the famous archaeologist V. Gordon Childe in 1928. He immediately recognized why the first Orcadians had been attracted to the site, despite its exposure to harsh conditions of the North Sea. The ecotone by the "sandy sheltered bay with a rich and grassy hinterland [was] attractive alike to the fisher, the pastoralist, and the cultivator." By locating first their middens and later their village well back from the shore, they gave themselves almost seven hundred years of what must have been considerable peace and plenty. No weapons have been found at Skara Brae, and there is no evidence of famine or epidemic disease. As Childe pointed out, the people of Skara Brae left a legacy of foodways and domestic architecture that can still be found on the islands. The so-called black houses that island farmer-fishers occupied well into the twentieth century were laid out in a manner similar to Stone Age dwellings. Beds were no longer constructed of stone, but they were located on either side of the entry as they had been five thousand years earlier. There is no greater compliment than imitation, and the continuity of this and other coastal civilizations is truly remarkable when compared to inland societies dependent on a single ecosystem.[63]

The small size of the community prevented it from overexploiting its ecotone. Farming, herding, fishing, and gathering complemented one another perfectly, precluding any need for specialization or class divisions. In time, however, the accumulation of surpluses led to exchange with other Orcadian Stone Age communities. The temporal and spatial scales of the Orcadian edge species began to expand, and so too did their cultural sophistication. The need for marriage partners probably led to alliances with other Stone Age villages; and in time these entered into joint building projects, like the standing stones at the Ring of Brodgar and the great chamber at Maes Howe. These connections may ultimately have led to the abandonment of Skara Brae itself, but ultimately generated a thriving island civilization connected to an ever widening world.[64]

Even five thousand years ago, Orcadians were sustained by outside worlds that they could not have possibly have been aware of. Driftwood from North America's vast forests is known to have washed up on Europe's shores, providing fuel and roof timbers that their treeless island could not. We have seen how, time and again, the sea that seemed so alien proved so giving when inland resources failed. Shores were humankind's first Eden. Landlocked gardens came along much later, for initially agriculture, hunting, and gathering were inseparable activities. Humans came only slowly and reluctantly to abandon ecotones for monocultures. Even as late as AD 1500, 15 percent of the world's population were still hunter-gatherers. Farmers were not our progenitors but children of those who developed their green thumbs at the shore or along watercourses. Skara Brae reminds us yet again that, as Rowan Jacobsen has put it, "we were made for—and made by—that thin world where land meets sea."[65]

2 · COASTS OF THE
ANCIENT MARINER

… living around the sea like ants or frogs around a marsh …
SOCRATES IN PLATO'S *PHAEDO*[1]

Homo sapiens launched their epic journey from the coasts of Africa, moving along the shores of Arabia and India before branching out to populate the entire globe. For the next fifty millennia, even the most venturesome mariners rarely sailed out of sight of land. To the ancient Greeks, the Mediterranean was more like a pond than an ocean. Fernand Braudel described its peoples as "moving crab-wise from rock to rock," from island to island, peninsula by peninsula. The Italians called this *costeggiare*; the English know it as coasting; for the Portuguese it is *cabotage*. Even after the oceans were crossed, most ships continued to hug the shores. Yet those voyages have gotten little attention from maritime historians, who are obsessed with the deep sea, with blue-water navies rather than the much more abundant brown-water vessels.[2]

Our origins lie with what Rachel Carson called the "great mother of life, the sea," but our subsequent history has been more amphibious than aquatic. We have evolved alongshore rather than offshore, for the real home of humankind is where land and water meet, the birthplace of civilization. We normally associate that with the development of agriculture in the Middle East and India ten thousand years ago, but new research indicates that Stone Age peoples were cultivating crops and husbanding animals much earlier, often in places where a mix of land and water offered the greatest yield for the least effort. As it turns out, foraging and farming were indistinguishable from one another for millennia before and after the so-called Agricultural Revolution. Furthermore, what Felipe Fernandez-Armesto has correctly identified as *seaboard civilizations* developed independently of interior ones. Their rise remains a strangely neglected historical and geographical subject.[3]

We readily apply the term *civilization* to lands like Egypt, China, and Mesopotamia but are strangely reluctant to bestow it on people like the Phoenicians, the Norse, the Swahili, or any of the less well known coastal or island peoples, including the Aleuts, Malaccans, Caribs, and Tongans, who are every bit as qualified to be called civilized as their inland neighbors. Seaboard societies were different from their landlocked neighbors but in no way inferior to them in economic as well as cultural accomplishments. What sets them apart and should make them of paramount interest are their environmental circumstances at the edge of land and water. Not exclusively agricultural, they are not wholly marine either. Rather, they manifest *amphibiousness*, an ability to exploit both sides of the tide line, to live not just *by* the sea but *with* the sea in a sustainable relationship.[4]

Seaboard civilizations emerged from marine hunter-gatherer societies that had populated every part of the globe at the end of the last great ice age. They developed slowly and quietly, leaving behind few of the monuments and written records that have made landed civilizations so much easier to study. But now, thanks to archaeological sources, we know that peoples occupying coastal ecotones had access to abundant material and cultural resources, which allowed them to adopt a sedentary existence earlier than inland foragers did. The coasts allowed populations to grow and develop more complex social and economic relationships, including trade alongshore and inshore. As we have already seen, the shore was conducive to precious cultural development. And in time, coasts would also accumulate considerable wealth and authority, leading to *thalassocracies*, states that ruled by sea rather than by land, with a reach beyond that of any territorial empire.[5]

In the West, beginning with the Phoenicians, followed by the Greeks, the Norse, and the early modern naval powers of northwestern Europe, seaboard civilizations established trading enclaves and colonies on distant shores, ultimately replicating themselves over wide areas. While historians have tended to associate empires with land, the most extensive empires in human history, the Dutch and the British, were seaborne. Today, the last of the great thalassocracies, the United States, still uses its island bases and coastal enclaves to secure its economic and political interests around the world.

There is a striking degree of continuity in seaboard civilizations over the past fifteen thousand years, and perhaps even earlier. They are a missing link in the narrative of world history, which has remained landlocked for too long. The setting of the ancient mariner is for the most part brown water rather than blue water, but even when coasting was supplemented by transoceanic voyaging, as it was first in the Indian Ocean,

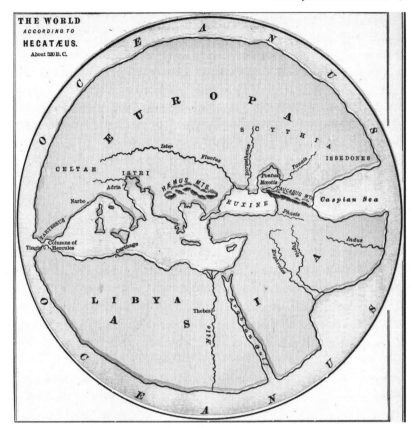

FIGURE 9. World as pictured by Hecataeus, 500 BC.

then in the Pacific, and later in the Atlantic, the greater part of marine activity remained inshore rather than on the deep sea. The Greek geographer Hecataeus imagined land to be a great island, Orbis Terrarum, surrounded by an impassable river, Oceanus, and this vision was to dominate geography until the fifteenth century. As Al-Idrisi, the great Islamic geographer of the twelfth century, noted: "No one knows what lies beyond the sea . . . because of the hardships which impede navigation; the depth of the darkness, the height of the waves, and the violence of the winds. . . . No navigator dare cross it or penetrate the open sea. They stick to the coasts." Even today, most marine activity is still concentrated along coastlines.[6]

But one coast is not like another. They vary in geology, biology, meteorology, and a host of other features. Any given coast can have a multitude of microclimates and environments that make it very difficult to generalize. And no coastal people is quite like another, not only because of the different conditions they live with but also because of the variety of adaptations that humans are capable of. Each coastal people has a different social structure and culture. My focus here is on the unique coastal culture that developed in Europe beginning with the Mediterranean, but in order to highlight its peculiarities, I'll begin at the shores of two very different seas, the Indian Ocean and the Pacific.

The Oldest Shore: The Indian Ocean

When we speak of seaboard civilizations, those of the Mediterranean come first to our Eurocentric minds. In ancient and medieval world maps originating in the West, the Mediterranean is always the central focus; and Fernand Braudel's classic treatment of it has also been the model for all other historical and geographical treatments of ocean basins. Yet the Mediterranean is small by global standards and by no means the oldest of the seven seas to be navigated. That honor belongs to the Indian Ocean, the world's third largest body of water, which has been traversed by humans for at least five thousand years, as compared to the Pacific's two thousand and the Atlantic's brief five hundred years of repeated passages. Of course we must acknowledge that oceans did not assume their present shapes until about seven thousand years ago. When the seas were as much as three hundred feet lower than they are now, many seas were more like straits or rivers, easily crossed on rafts or canoes.[7]

But oceans do not have to be crossed to be significant in the history of humankind. We have made heroes of transoceanic voyagers, forgetting many astonishing feats of navigation accomplished alongshore. It is coasts, not open waters, that pose the greatest danger to mariners, a fact lost on most landlubbers. We need to pay more attention to coasting, which, until very recently, constituted the greater part of the world's maritime traffic.

If we focus on seaboard civilizations, then the Indian Ocean shore must be our starting point, beginning 125,000 years ago when interior *Homo sapiens* arrived on what are now called the coast of Eritrea. It would be perhaps another 75,000 years before these coastal folk crossed the waters at the southern end of the Red Sea. As they made their way to India and beyond, they remained marine foragers, moving laterally along the shore in search of resources, trading over relatively short distances. Before it was a unified basin, the Indian Ocean was a series of discrete

FIGURE 10. Ship's boat arriving on beach, Madras, India. Courtesy of National Maritime Museum, London.

seas—the Red Sea, Bay of Bengal, Arabian Sea—each with its own coasts and distinctive seaboard civilizations.[8]

When long-distance trade began, it too was largely a form of coasting, initiated, however, from the great agrarian civilizations, Mesopotamian and Egyptian, which lay to the north and were seeking goods available farther south in East Africa and the Indian subcontinent. India itself was self-sufficient but receptive to these initiatives. Africans also welcomed traders from the north but rarely took to the sea on their own. Trade in the Red Sea began as early as 5000 BCE. The connections between Mesopotamia and the Indus Valley were secure by 3000 BCE, and it was the intensification of this intracoastal trade that led traders to decipher the monsoon system between 3000 and 1000 BCE, which led to the world's first regular transoceanic passages, moving across rather than around the Indian Ocean basin.[9]

Humans first went to sea in the Indian Ocean, but this does not mean that a blue-water culture developed there. Both India and Africa were to remain largely agrarian economies for a very long time, their coastal populations more attached to land than to sea. Their interior states showed no interest in projecting their power seaward or even directly controlling coastal trade. They were content to allow coastal peoples to mediate between land and sea, allowing them a certain autonomy culturally as well as politically and economically. What unity the Indian Ocean had was not imposed from the interior but "created by the movements of men, the relationships they imply, and the routes they follow." Along these routes came new peoples, and new religions—Buddhism, Hinduism, Jainism, and ultimately Islam—spread along the coasts more readily than they penetrated the interiors. Universal faiths mixed easily with indigenous religions, ultimately creating distinctive coastal cultures like the Swahili of East Africa. Some were more seafaring than others. Hindus regarded the ocean as polluting, and its higher castes would not venture across what they called the "Black Water." But these prohibitions did not inhibit lower-caste peoples, who constituted the bulk of the fisherfolk and seamen in India as well as elsewhere.[10]

Most of the peoples around the Indian Ocean were coasters rather than deep-sea voyagers. The only truly seafaring people in the Indian Ocean came from the east, not the north or west. They probably originated in South China or Taiwan about six thousand years ago, voyaging to southeast Asia and then moving on to settle Oceania, but not before moving westward by 1000 BCE to find the uninhabited island of Madagascar, which they made their own economically and culturally. From Madagascar they sailed in outrigger canoes, bringing bananas, coconuts, and sugar to East Africa for the first time. Still, this stupendous feat of long-distance sailing did not lead to dramatic breakouts to other oceans. The mariners who had crossed the Indian Ocean continued to hug its shores. The Indian Ocean remained the realm of small, relatively isolated coastal societies that never reached the levels of the inland civilizations in terms of power, urbanization, or cultural sophistication, but were fully civilized by any measure.[11]

When the Greeks and then the Romans succeeded the Phoenicians, Egyptians, and Persians in the Indian Ocean trade, they used the same routes and ports, doing very little to change the nature of either coastal India or Africa. Even the arrival of Muslims around 1000 CE did not disrupt this assimilative pattern. As Michael Pearson puts it, peoples of the Indian Ocean did not so much convert to as accept Islam. It was not until the arrival of the Portuguese in the fifteenth century that the continuities of the previous millennia were challenged, and, even then, the intrusion of this new maritime element did not quickly displace the ancient coast-

ing cultures that can still be found in East Africa and along India's western shores.[12]

Around the Pacific Rim

Another ancient coasting culture existed around what is known today
as the South China Sea. For some two thousand years its rim connected
South Asian peoples. Before the existence of territorial states capable of
unifying this vast and diverse networks of rivers, deltas, archipelagos,
and seas, it was a kind of waterland held together by trade and migration among the multitude of ethnic groups. As we have seen, peoples of
this region moved west into the Indian Ocean and south into the Pacific,
where they would become the Austronesian mariners who would ultimately voyage east across the Pacific in the greatest feat of seafaring that
the world had seen before the fifteenth century.[13]

The Pacific is the largest of the great oceans, twice the size of the
Atlantic. Those who first ventured there apparently had no name for it
and, like other ancient peoples, thought of it as a series of seas—South
China, Japan, Java, Banda, Celebes, Sulu, Timor—named for the bordering mainlands. Like other oceans, it was named long before it was fully
known. Ferdinand Magellan baptized it Mare Pacificum (peaceful sea),
not knowing anything of its extent and vastly underestimating its violence. To the Polynesian navigators who arrived long before him, the Pacific's awesome vastness was minimized somewhat by its ten thousand
islands, many grouped into archipelagos, which felt to their inhabitants
to something like watery mainlands, connected rather than separated
by water. Understood to be a sea of islands rather than islands in a far
sea, these archipelagos made the Pacific seem more manageable. When
European explorers arrived in the sixteenth century, they too focused on
the archipelagic, dividing the Pacific into three main regions, which they
named Polynesia (meaning many islands), Micronesia (small islands),
and Melanesia (black islands, named for their darker-skinned inhabitants), while imagining most of the Pacific as a great void.[14]

Before the 1960s, it was believed that the archipelagic Pacific was originally populated from east to west. This is now entirely discounted by archaeological and genetic research, which traces the peopling of the Pacific
from Southwest Asia to New Guinea and Australia back forty thousand
years to the Ice Age, when sea levels were much lower and there were
only narrow straits to be navigated. The foragers who made this journey
to the Australian and New Guinean coasts settled where resources were

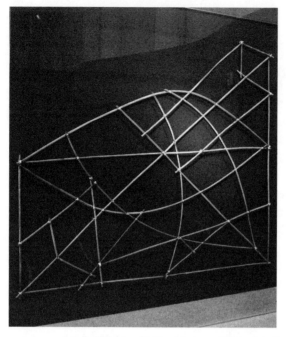

FIGURE 11. Marshall Islands *rebbelib*, stick chart with islands indicated by cowrie shells, swells by lines. Courtesy of Wikipedia.

most abundant. By 30,000 BCE they were again on the move, this time to the Solomon Island chain off New Guinea. They retained most of the characteristics of their forager ancestors, for islands are the most coastal of all land forms. But in time they began to cultivate jams and taro root, an agriculture compatible with marine hunting and gathering.[15]

Migration resumed about 2000 BCE with the arrival from the north of the so-called Lapita peoples, who had a superior level of pottery production and boatbuilding skills. By 1000 BCE, remarkable feats of navigation had brought them to the farthest eastern reaches of the islanded Pacific, to the Hawaiian Islands, to Easter Island, and to what is now known as New Zealand. By this time they had developed well beyond a foraging existence, carrying with them not only plants and animals but also sophisticated political and religious systems. They constituted a rare instance of a maritime society capable of transoceanic voyages but never seeing itself as anything but navigators within a sea of islands. Sometimes these argonauts of the Pacific even forgot their seafaring skills and became purely insular. Australian aboriginals turned their backs to the sea and became inland foragers; Easter Islanders became a wholly isolated population, doomed by their inability to connect with the larger world.[16]

There is no conclusive evidence that any argonauts of the Pacific made it to the shores of the New World, but this should not be allowed to obscure the fact that until the fifteenth century they were the world's premier seafarers, covering vast distances, colonizing distant shores, and setting up regional trading systems of great richness and complexity. Had they reached the western coasts of the Americas, they would have found another ancient seaboard civilization, but one very different from their own. Until the arrival of Columbus, the inhabitants of the Americas had been living in isolation for perhaps fourteen thousand years. These continents constituted their own biota, with their own disease environment, so that inhabitants were unimmunized against the diseases that existed in other world regions. Had the argonauts of the Pacific reached American shores, they would no doubt have set off epidemics at least as devastating as those that ravaged the American eastern coasts in the sixteenth century. For the peoples of the west coast, the day of reckoning came three hundred years later. By then the archipelagos of the Pacific had already been devastated by diseases brought by European explorers.

The Mediterranean: Ants and Frogs around a Pond

Peoples of the Indian Ocean and the Pacific developed orientations toward the sea very different from those that would emerge around the Mediterranean and on the Atlantic's eastern edge. In Southeast Asia some interior peoples, having been driven by aggressive neighbors to the coast and then offshore, came to be designated as "seapeople." The Moken of Thailand and Burma call themselves the "sea drowned" and live aboard their *kabangs* much of the time. But they do come on land to trade and seek protection from storms and tsunamis. They call the latter the Laboon, "the wave that eats people," and developed their own early warning systems that have served them well for centuries. Other coastal people learned to build on stilts or create amphibious dwellings. Those living around the Indian Ocean's edge remained among the world's preeminent coasters.[17]

It was the peoples of the Pacific who ventured farther offshore than anyone had ever dared to go. They felt much more at home at sea, investing it with a sense of time and place that Europeans would reserve to land alone. For the Greeks the sea was always alien and exotic, a place "to bring death, to take things away, and make things disappear." This orientation began in the ancient Mediterranean, or rather, around the ancient Mediterranean, whose shores had attracted hominid foragers for as many as 125,000 years and perhaps much longer. At first, these coasters had been highly mobile, but eventually they settled down to form complex societies and ultimately impressive seaboard civilizations. Socrates said they were like "ants or frogs around a pond," a description that still fits the peoples of today's Mediterranean.[18]

If there was something about the Mediterranean that set it apart from the Indian and Pacific Oceans, it was the narrowness of its coasts. Between 7000 and 4000 BCE its waters rose as much as 150 meters, flooding what had been extensive coastal plains and creating in its shallower parts innumerable near-shore islands. On the north and west, mountains came right down to the sea; in the south and the east, the coasts were hemmed in by equally forbidding deserts. Those who settled on the shore were cut off from the hinterlands, but on the northern side they gained access to innumerable near-shore archipelagos. Apart from the Black Sea and a few great rivers that drained into the Mediterranean, there was no easy access to the interior. This is why the Greeks called it the "sea between lands." Here the sea was the center and land the periphery, water the interior and land the exterior. For its peoples "places linked by sea are always 'close,' while neighbors on land seemed, in terms of interaction, quite distant."[19]

Not only were Mediterranean coasts, particularly on the northern and western sides of the pond, shallow, but they were extremely irregular. Long peninsulas extended far out, belonging more to the sea than to the land. The largest of these—Italy and Spain—constituted worlds of their own, more like islands than parts of the mainland. They were connected by waters, which often constituted their own separate seas rather than being part of the larger body of water we now know as the Mediterranean. The Adriatic and Aegean were among the first seas to be sorted out, and they were subdivided into even smaller bodies of water. These took their names and identities from the lands that bordered them. Opposite coasts often had more in common with one another than they did with their own hinterlands. The ancients learned to treat these inland seas as we would treat any territory. The Romans claimed the Adriatic as part of their empire, even as they held that the rest of the Mediterranean was open to all.[20]

As Felipe Fernandez-Armesto reminds us, "strictly speaking oceans do not really exist: they are constructs of the mind, figments of the cartographer's imagination, landlubbers' ways of dividing up maritime space according to the lay of the land." For Predrag Matvejevic, "the Mediterranean is not merely geography" but rather a set of social practices and cultural perspectives associated with that body of water. Ancient mariners experienced the Mediterranean in its particulars long before they knew it as a whole. It was initially known from the shores of the Levant as the "Great Sea," a term often used by the Greeks. The ancient mariner did not sail by compass or by charts, but by local knowledge gathered through firsthand experience and passed on orally. As it was for their Polynesian and Native American counterparts, water was a "place, not a space, its mobile surface full of portents, clues, and meanings." Ancient mariners knew their local seas as landsmen knew their neighborhoods. Most of their voyages were more like a landsman's saunterings, undertaken without fixed schedules or destinations. Because they knew themselves to be at the mercy of wind and current, they zigged and zagged, rarely navigating between fixed points but meandering along the coast, stopping frequently to eat, sleep, trade, and, on occasion, plunder.[21]

Until the age of steam, sailing a straight line was an impossibility in any case. Tim Ingold points out that the very notion of the straight line is "an virtual icon of modernity, an index of the triumph of the rational, purposeful design over the vicissitudes of the material world." The idea of a continuous *coastline* did not emerge until the eighteenth century, for the shore was known from personal experience, not through strokes of a cartographer's pen. Ancient coasts were discovered first by sea and only later from land. They were not lines but a series of certain disconnected points that had always been of greatest interest to sailors, namely safe harbors and hidden hazards. Before a line was drawn on skin or parchment, the mental maps passed on by memory from generation to generation consisted of a series of particulars vital to alongshore seamanship. The earliest Mediterranean charts, the *periploi*, were essentially route maps, "a sequence of harbors and natural features." They largely ignored what lay offshore, for the sea was not to be crossed but to be navigated around. It is not by accident that the term *periplous* meant "sailing around."[22]

The ancient Mediterranean did not have coastlines as we now understand them. Before there was a coast, there were only harbors, coves, fishing spots, and landmarks. A mariner did not set sail for a coast as such but for particular ports or landings. These were the first to be charted and named. What lay between went nameless or was called, as in Newfoundland today, the "strait shore," of no interest to ancient mariners. It was the imperatives of the sailor rather than the preoccupations of the landlubber that first shaped humankind's image of coasts; and in the view of the ancients, it was the sea that shaped the land. As the Roman geographer Strabo put it: "It is mainly the sea that gives the earth its outline and its shape, fashioning gulfs, the high seas, straits, and equally isthmuses, peninsulas and capes." Coasts belonged to the sea and encompassed the islands that lay opposite them. In the case of ancient Greece, we find instances where the mainland was defined "in terms of its relationship to an offshore island rather than vice versa." The coast was neither land nor sea but a combination of both, a much broader thing than our contemporary understanding of coastline would suggest.[23]

In the ancient world, the marine environment was understood as a multitude of small seas rather than the large bodies we now call oceans. Human beings felt comfortable with the idea of seas long before they could grasp the immensity of oceans. The notion of sea was applied to any body of water bordered by lands. It also applied to landlocked bodies of water, fresh or salt, such as the Sea of Galilee, the Caspian, or the Dead Sea. The ancients made no clearer distinctions among bodies of water than they did among landforms. Continents were not distinguished from *insula*, a term applied to any isolated place inland as well as offshore. Not until the sixteenth century were islands defined exclusively as lands surrounded by water. Lakes, estuaries, rivers, and seas all blended into one another. Greek maps depicted the Mediterranean as like a great river, flowing from the Black Sea out through the Pillars of Hercules. They deliberately underestimated its width, perhaps to calm those who feared losing sight of shore.[24]

The notion of the Seven Seas is applied today only to waters of an oceanic scale, but in the ancient and medieval worlds it could include just about any body of water, from lagoons to river systems. In the Roman era, the waters off the west coast of Italy and bordered by Corsica, Sicily, and Sardinia were known as the Tyrrhenian Sea, which the inhabitants of the mainland came to call Mare Nostrum (Our Sea). A self-contained sea was something you could get your mind around, a manageable unit of voyaging, where the mariner was rarely out of sight of land. As Braudel puts it, "Mediterranean lands were a series of regions isolated from one another, yet trying to make contact with one another." The numerous seas created the incentive for the establishment of vigorous trading networks. Hemmed in by mountains and deserts, these seaboard civilizations quickly became thalassocracies, pursuing conquest and colonization from peninsula to peninsula, from island to island, until empires stretched all around but not necessarily *across* inland seas.[25]

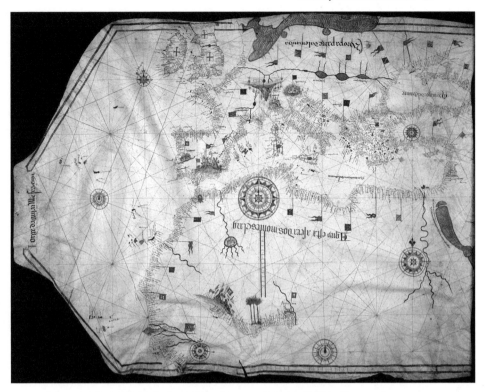

FIGURE 12. Portolan chart by Jorge de Agulon, 1492. Courtesy of Wikipedia.

In the ancient world, large bodies of water were known for the territories they bordered. The term *atlantic* is rooted in Greek mythology and originally meant the waters nearest to North Africa's Mount Atlas. It would take many centuries before the term was applied to the waters outside the Pillars of Hercules. Initially these were called Oceanus and understood to be more like a river encircling the known world. They eventually lost their riverness and came to be likened to the Mediterranean, sometimes known as the "Greater Sea," then the Great Outer Sea, then the Sea Ocean or the Ocean Sea, finally the Western Ocean. The term *ocean* was commonly used to denote seas that were huge and unfathomable. During the Middle Ages it was common for what we know as the Atlantic to be called by the nearest coast—the German Ocean, the Spanish Ocean. Not until the seventeenth century was the name Atlantic commonly used. When confronted with the unprecedented scale of the Pacific, Ferdinand Magellan chose to call it an ocean in the 1520s. In time, the multitude of seas would be replaced by the seven oceans.[26]

Seaboard Trading Empires

Mediterranean seaboard civilizations developed slowly, by movement alongshore or by island-hopping rather than by long voyages offshore. Islands were already important in the prehistorical Mediterranean. They offered places to trade with the mainlands, and when agriculture developed in the Levant in 9600–6900 BCE, it was first transferred to the island of Crete about 7000 BCE before moving to the European mainland a few hundred years later. And so it went all around the Mediterranean. Coastals confronted with barren or hostile interiors island hopped in a similar manner. The Phoenicians, a Canaanite people who turned their backs on the deforested Levant, colonized North Africa and were eventually displaced by the Carthaginians, who ultimately ventured into the Atlantic to found places to trade along its coast and on isles off North Africa and Iberia. While they were as close to a purely maritime people as the ancient Mediterranean produced, they too were coasters, hugging and colonizing the shore.[27]

Ever since humanity had begun to trade, it had chosen to do so at the edges of territories, thought of as neutral ground, where fair exchange could be guaranteed. Before there were permanent city markets, there were seasonal fairs held on the borders of royal domains and crossroads. Coasts were among those obvious edges that favored exchange, and before there were fixed ports there were landings where trade was conducted. Herodotus describes the way the Carthaginians traded with the locals on Africa's Atlantic coast:

> They land their goods and lay them out on the beach piece for piece. This done they return on board of their vessels and make smoke signals. When the natives perceive the signals they repair to the beach, deposit gold for the goods, and retreat inland. Thereupon the Carthaginians land again on the shore to consider the offer. If they deem the amount of gold an appropriate equivalent for the goods, they gather it up and sail home. But if it is not enough, they board their vessels again and wait events. Hereupon the Libyans return to the beach and add more gold to their previous offer, until they, the Carthaginians, are satisfied.

In other places, this kind of exchange without direct contact was called dumb barter or silent trade.[28]

The Greeks called places of trade *emporia*, not to be confused with the city, the *polis*. Separating the exposed port from the fortified city allowed Greeks to exploit natural landings and thus to better defend the polis from foreign and natural enemies. Plato believed that cities should be physically removed from the sea, "for the sea, though agreeable, is a dangerous companion, and a highway of strange morals and manners as well as of commerce," which was thought of as corrupting of civic virtue. The ancients often located markets outside city walls, in a kind of neutral ground that facilitated exchange with other city-states. It was also there that strangers were allowed to gather and mingle. City-states granted concessions to foreign traders, for whom the *emporium* was a kind of self-governing space, often with its own customs and languages distinct from the city. Later, enclaves known as *funduq* became more permanent all around the Mediterranean, but initially, as in the case of Athens, the market was the shore itself, a practice also followed in the Indian Ocean and, later, in northern Europe. Only when markets were incorporated within city walls and trade was removed from the edge to the interior did the permanent port fully displace the beach as the locus of trade. Romans relied less on natural landings than did the Greeks, but their engineering feats made their purpose-built ports vulnerable. When they constructed the Ostia harbor at the mouth of the Tiber, they encountered the kind of silting that would frustrate European port builders for centuries to come.[29]

The Greeks were comfortable with the coast but ambivalent toward the sea. Their voyages were dominated by the notion of *nostos*, the hope of return. They preferred, if possible, not to take their meals or sleep on ships, and they fought their sea battles mainly within sight of land. The coast was their home, and as Alain Corbin has pointed out, "in ancient epochs, shore kept alive the dream of fixed abode prescribed by the gods or provided a focus for hope of return." The sea itself was never the destination but only a means of returning home. The ancients had no concept of exploration or discovery, except to chart islands or coasts, and the sea interested them only as it touched on land and connected one point of land to another. Like Ulysses, they never set sail with anything but their home port in mind, for they took no pleasure in the sea itself, which for them was a threatening nonplace unless filled with islands or contained within bays sheltered by peninsulas. That the Mediterranean was bounded on all sides but one, and was open to the Atlantic only through the narrow Pillars of Hercules, was a great comfort to ancient mariners.[30]

Most navigators chose to stay close to shore, taking comfort in the presence of the numerous archipelagos that blessed the northern shores of the Mediterranean. Today we think of islands as remote, belonging to the sea rather than to land, but the ancient Greeks thought of the world as terraqeous, equal parts land and water. As we have already seen, the sea was for them an interior. We say we are going out to sea, but to them the hinterland was the outer space. This "inside-out" geography challenges our modern understandings, but it is crucial to appreciating the nature of ancient coasts and coastal peoples.[31]

Mediterranean Thalassography

Possession of an archipelago was the key to both political and economic power in the Mediterranean right through the early modern period. Coastal people occupied a narrow margin with mountains or deserts to the rear and, in the case of the northern shores, a sea of islands at their front door. They lived in a kind of waterland that has no counterpart today but was common enough in earlier periods. Peninsulas surrounded on three sides by water were originally thought of as "almost islands," for they too belonged more to water than to land. In many old European languages the term *island* combined the term for water (*is*) with the term for land, suggesting an amphibious condition. Waterlands included not only islands but also wetlands. Islands were ideal places for exchange, and when they did not exist, trading peoples created them. The earliest inhabitants of what is now Venice were fishers occupying a marshy tidal lagoon. In time, they would create a metropolis built on pilings that by the eighth century would come within the orbit of the Byzantine empire and eventually established its own colonies around the Adriatic.[32]

The notion of *archipelago* originally embraced both land and water. The Aegean Sea, bordering both the Balkan and Anatolian peninsulas, was initially know as Archipelago. It was only later that the term came to be applied exclusively to the islands, and ultimately to any group of islands. Eventually *islands* came to mean lands surrounded by water, but for a very long time the term was applied to any isolated place, including entirely landlocked territories.[33]

Islands loomed large in the ancient world. In our modern continentalized understanding of space, islands isolate and diminish, but in the amphibious world of the ancient Mediterranean, islands connected and enhanced. When the Phoenicians broke out of the Mediterranean into the Atlantic, the first thing they looked for were islands where they could set up trading stations. Islands on the African and European west coasts would play a disproportionate role in the development of cultural as well as economic exchange for centuries to come, for they were the nodal points in a world of movement that had been central to the life of pre-historic foragers and ancient mariners alike. This was an economy and culture that, in contrast to the agrarian interiors, lived by movement and perished by stasis. Coastal societies are best described by their routes rather than their roots; perhaps this is why coastal peoples have been so invisible to historians, who find mobile populations hard to pin down.[34]

Like islands, Greek city-states faced the sea, more connected to it than to their hinterland territories. The same was true of Venice and other coastal trading centers. In the Mediterranean, a unique form of empire developed, the thalassocracy—one that depended less on domination of the land than on mastery of sea lanes and coastal enclaves. Thalassocracy had various purposes, more mercantile in the case of the Phoenicians, more military in the case of the Greeks, but all depended on sea rather than land power. Greek thalassocracies spread island to island, penin-sula to peninsula. A strategy called *epiteichismos* was to plant enclaves on alien coasts, in such a way that Cicero could say, "The shores of Greece are like hems stitched on the lands of barbarian peoples." Greece was where Greeks were. It was less a territory than a collection of shores. The Ro-mans were a more interior agrarian people, but their cities were equally insular, set apart from the countryside. The notion of a territorial state fo-cused on the lands within fixed borders was also unknown to them. Like the Greeks, they were empire builders, focused not on contiguous lands but on networks of enclaves possessing commercial and military value. Rome's empire consisted of islandlike cities connected, in this case, by roads as well as seas, but consistent with the ancient presumption that the world is by nature islanded. Theirs was a distinctly archipelagic rather than continental spatiality. And this would persist for centuries before giving way to what Denis Cosgrove has called a "land-based, territorial-izing vision," only in the nineteenth century.[35]

The ancient Greeks understood themselves to be an insular people, on land as well as at sea; it has been said that Greek city-states were like "is-lands on dry land." Insularity was regarded as a strength, and water was an opportunity rather than a barrier. Thales, a native of seventh-century BCE Militos on the Anatolian coast, was the first to define water as the basic element of all life, and his students thought of the earth as a disk floating on primordial waters. It was another native of Militos, Hecataeus, who drew up the first world map around 500 BCE.[36]

In time, the Greeks and Romans would explore the western reaches of the Mediterranean and the Atlantic coasts as far north as the British Isles, which they called the Tin Isles for the metal they traded for there.

Hecataeus imagined the earth itself to be an island, Orbis Terrarum, surrounded by a raging river that he called Oceanus. He had no concept of continents but instead thought of earth as an island divided into three parts that we can readily recognize as Africa, Asia, and Europe. And he placed the Mediterranean, together with the Black Sea, at the very center of the earth island. Like all good cartographers, he placed his own home, Militos, at dead center.

The Greeks had already gone some way in transforming the eastern Mediterranean into one great pond, calling it "the Sea over by Us," but the Romans would go further. By 30 BC, their empire extended to all its shores, and they were ready to transfer the notion of Mare Nostrum from the Tyrrhenian Sea to the entirety of the Mediterranean.[37] But a sharp distinction was made between the inner sea and the external western ocean. The Mediterranean was known and bounded; Oceanus, however, was what the Greeks called *aperion*, infinite, mysterious, and terrifying. If the Mediterranean was home to the Romans as well as the Greeks, that which lay outside the Pillars of Hercules was an entirely different matter. It would remain an abyss for centuries.[38]

The idea that water represented chaos while land represented order was deeply rooted in the mythical geography of the ancient Middle East and subsequently elaborated and exaggerated first by Judaism and then by Christianity. The Old Testament horror of floods and its treatment of the sea as a barrier rather than an opportunity was deepened by Christians, who added to the pagan world's view of the ocean as a terrifying void by introducing an active agent, the newly invented figure of Satan. Beyond the confines of Mare Nostrum pagans too saw nothing but death and destruction, relieved only by the existence of Elysium and the Garden of Hesperides, thought to exist in the near Atlantic on what were known as the Isles of the Blest or the Fortunate Isles, the place of dead heroes, inaccessible to ordinary men. As Hesiod described them, on "the Islands of the Blest, bounded by deep-swirling ocean, they lived untouched by toil or sorrow. For them the grain-giving earth thrice yearly bears fruit as sweet as honey."[39]

If Christians imagined ancestors either in heaven above or in hell below, pagans provided a place for theirs in the sea. For them the edge of the sea was a *limen*, a boundary between the world of the living and the dead, a place of immense opportunity but also of great danger. There was a place to communicate with ancestors but also a haunted landscape. Stone and Bronze Age coastal peoples sometimes launched their dead from the shore or buried them on near shore islands, ensuring them an eternal life but also preventing them from returning to disturb the living. When burial at sea was not possible, the Norse were in the habit of interring in ship graves, another variation on the same theme. Mythic isles continued to provide consolation in the face of death for coastal peoples long after Christianity became the official religion of the Roman empire in the fourth century CE.[40]

Along North Atlantic Shores

The Atlantic poses a paradox: it was the last of the oceans to be mastered but arguably has been the one that has had the greatest influence over time. Humans were late in reaching both its northwestern and northeastern shores because of the great masses of snow and ice that covered them until ten thousand years ago. Retreating glaciers and rising waters resulted in exceptionally variegated coasts, with the greatest coast-to-inland ratios of almost any place in the world. The Atlantic edge was also distinguished by the amount of "drowned lands," the numbers of peninsulas and near-shore islands, and the depth of watersheds drained by great rivers that emptied into large estuaries. Until seas attained their present levels around 6500 BCE, what we now know as Europe extended westward to encompass the British Isles, including Ireland. Between Europe and Britain there existed forests and meadowlands that archaeologists have called Doggerland, after the now submerged Dogger Banks. The Baltic was even slower to gain its current contours, around 5000 BCE. What ultimately emerged in the Europe that Fernand Braudel called the western cape of Asia was characterized by great geological and environmental variation. This proved a great inducement to movement and to trade, a characteristic of all coasts, but one that was particularly pronounced on the European littoral.[41]

The first postglacial coastal foragers arrived in northwestern Europe between 9000 and 7000 BCE. There they found biodiversity greater than the Mediterranean's, complete with sea kales, sea turnips, parsnips, seaweed, and, of course, an abundance of shellfish. As they moved along-shore, they made particular use of estuaries, where archaeologists have found huge shell middens but also evidence of fishing and birding. Small islands just off the coasts were often the first places to be used by foragers. In a pattern repeated all along the Atlantic edge, the island of Gadir at the mouth of Río Gaudalete in what is now known as Andalusia was already settled by marine hunter-gatherers when it became a Phoenician trading post in the eighth century BCE. In the current Netherlands, foragers moved to the coast in summer, gathering foods and grazing animals on the rich marsh grasses there before retreating to higher ground in the winter. By 800 BCE they were settled on islands of their own making, farming and trading from what today are called polders.[42]

When agriculture arrived in western Europe beginning in 5000 BCE, it too came largely by sea, spread by the same marine foragers. Southeast England was populated by sea by about 4300 BCE by hunter-gatherers who carried elements of agriculture and husbandry with them, even though they did not immediately become full-time farmers. Using the navigational skills acquired over millennia, foragers were coasting around Ireland and western Scotland, arriving at the Orkney Islands by 3800 BCE. Often it was from the isles that the British mainlands were first inhabited. For a very long time, hunting and gathering seem to have mixed with planting and husbandry. Prehistoric British hunters cleared woodland and created water holes to draw their prey to them. Before they were gardeners they were gamekeepers. The same was true of marine foragers, who felt no need to turn to farming as long as the coastal ecotone was so productive.[43]

Like marine foragers elsewhere, these first coastal Europeans were highly mobile and predisposed to exchange, often on islands just offshore. As Barry Cunliffe points out, "they could be safe places, extraterritorial, where by agreement foreigners could stop over to create ports-of-trade." In the case of Atlantic Europe, trade preceded permanent settlement, but it was also the case that marine foragers developed more complex social organization than did their inland counterparts. And, strange as it may seem, it was these highly mobile people who were the first to take up more sedentary life forms, while the hinterland foragers stayed on the move much longer.[44]

As had been the case in the Mediterranean, the Atlantic coast was first discovered by sea and for a very long time remained more connected to it than to its own interior. On the broad coasts of northwestern Europe, the line between sea and land was never deeply etched, and like the archipelagic cultures of the Mediterranean, the coast incorporated the nearshore islands. But in contrast to the Mediterranean, the Atlantic edge was both a seaboard and a riverine civilization, because it was less hemmed in by mountains or deserts, and it extended well back from the sea, as far up rivers as the tides reached and often beyond. In Britain, the Netherlands, and the lands of the Baltic, "the influence of the sea in the past extended much further inland than the coastal margins." As long as boats were shallow draft, ports were more likely to be located well upriver, safer and with greater access to inland trading networks. As we have seen, foragers made no sharp distinction between fresh and salt water, moving forward and backward across the tide lines on a seasonal basis. This would remain the case in Atlantic Europe until nearly the modern era, when deep-draft ships meant for ocean going dictated locating ports on the coast itself.[45]

Atlantic Europe had many seas, named for the nearest landfalls, more like what we would call gulfs or straits than great oceans. The discovery of a large boat at Dover thought to date two thousand years prior to the arrival of the Romans suggests a series of "sea highways" that had no counterparts on the still impenetrable land. The shallow seas of the Baltic had many coastal archipelagos similar to those in the Mediterranean. Aland, the name of a cluster of islands that lies today between Sweden and Finland, originally meant "waterland," a distinctive seascape set apart from both the mainlands and the Baltic itself. In northern Europe water also defined territory, because with the collapse of the Roman empire, the interior fragmented and states near the coasts organized around water rather than land. What H. C. Darby called the medieval "sea-states" emerged, creating a "rim of states which, at various times, utilized its marginal seas as so many bases for political units."[46]

Opposing coasts had more in common with one another than either did with their own interiors, but medieval thalassocracies, including the one created by the Normans, stretched alongshore from the North Atlantic edge to the western Mediterranean. The Venetians consolidated a sea-state in the Adriatic begun by the Romans, while during the twelfth and thirteenth centuries Sweden dominated the northern rim of the Baltic. The late medieval English used their sea power to dominate western France, turning the channel between them into what was known for a long time as the English Sea, while the Byzantine empire's control of the islands and shores of the eastern Mediterranean was far stronger than its dominion over its hinterlands. The doctrine of Mare Claustrum, endorsed by the medieval papacy, legitimized the sea-state until the sixteenth and seventeen centuries, when sovereignty was finally vested exclusively in territory and oceans were declared Mare Librum by Hugo Grotius. Even then, however, the notion of sea territories persisted, for European empires invariably extended their power along sea lanes even when they did not claim sovereignty over the Atlantic Ocean as a whole.[47]

The attachment that Europeans had to their coastal seas did not extend to what the ancients called Oceanus, the raging river that surrounded the earth island in which Europe was a backward western periphery. Northern Europeans were no more eager than the Greeks or Romans to test the poet Pindar's warning that "what lies beyond cannot be trodden by the wise or the unwise. One cannot cross from Gadir towards the dark west. Turn again the sails towards the dry land of Europe." Before 1500 Europeans were, with the exception of the Norse, a coasting rather than a deep-sea culture, preferring to sail within sight of land, comforted by the presence of islands and peninsulas that buffered them from the ocean itself. Their earliest charts, the *portolani*, were, like the *periploi*, focused on landmarks and harbors, providing little information about the ocean as such.[48]

Origins of a Coastal Culture

Northern Europeans inherited the Mediterranean's coastal culture, including its mythical geography. Sea and land continued to be seen not just as different elements but as different worlds. Land stood for order, sea meant chaos. Pagans associated land with life, the sea with death, and the coast with mysterious supernatural occurrences. Christianity was equally sea-fearing, associating the ocean with the realm of Satan. God's influence was stronger on land than at sea; farmers were thought more pious than sailors. This sharp dichotomy between the terrestrial and marine worlds made the coast itself a very special place, however, a threshold like no other. As Barry Cunliffe has put it: "If then, the domains of land and sea are conceived of as separate systems subject to their own very different supernatural powers, the interface between them was a liminal place, and as such was dangerous."[49]

Thresholds are always precarious but seductive places, freighted with dread as well as invested with great expectations. They were associated with both arrivals and departures, the beginnings of life and its ending. While day-to-day crossing of the tide line in quest of subsistence was rarely ritualized, long-distance voyaging was treated as a passage from one world to another and invested with great symbolic meaning. Voyages across waters were viewed as transformative. Elite voyagers were invested with great prestige, while dead heroes were imagined to have been transported to an eternal life on legendary islands like the Isles of the Blest, which were thought to lie beyond the Pillars of Hercules. The Celts and Norse had imagined the dead to exist offshore, and they too salted the far sea with legendary isles, to which Christians added their own stock of both hellish and paradisiacal apparitions in subsequent centuries. The sea was the place where they preferred to locate their dreams of peace and plenty, usually on Edenic islands whose allure would eventually overcome the fear of the oceanic waters that surrounded them. But in the meantime water was a place of no return, a depository of all that was unwanted on land, not just the wastes generated by everyday life but the bodies of deformed babies, suicides, and deviants. As both paganism's place of no return and Christianity's Satan's playground, the sea was stocked with dangers, which provided cautionary tales for credulous seamen.[50]

Near-shore islands were themselves thresholds where strangers could come and go freely, thus facilitating trade and communication between territorial groups that were otherwise hostile to one another. As *limen*, islands provided passages between worlds. Believed to exist outside of time, they were burial places for the dead. The Phoenicians and the Greeks had used them in this way, and for centuries the coastal societies of Europe treated them as "liminal places, neither entirely of land nor of the sea . . . endowed with unusual power in the minds of those who lived at the interface between land and ocean." Ancient coasts were replete with hybrid shape-changing creatures. In the folklore of the North Atlantic, seals were thought to shed their skins in order to become human. Selkies or selchies, as they were known in the Orkney and Shetland Islands, were believed to establish romantic relationships with humans, unions that usually ended in tragedy when the seal creatures reappropriated their skins and returned to the sea.[51]

Selkies were in many ways similar to mermaids and sirens, animal-fish hybrids whose legends go back at least five thousand years to Babylonian mythology. It was on coasts, where the aquatic and the terrestrial overlapped, that hybridity was most easily imagined. Before humankind ventured into the deep oceans, mythical creatures, the mermaid and the merman, first appeared in the half-known world of the shore. The almost human features of certain animals like the manatee made them objects of perpetual fascination. The Greeks knew them as sirens, accounting for their scientific name, *Serranus*. When Columbus encountered manatees in his Caribbean reconnaissance, he recognized them as creatures from ancient literature.[52]

Richard Ellis has shown how various sea mammals took on mythological dimensions before ultimately being identified as actual animals. However, because they originated in the human imagination, they have tended to live on as long as the fears and desires that generated them persist. They simply migrated from folklore to film, from religion to literature. Mermaids and mermans were expressions of the attraction of the sea but also cautions about its dangers. Before the eighteenth century, coasts were primarily what Yi-Fu Tuan has called landscapes of fear.[53]

Belief in mermaids seems to have reached a crescendo in the late eighteenth century, when fakes, constructed of monkey bodies and fishtails, many of them manufactured in Asia, flooded Western markets. Circus impresario J. T. Barnum exhibited his "Feejee Mermaid" in New York in the 1840s, but by that time the appeal was already fading, as it had become apparent that what had been taken for sirens were actually the Atlantic manatee and the Pacific dugong. By then, coasts were becoming much better known, and the realm of the mysterious and horrific moved well offshore. The new sea monsters—the sea serpent, the great whale, and the killer shark—were all deep-water creatures. In the twentieth century, when the deeps were more thoroughly explored, these were transformed from objects of fear into endangered species to be feared *for*. The landscape of fear has shifted once again, this time to outer space.[54]

Coasts have always been the places that humans have turned to explore the mysteries of life and death. Not surprisingly, they have long been associated with the sacred. The coast of Peru was the site of elaborate burial rituals as early as five thousand years ago, and chambered tombs existed on the shores of northwestern Europe long before the Egyptians built their pyramids. The intersection of land and sea appears to have stimulated human symbolic activity from the very beginning. Both pagans and Christians believed that islands and promontories were "sacred to the gods." Places like the islet of Hieronisos off Cyprus hosted the cult of Apollo before it became a shrine to St. George. Other Mediterranean islands were sacred to pagans, then to Christians, and ultimately to Islam. On the edge of the Atlantic, the isle of Lavret in the estuary of the Loire was said to have harbored a prehistoric women's fertility cult. Such places were later used by Christian missionaries and pilgrims. The pagan shore was the location of numerous rites meant to bless the seafarer and propitiate an animate sea which was thought to have a mood and a will all its own that no human being should challenge unaided by the gods. All along the Atlantic coasts, priests still annually bless fleets, even if this is now more for the benefit of tourists than for the moribund fishing industry. As a place of mystery and magic, nothing has ever quite rivaled the shore.[55]

Atlantic Borderlands

Of course, coasts opened the way not only to trade and cultural development but also to invasion and conquest. Europeans had been fortifying their headlands for centuries, but their shores remained porous, without defensible borders. Pirates and raiders had been around for millennia, but nothing matched the intrusive power of the eighth-century Norse, perhaps the most successful of all Europe's ancient coastal societies, one that had been in the process of development from the moment that foragers arrived in Scandinavia. From the beginning, the Norse had been an amphibious people who were as much at home on water as on land. Until the thirteenth and fourteenth centuries, their homeland was a region without roads, where everything moved by water and the central symbol was the boat, which not only transported the living but delivered the dead to the next world. The Norse built houses and churches in the form of ships; they consigned their dead to vessels buried in the famous ship graves that still distinguish the Scandinavian landscape from any other. What Gunilla Larsson has called a "maritime" culture extended deep inland, as far as the rivers would take shallow-draft boats. It lasted until the thirteenth century, when the region was finally feudalized, power shifting from water to land, and "the ship as a key symbol was replaced by a knight on a horse."[56]

Larsson is right to note that marine culture permeated deeper inland there than at any other place in northwest Europe. Nevertheless, the Norse are best described as a coastal rather than a maritime people, for they remained deeply attached to land even as they ventured on water. To be sure, they were remarkable sailors, but like all ancient mariners, they were quite sedentary, developing their own modes of agriculture and animal husbandry. As pagans, they regarded the shore as a *limen*, a place to offer sacrifices to water deities and conduct rites to enable their ships pass from the familiar world of land to the dangerous domain of the sea, rites that were replicated in their funeral ceremonies when the ship provided conveyance between the world of the living and that of the dead.[57]

Until population pressures pushed them from their coasts in the eighth century, they remained farmer-mariners, more noted for their trading skills than for their raiding prowess. On places like the Island of Gotland in the western Baltic, farms extended right down to the shore, and their inhabitants moved easily between fishing and farming. Later, when fishing on the Norwegian coast became more commercialized, there was greater division of labor, but the presumed right of all peoples to act as marine foragers was never challenged in Scandinavia.[58]

Even after they launched themselves farther from home, the Norse voyaged, as did the Polynesians, with the seeds and animals necessary to recreate a viable agrarian existence. In this respect they were the Phoenicians of the North, moving from coast to coast, island to island,

FIGURE 13. Tjelvar's shipgrave, Boge, Gotland. Photo by Owe Ronström.

reproducing their culture wherever they went. The Norse moved north and south, east and west, using the river systems of what is now Russia to reach all the way to the Bosporus, while sweeping down on the British Isles and mastering the coasts of France before moving into the Mediterranean. By the ninth century they were extending their range far into the North Sea itself, colonizing the Faeroe Islands in 800, arriving in Iceland in the 870s. Irish monks probably preceded them by some years, but they were no match for the pagan Vikings, who would move on to Greenland a century later, reaching the shores of Newfoundland around the year 1000.

The navigational feats of the Norse match those of the argonauts of the Pacific, who were already completing their settlement of remote Oceania about the time that the Vikings were pushing off from their native shores. But it would be wrong to think of the Vikings as anything but an exceptionally amphibious seaboard civilization bent on exploring the coasts and islands of the North Sea. In Norse cosmology, the world was composed of two concentric circles. The inner one (Midgadr) was fit for humans, the outer circle (Utgadr) belonged to monsters. Separating them was their version of Oceanus, know as Uthaf, which they placed to the west, beyond what they thought was a vast inland sea stretching from the coasts of Scandinavia all the way to what we now think of as the shores and islands of North America.[59]

The Norse version of Mare Nostrum contained not only the British Isles but also the Faeroes and Iceland. They appear to have imagined it as being bordered on the north by what they called the "Cold Coast," an extension of the Norwegian shore imagined to reach Greenland, and to the south by a northern extension of Africa that was called Vinland. To the west were Helleland, positioned roughly where we would place Baffin Island, and Markland, where Labrador should be, with Skralinge Land and Vinlandia occupying the location of Newfoundland. While we have no texts or maps from the Viking period itself, a later manuscript expresses what may have been the contemporary understanding: "To the south of Greenland lies Helluland and then Markland; and from there it is not far to Vinland, which some people think leads to Africa." The Skalholt Map, drawn by Bishop Thordu Thorkaksson in 1570, clearly represents an enclosed body of water, a Norse Mediterranean.[60]

There is no indication that Leif Erickson and his companions understood themselves to have crossed an ocean or discovered a New World.[61] The Norse were simply mastering an inland sea, coasting and island-hopping in the manner of ancient mariners everywhere. What they managed to do had already been done in the Indian Ocean and in the Pacific: mentally enclosing a body of water, taming its terrifying terrible vacuity by endowing it imaginatively with embracing coasts and filling it with islands. They made voyages longer than those attempted by Europeans before but not qualitatively different from those accomplished by other ancient coasting peoples.[62]

It would be another five hundred years before Europeans were ready to take on transoceanic travel as such. As in turned out, the Viking voyages were a kind of interlude that found no imitator during the later Middle Ages, when the Atlantic remained a formidable mental as well as physical barrier. Europeans became more comfortable as seafarers, but they showed no desire to be oceangoers. Their *mappaemundi* continued to locate them on an earth island girdled by a vast sea that only gradually lost the features of an angry, impassable river. In the course of the late Middle Ages the void that had been the Atlantic was gradually filled with legendary islands. But these remained as far off-limits as they had been in Pindar's day.

When the eastern Mediterranean was closed to them in the fourteenth century, thus cutting them off from trade with the Far East by way of the

FIGURE 14. Skalholt Map by Bishop Thordu Thorkaksson, 1670. Courtesy of Wikimedia Commons.

Indian Ocean, Europeans began to explore other possibilities, including coasting around Africa. In the course of their exploratory voyages along west Africa, the Portuguese discovered by accident the near Atlantic isles of Madeira and the Canaries, but once again, this was an extension of ancient coasting and island-hopping rather than a new departure in maritime adventure. Then came the extraordinary voyages of Columbus and the unintended discovery of a New World, which would ultimately wholly discredit the idea of Oceanus encircling Orbis Terrarum, establishing once and for all the existence of the Atlantic and Pacific Oceans and beginning the era of transoceanic travel. Yet Europe remained a seaboard rather than an oceanic civilization. As we shall see, European explorers brought a littoral mindset to the New World, where they met other coastal peoples who were in many ways more like them than different. In most respects, early modern seaboard civilization was the continuation of ancient coasting, now extended aggressively around the Atlantic and Pacific rims by northwest European thalassocracies more dynamic and powerful than anything the world had previously known.

3 · SEA FRONTIERS OF THE EARLY MODERN ATLANTIC

The river is within us, the sea is all about us; The sea is the land's edge also ...   T. S. ELIOT, "THE DRY SALVAGES"[1]

Foragers were still foraging when the next phase of North Atlantic coastal history—a transoceanic phase—began in the late fifteenth century. Conventional history emphasizes change at the expense of continuity. We are told that the voyages of Columbus opened a new era, yet in fact the vast bulk of marine activity continued to involve sailing along rather than across the newly discovered seas. The exploration of the New World proceeded island to island, peninsula to peninsula, using vessels not that different from those used for millennia. As we shall see, the fisheries of the early modern era were outgrowths of their medieval predecessors, transoceanic trade was an extension of coastal commerce, and the imperial practices of the early modern European empires look much like those of ancient and medieval thalassocacies.

When they could manage it, early modern mariners preferred to sail around rather than across oceans. They voyaged in the manner of the old *costteggiare*, hugging the shore as much as possible. Their rare ventures offshore were encouraged by the mistaken belief that the sea was filled with islands, providing short, safe passage. When Columbus blundered into the New World, he failed to see that its lands were not another archipelago, easily traversed by water, but an impassable landmass. It would be a very long time, almost three hundred years, before Europeans realized the full extent of the Americas' continental character and grasped the fact that they might have to abandon the ways of seaborne empires for those of territorial states. In the interim, however, they created a new kind of seaboard civilization, one that extended around the rim of the North Atlantic, populated by coastal peoples who had more in common with one another than with their hinterland neighbors.[2]

Brethren of the Water, Souls of the Edge

Justifiable fear of sea-wrought damage caused northern Europeans to live lightly on their Atlantic edge. Coasts are the most ambiguous and unstable of all geographical features. Since the great upwelling at the end of the last ice age, the sea has risen periodically, initially in the early Roman period and then twice during the Middle Ages. During the second of several medieval high-water periods between 1099 and 1570, storm surges inundated 286 towns and villages in the North Sea basin. Perhaps the best known is Dunwich on England's East Anglian littoral, in the twelfth and thirteenth centuries a major port with a population of three thousand people, famous for the wool trade and its eight churches. Then, beginning with a great storm in 1286, its harbor was destroyed and whole neighborhoods were lost to the sea. Two subsequent storm surges, one in 1328, another in 1347, destroyed Dunwich's economic viability but not its political privileges. Until these were abolished by the Reform Act of 1832, the town was a notorious "rotten borough," sending two members of Parliament to Westminister. Today Dunwich is a village of about three hundred people, still losing ground to the North Sea. Everywhere in the medieval era storms took lives as well as lands. In what the Dutch call the "Grote Mandrenke," the great drowning of 1362, between eleven and thirty thousand people were swept away.[3]

It was not just water that drowned good land. A sandstorm around 2500 BCE may have caused the abandonment, after more than six hundred years of habitation, of the remarkable Orcadian Neolithic village of Skara Brae on the edge of the Bay of Skaill. In northern Jutland, near the Danish resort town of Skagen, the tower of a church—known locally as the Buried Church—rises quite unexpectedly from the dunes. It was erected around 1400 but was abandoned in 1591, when a combination of deforestation and overgrazing, coinciding with violent winds, caused old Skagen to be flooded with sand. The Scottish village of Culbin suffered the same fate when local thatchers overharvested the marram grass that held the local dunes in place. As late as the 1840s a church on the Cornish coast had to be dug out after a storm. From Holland east to the shores of the Baltic, many villages lie beneath what to sun worshipers and bathers now seems a wholly benign landscape.[4]

Even as coasts expanded and contracted with rising and falling sea levels, coastal peoples had adapted by moving both inland and coastwise. Northern Europeans found it easier to retreat from the sea than did Mediterranean populations hemmed in by mountains and deserts.

Northwestern Europe's broad and gently sloping watersheds gave access to huge interiors that could be navigated by shallow-bottomed boats carrying trade great distances up rivers and through lakes. Mediterranean peoples made good use of their archipelagos, while northern Europeans had the advantage of a vast waterland of rivers and lakes. They farmed and fished, built settlements and trading posts, but were always ready to move on when waters threatened.

Water was the lifeline of this edge species. They had learned to cope with the coastal flooding that refreshed their meadows, offering a haven to wildfowl and fish and renewing the supply of peat they relied on for fuel. The extent of flooding in the area of southwest England known as the Somerset Levels is recorded in the place-names of its dry places—Isle of Avalon (Glastonbury) and Isle of Atheney—which are now completely landlocked but in the Middle Ages were often surrounded by water. In the Fenlands on the east coast, the Isle of Ely (Island of Eels) was literally an island until the seventeenth century, when the wetlands were finally drained.

Water also gave access to the deep interior, to trade, and thus to a bounty not available on the shore itself. Life depended on keeping rivers and watercourses open; when these silted up, canals were built. Cities were almost always located on rivers or estuaries, often on islands that provided access to water on all sides. As these cities grew in size, canals were dug to make their centers even more accessible. Venice, Amsterdam, and Stockholm were all archipelagic by design, canalized by the efforts of their inhabitants. All experienced the threat of flooding but also embraced the sea, a practice that later port cities, with firmer linkages to the hinterland, abandoned.[5]

The best defense had always been retreat. Since 500 BCE, lowlanders situated along the North Sea had learned to keep dry by building mounds called *terps* or *wieden*. Serious dike building began only in the thirteenth century, with windmills to pump out water coming about two hundred years later. To those sixteenth-century coastal people who inhabited what is now the Netherlands, it seemed that the sea "sleeps neither by day or by night, but charges savagely like a lion to devour the entire land." But the efforts at diking and draining were just as great a danger to land as the sea itself. The removal of water caused the peaty land to shrink and subside, causing even more flooding. As the Netherlands urbanized in the late Middle Ages, wetlands nearest the cities were drained, requiring even more herculean efforts to keep the sea at bay.[6]

FIGURE 15. Drowned church, Skagen, Denmark, abandoned 1775. Courtesy of Wikipedia.

The technology of drainage spread gradually throughout Europe and ultimately to the New World. The English shore opposite the Netherlands constituted another wetland, the Fens, which had been inhabited by hunter-gatherers since the Stone Age, water people who wanted nothing to do with drainage schemes that would destroy their precious ecotone.

These people had earned the reputation of being the "Fen Tygers," were said to walk on stilts and "apply their mindes, to grasing, fishing, and fowling." They were very different from those who were known as the Upland-men, inland agrarians who regarded them "a kind of people according the nature of the place where they dwell, rude, unciville, envious." Absentee landlords regarded flooded lands as "utterly wasted" and moved to have them drained. By the 1630s they were ready to bring in Dutch engineers to assist them in what they called their "Adventures." In the process of draining and enclosing, this massive project displaced the inhabitants of the wetlands, who regarded the marshes as a great common to which they had time-honored use rights. The displaced turned to the courts but in 1641 also "took arms, and in a riotous manner, they fell upon the Adventurers, broke the sluices, laid waste to their lands, threw down their fences, spoiled their corn, demolished their houses, and forcibly retained possession of the land." They were particularly hostile to the Dutch engineers, but it is clear from their protest songs that these lowlanders felt their whole way of life threatened by the Upland-men.[7]

> Come, Brethren of the water, and let us all assemble.
> To treat upon this matter, and make us quake and tremble:
> For we shall rue it, if 't be true, that Fens be undertaken,
> And where we feed in Fen and Reed, they'll feed both Beef and Bacon.

Whole communities rose up against the enclosures, "a crowd of women and men, armed with sythes and pitchforks, uttered threatening words against any one who would drive them from the fens." In the name of agricultural improvement, the adventurers were on a mission to tame not only the forces of nature but also the stilt walkers, whom they regarded as little better than pagan savages:[8]

> I sing Floods muzzled and the Ocean tam'd
> Luxurious Rivers govern'd and reclam'd
> Water with Banks confin'd as in a Gaol
> Till kinder Sluices let them go on Bail.

> There shall a change of Men and Manners be;
> Hearts thick and rough as Hydes, shall feel Remorse
> And Souls of Edge shall understand Discourse,
> New hands shall learn to Work, forget to Steal,
> New leggs shall go to church, new knees shall kneel.

It is no wonder that many fenlanders were republicans during the English Civil War. Coastal people had long had a reputation for being beyond God's as well as man's law. A hundred years later, the Fens were still considered by the great agricultural reformer Arthur Young to be "so wild a country [that] nurses up a race of people as wild as the fen; and there the morals and eternal welfare of numbers are hazarded and ruined for the lack of enclosure." As late as the mid-nineteenth century, these coastal people were infamous for their unruliness, and the Souls of the Edge were still thought to be beyond the pale of civilization.[9]

Facing the Atlantic

Initially, Europeans relied on a strategy of defense in depth to protect themselves against the sea and enemies who might come by sea. They located their ports well inland, in fresh rather than saltwater locations. In the early Middle Ages, Sweden's most important entrepôt was Sigtuna, now a small landlocked town west of Stockholm. Located inland on Lake Malaren, it gave access to both the Baltic and the interior, making it a royal and commercial center from 1000 to 1300. Then it gave way to Stockholm, a cluster of Baltic islets that were not even mentioned in the historical record until 1252. By the fourteenth century Sigtuna was in eclipse, becoming what it is today, a small tourist town of no great economic importance. The association of ports with upriver locations persisted into the early modern period, however. In the New World as well as the Old, trading sites were initially located upstream, often at the "fall line," where upland regions met the coastal plains. These became ports, some of them, like Albany, New York, and Richmond, Virginia, far upriver. Rapids and falls blocked river traffic beyond them but provided ideal spots for mills and industrial enterprises. In the case of New Hampshire, fall-line mill towns like Durham and Exeter were initially more important than seaside Portsmouth. In California, the ports of Sacramento and Stockton lay far inland, as important as San Francisco in the early days of the Gold Rush.

Movement toward the sea has been a long, complicated process, but we can detect its beginnings in the late Middle Ages, when entrepôts everywhere were moving toward the coast as a result of the damming and silting up of rivers and the inability of larger seagoing craft to reach far inland. York, Ypres, and Ghent gave up their status of ports to become landlocked trading centers. As we have seen, markets had long been associated with edges and particularly with shores, which were considered

neutral venues where trade could be conducted freely. From the thirteenth century onward, a northern trade in herring developed initially
not in ports but on the shore of Falsterbo, now a part of the southern
Swedish province of Scania. A part of the domain of the Danish king,
this beach was open to foreign traders who came there in both spring
and fall, anchoring offshore but setting up temporary villages called *fitten* where they would conduct their business. At its peak, the seven kilometers of Falsterbro beach attracted representatives of thirty-five trading
cities and corporations, together with a horde of victualers, entertainers,
and prostitutes. In the interim Falsterbo was, like inland market sites, an
abandoned place, with only the empty *fitten* to suggest its importance to
the international fish trade.[10]

In time, entrepôts like Falsterbo strand gave way to more permanent
trading places. Initially places outside the walls of cities, they became port
cities with permanent infrastructure, deep harbors protected by break-
waters, waterfronts with service facilities, warehouses, and sailor towns.
As ports came to be associated with the edge of the sea, the old strategy
of retreat gave way to a new, more aggressive posture—new harbors were
built and piers thrust outward. By the sixteenth century Europe's Atlantic
edge was no longer the end of the Old World but the beginning of a New
World that had begun to encompass the Atlantic and beyond.[11]

Still, Europeans remained more sea-fearing than seafaring, stubbornly
coastal. In the late Middle Ages, European alongshore trading intensified.
In a similar manner, fishing, which until the late Middle Ages was almost
entirely a freshwater operation, began to migrate coastward. Once again,
changes in land use, particularly the building of mill dams, along with
silting due to deforestation, and pollution of water caused by animal and
human populations, so altered the environment that Europeans began to
turn from fresh to salt water for the supply of fish that in the course of the
Middle Ages had become a central part of the diet required of practicing
Catholics. Populations recovering from the visitation of the Black Death
in the fourteenth century began to encroach again on coastal wetlands.
The foragers who had occupied these waterlands for millennia fought
back against drainage and enclosures, but they were now confronted with
increasingly powerful royal and ecclesiastical establishments.

The erosion of the hunting and gathering rights of ordinary people has
a very long history. Until the Norman Conquest of 1066, English people
had access to all tidal waters. When this was abridged by the Norman
kings, who licensed the fishers, a struggle ensued, leading to the revo-
cation of the crown's privilege in the Magna Carta of 1215. The coastal

peoples had their victory, but their rights were limited to swimming fish, not shellfish. In subsequent centuries, great landowners continued to encroach on customary use rights, producing a perpetual resistance by coastal and river peoples.[12]

By 1500, coasts and interiors were more sharply differentiated, not just economically but socially and politically. The interior was by then thoroughly feudalized, controlled by increasingly powerful landed aristocracies and kingdoms, its trade dominated by urban merchants who were eager to monopolize commerce previously carried out uncontrolled and untaxed by coastal peoples. But just as the land had refused to be swallowed by the sea, the sea did not yield easily to the land. The coast was largely independent not only of aristocratic and royal control but also of guilds and urban corporations. Coastal Europeans were by then what Barry Cunliffe has called a "cosmopolitan brotherhood," the product of millennia of alongshore free movement of trade and peoples. Efforts by interior lords to redefine free trade as smuggling were met by resistance from the Souls of the Edge. They continued to operate out of small, often temporary landings, many of them located on islands that maintained their extraterritorial status and independence. The coast during the late medieval and early modern periods has been rightfully described as a "zone of transition or of transmission, an 'open' frontier to a wider world, far less regulated and controlled than the feudal demesne or the core areas of the bureaucratic-military state."[13]

Holding Helm and Plow: The Rise of the Protomaritime Economy

Our current inclination is to draw a sharp line between land and sea, but such a distinction wholly distorts the past, especially the early modern period, when most fishers were farmers, with, as the Swedes say, "one boot in the boat and the other in the field." Orcadians were said to be farmers who fished, while on the Shetlands farmers were known as "fishermen with a plough." Inland farmers became increasingly market-oriented and specialized, but those at the coast mixed occupations, combining fishing, gathering, and gardening, taking advantage of the full range of resources offered by the coastal ecotone. During the Middle Ages, feudal lords encouraged their tenants to take up maritime pursuits by requiring rents in both kind and cash from fishing. The church also pushed smallholders toward the sea by demanding tithes from the same source. But the peasants involved rarely lived on the coast itself, but came down to the sea only seasonally. On the South Devon shores, they kept what were called "cellars" where they stored their boats and gear, continuing until the fifteenth century to live inland, where they felt secure both from storms and from pirates.[14]

Until the late medieval period in England, "most fishing was still firmly in the hands of farmers who fished on a part-time basis." Women as well as men participated in a range of activities that were variable by both season and location. This flexible economy is best compared to inland protoindustrialization emerging in the same period. At that point farming was combined with craft and resource production—mining, weaving, smithing, and tanning—all of which took place in a household rather than factory setting, often involving all members of the family, women as well as men, children and adults. What might be called a *protomaritime* economy was developing around the rim of the North Atlantic. Like the protoindustrial development, it was largely decentralized, taking place outside major cities and ports, organized by ordinary people in pursuit of a better life than they had as peasants exclusively working the land.[15]

The coast was a kind of frontier, less regulated than the interiors and providing people with a greater degree of freedom to explore new possibilities. If in earlier periods the coast extended far inland, now it moved seaward, encompassing near-shore islands. In the fifteenth century the Portuguese began turning their backs on the Iberian interior, exploring the coast of Africa and, in the process, discovering by accident the Madeira and Azores. The Basques, Bretons, and British also turned to the sea, not in search of new lands but to find new stocks of fish for flourishing inland markets. Notably, it was not so much the lure of the sea but the push from the land that initiated this fundamental transformation. What was emerging was not so much a maritime society but a more dynamic and innovative edge species, one that was about to make itself at home throughout the entire North Atlantic rim.

By the late Middle Ages, poorer peasants were concentrated along the coasts. Population growth in the sixteenth and seventeenth century pushed many from the interiors. Later, enclosures and clearances would cause still more to move to the shores and into the protomarine economy. The poor rented or squatted on small pieces of land that could not by themselves yield a livelihood. Inland, the impoverished smallholder would turn to protoindustrial pursuits to survive. On the coast, the poor turned to the sea to supplement the land. Their numbers grew and the density of coastal settlement increased, with more sedentary fishing communities replacing the older temporary sites. but not in the way that one might imagine. The concentration at the coast did not necessarily result in the kind of close-knit fishing villages that are the legacy of the eighteenth and nineteenth centuries. Before then a generally scattered pattern of settlement persisted. In many places on the Atlantic shore "there are no villages. Every fisherman lives in a house apart. Collectivity does not extend beyond the family."[16]

The fisher-farmers spread laterally along the coast, concentrated around landings accessible to small boats rather than around the deep-water harbors necessary to larger craft. The specialized fishing village did not emerge until the eighteenth century, when farming and fishing finally began to differentiate and land and sea were rent apart. Early ports must be understood as places of "change, flux, and unpredictability. [For] it is what they were built on." Later, the myth of fishing folk as a distinct, rooted people, as a race part, emerged to obscure the prior history of the protomaritime edge species that exploited both sides of the tide line. One of the best descriptions of such people comes to us from a condescending report on the people of Thanet, a Thameside community just downriver from London, who were described as "amphibious animals, who get their living both by sea and land . . . equally skilled in holding helm and plough, according to the seasons of the year."[17]

The myth of a separate fisher folk arose simultaneously with the myth of the professional mariner, products of the emerging romance with the sea already visible in the eighteenth century but emerging full-blown in the nineteenth century. We tend to exaggerate the proportion of full-time mariners in the early modern world. Seafaring had always been part time, taken up seasonally by men (and sometimes women) who were firmly attached to the land, often as a phase of life rather than a lifelong endeavor. When full-time commercial sea fishing was taken up, it was, out of necessity, the fate of the poorest of the poor, landless or unmarried young men, who had no farm or craft to fall back on and whose access to a household and family of their own depended on spending years in celibate service or indenture either waiting for an inheritance or saving for a homestead.[18]

Those who fished were never a race apart but a motley crew, not at all conformable to the stereotype of the seafarer that nineteenth-century fiction writers conjured into existence. It is an error of retrospect to label fishers "traditional," either closer to nature or survivals of archaic culture; in fact, coastal communities were more dynamic than many of their inland neighbors. Anything but traditional in habit and outlook, fishing folk were the product of changes on the land which had given disinherited smallholders no choice but "to fish or starve." A comforting image of the emerging fishing village as a steady point in a rapidly changing world later appealed to nineteenth-century Europeans and Americans undergoing the wrenching experience of urbanization and industrialization, but the myth obscured the fact that the proliferation of fishing villages was largely due to the very same set of changes that were creating a huge demand for fish among city folk. Well into the nineteenth century, the entire rim of the North Atlantic would remain protomaritime, a fragmented world of tiny outports whose inhabitants had one boot in the boat, the other in the field.[19]

The Migratory Fishery

What then took Europeans offshore without removing them entirely from the land? Ironically, it was what was happening not at sea but on land, specifically the environmental crisis that was changing the relationship between land and water in the High Middle Ages, first inland and then on the coasts themselves. In the early Middle Ages interior Europe was still heavily forested, and its streams "ran clear, cool, and stable." There were apparently sufficient freshwater fish to satisfy subsistence needs and even support a bit of recreational fishing. The banks of rivers and the shores of lakes offered an exceptionally rich edge. When asked by an English abbot why he bothered to fish in the sea, a local fisherman replied: "Sometimes I do, but rarely, because it is a lot of rowing for me to the sea."[20]

It was in the beginning in the tenth century that population growth led to massive deforestation. Arable land was less able to moderate runoff of rainfall, leading to local flooding and erosion. Rivers began to silt up, slow, and become warmer. Salmon were especially affected. In some cases, outlets to the sea were blocked, halting the spawning runs of anadromous fish. Even more detrimental were the dams that had been thrown across Europe's streams by millers and small industries to harness waterpower. So serious was the threat to salmon runs in Scotland that legislation in 1214 mandated that dams be opened periodically to allow the fish to pass. Similar legislation can be found throughout Europe, as concern with the decline of inland fishing rose in the thirteenth and fourteenth centuries. As interior Europe became more urban, pollution by human waste and activities like tanning and dyeing posed additional threats to fishing, not only for subsistence needs but also for the growing commercial fish market in the larger cities.[21]

Up to the eleventh century, European fishers had not even begun to tap the resources of the sea, except for subsistence purposes at the coast itself. But now declining inland fish stocks, combined with growing urban demand, changed all that. By the High Middle Ages, church prohibitions on meat and fresh fish eating on certain days—Fridays, saints' days, and the forty days of Lent—meant that dried fish was substituted on between 130 and 150 days a year. As Europe grew richer and more commercialized, people became habituated to fish eating. The result was the rise of urban fish markets, which could no longer be satisfied by freshwater catches. New forms of aquaculture organized around fish ponds stocked with warm-water fish such as carp failed to meet the growing demand. For the first time, then, Europeans developed a commercial sea fishery, beginning off the coast of Norway, where, on the Lofoten Islands, the process of drying cod was invented. From that point onward, cod became what Mark Kurlansky has called "almost a religious icon."[22]

In the eleventh century, Bergen became the center of the dry cod trade, supplying most of northern Europe and England. The Hanseatic League broke Bergen's monopoly two centuries later but failed to stop the English from fishing off their own shores. From ports on their northeast coast, the English challenged the Norwegians and the Dutch in the North Sea, setting off a series of cod wars off Iceland and elsewhere. Competition over diminishing near-shore cod stocks was causing northern European fishers, previously largely coasters with little deep-sea experience, to move farther and farther offshore. Fishers residing on the north coasts of England and Scotland began searching the North Atlantic for new fishing grounds. They soon faced competition from the Dutch as well as the Scandinavians; the formidable Basque fleet joined these from the 1540s onward.[23]

By the end of the fifteenth century, Bristol boats were looking for fish ever farther westward, not in the spirit of discovery or colonization but as part of market-oriented enterprise that now had a dynamic all its own. In 1497, John Cabot could report back to the Bristol merchants that he had sighted what he called "New Found Land." It was not the land itself but the fish in the sea around it that excited Europeans most and would continue to do so for the next two centuries. When Cabot's son Sebastian sighted Labrador in 1508, he named it Baccallaos, for "in the adjacent sea he found so great a quantity of a certain kind of great fish like tonnes, called baccallaos by the inhabitants, that at times they even stayed the passage of his ships." Once again, sea defined land for those who knew how to live by both in the manner of an edge species.[24]

The North Atlantic constituted what Jeffrey Bolster has called one great bioregion. Similar cold water, nutrient conditions, and fish species around its rim made it easy for Europeans to apply the techniques they had learned off their own shores to the seas to the north and west. The early modern European fishery was a migratory one, seasonal in nature, different from earlier hunter-gather practices only in the vast extension of movements involved. Migratory routes that had once extended for tens or at most hundreds of miles were now thousands. Time away from home, once measured in weeks, was now measured in months, and later, in the case of whaling, years. But the mentality of these latter-day foragers was similar to that of edge species in earlier periods. They operated in the same small groups, resisting organization by outsiders, remaining largely self-governing. Attuned to the movements of the sea and its creatures, always ready to follow the prey wherever it might lead, migratory fishers operated on the principle that the sea was open to all comers. To them, rights of access meant more than those of possession.[25]

Before the English colonized the North American mainland, they established seasonal trading posts and fishing camps on islands and coasts. Fishing boats would leave West Country ports in the spring and race to the most desirable harbors on the eastern coast of Newfoundland, where the first captain to arrive would be the recognized "admiral" for the season, allocating what were called fishing "rooms" and adjudicating disputes among competing crews. The first weeks onshore were spent constructing wharfs, rough wooden shelters, and the flakes on which the cod were dried. Most of the men would then take to smaller boats to hand-line cod while the rest would stay ashore to "make fish," splitting, curing, and drying the catch. By the eighteenth century, some men were left to protect the rooms during the winter, but permanent settlements were discouraged, and it was not until 1824 that property rights were recognized in the Maritimes.[26]

The Souls of the Edge skirmished over resources but showed a remarkable degree of cooperation when encountering other foragers on far shores. Electing an "admiral" to supervise each summer harbor, European migratory fishers from diverse places settled disputes without the intervention of royal power. The scene in Newfoundland was described by Lewes Roberts in 1638:[27]

> Five hundred sayle great and small doe from England yearly sayle to this coast . . . and arriving there about the middle of Aprill, unrigge their shippes, set up boothes and cabanets on the shore in divers creekes and habours, and there, with fishing provisions and salt, begin their fishing in shallops and boates, continue it till September . . . and this fishing ended and the cold beginning, they leave their stations and boats and, repairing

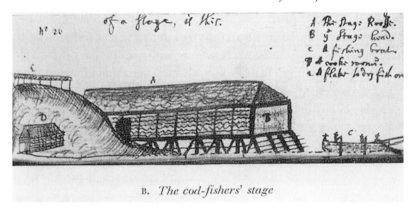

B. *The cod-fishers' stage*

FIGURE 16. Fishing stages at Ferryland, Newfoundland, drawn onsite by English surgeon James Yonge in the seventeenth century.

aboard their shippes, lade their fish and, rigging their vessels, returne to their native homes, where these fishmen winter and then become husbandmen, so their lives may be compared to the otter, which is spent halfe on land and halfe in sea.

Most fishing stations were private initiatives, with claims of royal sovereignty coming only later, almost as an afterthought. At times the English fished from shores that were nominally French, while French-speaking Acadians occupied lands under British sovereignty. The land itself was of interest, but to a people who lived "halfe on land and halfe at sea" only insofar as it gave access to the sea. As Donald Meinig puts it: "The seas were rich, the land poor. The main incentive to gain hold of land was to gain advantage in harvesting the sea." In Newfoundland and the Gaspe, interest in the interior was minimal, apart from timber for building the fishing rooms. Summer fishers had no time for farming and initially brought their food supplies with them. Later, when merchants became more involved with the fisheries, they operated a "truck" system in which fish were traded for food and trade goods from overseas.[28]

Even when permanent settlement became more common in the late eighteenth and early nineteenth centuries, fishing remained migratory, except that boats now departed from the coasts of New England and the Maritimes rather than England. British immigrants to Prince Edward Island were advised as late as 1819 that "the advantage of being situated on the sea-coast must be obvious, when compared with the miserable situation of those who have been deluded to quit their native land for the interior of the United States." On the shore and along the rivers they could expect to find land and access to fishing, as well as connections to trading networks that included Newfoundland and the West Indies. No wonder that the villages that began to cluster around landings and small harbors were called "outports": their only connection was by water, and they were often more attached to ports on far shores than to anything on their side of the Atlantic.[29]

Because they could sail directly to the Newfoundland fishing banks from Brittany and Normandy, the French had dominated the Newfoundland fisheries in the sixteenth century and early seventeenth centuries. They pursued a "wet" fishery, processing cod by salting and brining it, often without ever touching land. The English were masters of the "dry" fishery, which required seasonal fishing stations with drying racks known as flakes. By the 1590s the English were abandoning their old northeast coast ports for new ones in the West Country, which gave easier access to Newfoundland fishing. In time they would be able to oust the French from Newfoundland itself.

Due to the fact that cod preserved better than other North Atlantic species, it remained the great prize. Whaling had been practiced by the Norse as early as the ninth century, and in the High Middle Ages the Basques were taking right and gray whales for both their meat and oil in the Bay of Biscay. As in the case of cod, when the near-shore fishery was depleted they moved their operations ever farther west, ultimately installing themselves on the coast of Labrador, taking advantage of the migratory habits of bowhead and right whales through the Strait of Belle Isle. Whaling, like fishing, was migratory and seasonal. Basque whaling ships would leave the European coast in late spring, setting up stations from which small craft (*chalupas*) would pursue passing whales, bringing them back to harbors like that at Red Bay to be rendered into oil at what were called tryworks. The oil would then be transferred into huge casks aboard the ships departing for Europe. It is estimated that by the early seventeenth century, some twenty thousand whales had been killed, altering their migration patterns and causing the Basque to turn their attentions to cod fishing.[30]

Sealing also became commercialized at this time, again with the predictable results of driving seal colonies from the coasts where they had existed for centuries onto polar ice, where, until recently they were hunted for their fur. Walrus, coveted for the ivory of their tusks, would meet a similar fate. As long as these creatures were hunted by local arctic foragers on a subsistence basis, their survival was not in question, but once fishing and hunting had been commercialized, what Callum Roberts calls "the world's first fishery crisis" was virtually unstoppable. To be sure, the depredations of the fifteenth and sixteenth centuries were small compared to industrial-scale fishing today, but a pattern was established with consequences that no one at the time could have foretold.[31]

Alongshore Empires

Excessive focus on the voyages of notable explorers has blinded us to the ways in which the North Atlantic rim was created by the forgotten forays of hundreds of thousands of anonymous fisher-farmers, who never had any intention of settling on the far shore. If colonies were the end product of this process, they were by no means the original intention. Columbus voyaged with none other than commercial intentions. It is wrong to map the history of seventeenth- and eighteenth-century colonialism onto earlier periods. As had always been the case with earlier thalassocracies, the intention was to found defensible trading enclaves rather than territorial agrarian settlements.[32]

In very much the pattern of the ancient thalassocracies, European empires of the early modern period were sea-based rather than land-based. For three hundred years they controlled a series of ocean and river passages, along which were strategically located sea-facing enclaves rather than bounded interior territories. The initial discovery of the world was the discovery of the seas. "As by means of water-carriage, a more extensive market is opened to every sort of industry than what land-carriage alone can afford," wrote Adam Smith, "so it is upon the sea coast, and along the banks of navigable rivers, that industry of every kind began to subdivide and improve itself." Europeans brought with them the expectations of a seaboard and riverine civilization. Early explorations focused on estuaries as doors and rivers as passages to the interior, not as sites of permanent settlement.[33]

Europeans brought with them a diffuse body of geographical ideas, facts, myths, and experiences, and illusions that John Kirtland Wright called "geosophy." Since ancient times they had been imagining the world in insular terms, one great earth island surrounded by many smaller isles. Columbus had imagined himself island-hopping to East Asia, and it was a huge disappointment to find a land barrier blocking the way. But illusion did not yield easily to reality, and explorers continued to look to the northern latitudes for passages to India. The first generations of Europeans to set foot in the New World were water people—island, river, and

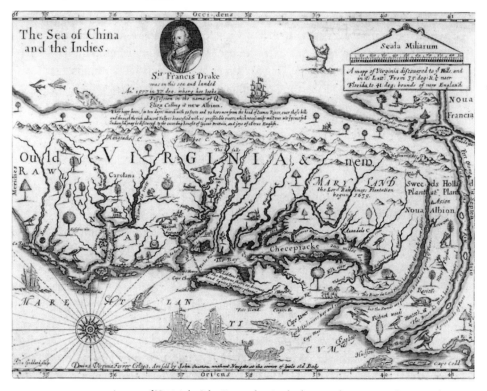

FIGURE 17. *A mapp of Virginia* by John Farrar, showing both east and west coasts. Courtesy of the Library of Congress.

coastal dwellers—and the Native Americans they first encountered were also an edge species, sharing much the same geosophy, imagining themselves on their own earth islands surrounded by encircling seas. John Smith's native Virginian informants believed the world "to be flat and round like a trencher, and themselves at the midst." They told him that to the west lay another sea. The Wabanaki people of Maine called themselves the People of the Dawn, living on the eastern edge of another great island.[34]

Reinforced by native geosophies, it is no wonder that Europeans believed themselves to have found an archipelago rather than a continent. Their geosophy told them that waters ran east to west, and the great rivers they encountered in North America were "indrawing seas" that would carry them swiftly to what was believed to be inland waters, often called the Western Sea, and then to the Pacific. The French explorer Cadillac was encouraged in this fantasy by cooperative natives who assured him that rivers and lakes would soon carry him to a point "beyond which they say, there is no more land." Jean Nicoll brought with him ceremonial garments of Chinese damask as gifts for the Asian potentates that he expected to meet among the Winnebago people on Lake Michigan. The explorer Verazzano was looking for a narrow isthmus like Panama in northern latitudes in 1524, when he mistook Pamlico Sound on the western side of Carolina's barrier islands (the Outer Banks) for the Western Sea. The idea that the passage to the Indies was only a few days' march remained an article of faith among Virginia colonists, who perceived themselves to be on an island. Their royal charter granted them lands "from sea to sea," as did those of Massachusetts, Connecticut, and Carolina. A map published in 1651 shows Virginia to be insular, with the Atlantic on one side and the "Sea of China and the Indies" on the other.[35]

As had been the case in the Old World, rivers and lakes formed a seamless waterworld, extending as many as a thousand miles inland. Early maps exaggerated the size and extent of bays and estuaries, promising water routes deep into the interior. The Hudson and the St. Lawrence fulfilled expectations, though the hopes that Virginia rivers would lead to lakes that drained west as well as east, leading to the Pacific, then called the East India Sea, were disappointed. For hundreds of years, and as late as the Lewis and Clark expedition of 1804, the continent would be explored mainly by boat, a reflection of not only the greater efficiency of waterborne transport but also the persistence of the belief that the New World was archipelagic rather than continental.[36]

As Wilcomb Washburn pointed out, "Europeans often looked over, or overlooked, the real land to which they came, anticipating the passage to the Pacific land that remained an ideal in their minds." One of the first things that Francis Billington did when he disembarked from the *Mayflower* in 1620 was to climb a tall tree with a westward view, reporting back that he saw "a great sea, as he thought." It turned out to be only a pond, which even today is called the Billington Sea. And when Europeans arrived on the west coast of North America they applied the same geosophy, though in a different direction, thinking archipelagically and seeking what they called the Strait of Anian, which was supposed to connect eastward to an inland sea. They explored every large estuary until finally giving up on the idea of an eastward passage. But they had more trouble giving up on the idea of California as an island, a fantasy that refused to yield to fact until the eighteenth century, when it, like the Strait of Anian, finally disappeared from world maps. Only then did Americans finally accept the fact that they were occupying an impenetrable continent rather than a navigable archipelago.[37]

"Europe's experiments in conquest, colonization, and commerce clung like ship's barnacles to the littoral of the world ocean or sought out offshore islands surrounded by sea moats," writes Stephen Pyne. This was an inheritance of the Mediterranean, where port cities had belonged more to the sea than to land. There, where people "feel closer to their cities than to their states and nations; indeed [where] cities are their states and nations and more," the territorial nation-state was slow to develop. Until the nineteenth century, the fruits of empire were best acquired offshore or alongshore rather than inland. New Spain was the exception that proved the rule. Continental "settlements were sponges that soaked up capital," a bad investment unless, like New Spain, they offered gold and silver. North America disappointed those who looked for quick riches, and when the Dutch, French, and English did settle, they did so on islands—Roanoke, St. Croix, Sable, James, Manhattan—or in places thought to be water-accessible on all sides, like Virginia and Massachusetts. The sea was their lifeline, and none of the northeastern colonies in the New World were anywhere near self-sufficient; when cut off from the Old World, they, like the Roanoke settlement, invariably failed.[38]

In many places dumb barter or silent trade was still conducted from the decks of ships, allowing European travelers to avoid direct contact with interiors. Permanent ports developed from temporary entrepôts that the Portuguese established on islands along the African coast and later throughout Asia. These served their commercial interests without involving them in the expense of defending onshore colonies. But it was the Dutch who perfected the alongshore empire throughout the world, using islands east and west, in Formosa, Japan, Ceylon, and Java as well as in the Americas. Donna Merwick calls them the archetypal "alongshore folk," who viewed the world not with the "eyes of a landsman looking for territory, but with the eyes of a seaman." She points out that Manhattan was, like the tiny Dutch trading post at Nagasaki, more a pied-à-terre than a formal possession. "The Dutch counted themselves to be people of islands and coastlines, drowned lands and shifting margins," whose cities were "isled," connected more by water than by land. They were generally distrustful of landsmen, even their own. New Amsterdam, founded in 1625, set its face to the sea and distanced itself from the interior as much as possible, resisting the impulse to farm because the merchants of the Dutch East India Company feared that would trigger confronta-

FIGURE 18. View of New Amsterdam by Johannes Vingboons, 1664. Courtesy of Wikimedia Commons.

tions with the local Indians. They had long contested the power of the sea and were reasonably comfortable with it. What they feared most, in Merwick's memorable phrasing, was being drowned by land. By the 1660s their worst fears were realized, and New Amsterdam was lost to the more powerful English landsmen who pressed in on them from the hinterlands. When the position of the island became untenable, they gave up all claims to it in exchange for the possession of another isle halfway around the world, the tiny Indonesian nutmeg island called Run, a decision that may puzzle us but made perfect sense to them.[39]

The first explorers of the North American coasts were more at home on sea than on land. Many were islanders with more coastal than deep-sea experience. Goods, people, and ideas followed similar alongshore routes. North American settlements communicated with one another by water. The Pacific coast developed later, but in a similar manner. First came the explorers, then the traders, and only much later the permanent settlers. Even then they tended to face the sea, dependent on it for replacements and resupply. As Dan Kelley puts it, "the Pacific Coast was explored more as an accessory to traffic with the Orient than as land worth knowing for its own sake." Oriented to far shores rather than its own hinterlands, the new United States was bicoastal from the beginning.[40]

The Inland Sea of North Atlantic Civilization

The waterborne empires of the sixteenth through the eighteenth centuries were more interested in access than possession. Apart from New Spain, they were not territorial in nature but "a network of collection centers and strategic points along critical traffic ways . . . fragmentary, shallow in continental impact, irregular in territorial hierarchy." Products of private, often regional initiatives rather than coordinated national policy, English settlements were often as different from one another as each was from Dutch or French settlements. Often at odds with the home country, they had their own foreign and military policies. Their populations were multiethnic, their languages were polyglot, and their culture was cosmopolitan. What they shared was what Meinig calls a "strand culture," facing the sea and more oriented to far shores than to its own immediate interior. They belonged to the Atlantic, what he calls the "inland sea of Western civilization."[41]

The notion of an inland sea was congenial to Europeans, who, beginning with the experience of the Mediterranean, felt more secure in bounded waters than on the open ocean. The newest version of inland sea encompassed much more than what today we call the Western world. It also washed the shores of Africa, whose cultures would have an immense impact on the Americas. And because it circulated east as well as west, it also bore the imprint of coastal Native Americans, without whom the European exploration and settlement of the New World would have been entirely different. Passages in the inland sea were never one-way. The tides of its history moved "not only westward upon the body of America but eastward upon the body of Europe, and inward upon and latterly along the body of Africa."[42]

Northern Europeans arrived on the American coasts by accident rather than by intention. They behaved as hunter-gatherers had always done, following their prey wherever this led them, practicing a kind of maritime transhumance, following fish rather than animals, on a seasonal basis, going farther and farther for longer and longer periods, but always returning to their home place when they had met their requirements. For more than a century, they showed no desire to farm. Thus the notion of the "Colonial" period, which supposes a territorial imperative, wholly distorts our view of the sixteenth and early seventeenth centuries, when northern Europeans "had no intention of being colonists—much less failed ones—but rather were migratory and sojourning members of their home society. They oriented themselves to North American spaces in relation to the needs of their home societies, rather than as spaces for new societies."[43]

Two quite different kinds of fisheries developed in the North Atlantic at the end of the fifteenth century. The French, Basque, Dutch, Spanish, and Portuguese, who were well supplied with salt, conducted their "wet" fisheries almost entirely offshore. They salted the catch onboard, brined and barreled them, and headed home, often without ever setting foot on dry land. The English preferred to dry their cod, but they did so only during the warmer season, returning to their home ports before winter set in. In many respects the American seaboard was a spatial extension of the European coastal life, still centered, despite the greater distances and the extended time away, on the home port. In migratory fishery, thoughts are always on return. As late as the 1970s, Spanish trawler men, fishing the waters of Newfoundland they call Terranova, told Joseba Zulaika that "there are only two terribly happy days at sea: the day you leave [Terranova] for Spain and the day you arrive home."[44]

On American shores, Europeans encountered other peoples who practiced a form of maritime transhumance on a smaller scale. Native Americans too had one boot in the boat, another in the field. They had been fishing and whaling alongshore for centuries, taking so-called drift whales that washed up on the shore but also sometimes going offshore in canoes. Their skills as fishers and farmers was the salvation of Plymouth settlers during their first starving years in the 1620s, when they taught the newcomers to plant maize and fish Massachusetts Bay. Native Americans were quick to learn European sailing skills and were soon using Basque-made shallops for both trading and fishing purposes. While there were some initial clashes, first encounters were generally amiable and mutually profitable. On his voyage of 1524, Verrazano encountered the sophisticated Narragansett people of present-day Rhode Island, who approached his ships without fear in the interest of exchange. Farther north he found the Abanaki less friendly, but he and other voyagers established the legend of a fabulously rich city of Norumbega, located somewhere in what we would call Maine, which Europeans continued to search for throughout the sixteenth century.[45]

As was the case in Europe, the coastal peoples of North America were numerous and, having learned the secrets of the ecotone, relatively powerful and prosperous. Their practice of burning forests created a mosaic

Bateau du port de Sⁿ Francisco.

FIGURE 19. Miwok boat made of tule reeds. *Bateau du port de San Francisco*, painted by Louis Chorus. Courtesy of the Bancroft Library, University of California, Berkeley.

of ecosystems with edge effects that were "ideal habitats for a host of wildlife species." And they exploited both sides of the shore, moving seasonally to take advantage of runs of anadromous fish—smelt in March, alewives, salmon, and sturgeon in April—and the arrival of cod and other ground fish in May. It has been estimated that a half of the annual food supply of Maine Indians came from such sources. It was said "they move . . . from one place to another according to the richness of the site and the season."[46]

Coastal Native Americans were by no means overwhelmed by initial contact, and in fact initially had the upper hand. The natives of what we now call New England "learned how to manage the European presence" and, like coastal peoples elsewhere, established themselves as mediators between the sea and the interior. Europeans did not involve Native Americans in their fisheries, but when that activity led to fur trading, they became increasingly dependent on them, for the native people had the interior contacts and controlled the riverways that delivered ever larger supplies of pelts. Native Americans remained welcoming as long as Europeans did not try to establish direct contacts with the inland hunters.

They would have continued to exercise their political and economic control of the coasts much longer had not diseases against which they had no defense had been introduced by their European contacts. By the early seventeenth century, when the Puritans finally decided to colonize the shore of Massachusetts, 90 percent of the natives were dead.[47]

The Canadian Maritimes remained unsettled for a much longer time. It is sometimes said by Canadians that their eastern shores were never meant to be inhabited. Residents of the United States came to think of their east coast as a seaboard, but Canadians do not. It is true that the Maritime provinces have always belonged more to sea than land, but we must be careful not to buy into the myth that we Americans were destined to be farmers and that our history "begins with the landing at James, [and] after the *Mayflower* drops anchor." In fact the true history of Canada and the United States begins not there but offshore and alongshore, for, as Benjamin Labaree has insisted, America is the most maritime of all the continents, although, beginning with the Native Americans, one boot has always been on land, the other in the boat.[48]

Sea Frontiers

The American coasts can be said to have been Europe's initial New World frontier. Like all frontiers, they were in constant motion, but unique in the way they faced two directions. Walter Prescott Webb has noted that a frontier "is not a line to stop at, but an area inviting entrance." Coasts ultimately invited entry to a continent, but initially they lured their populations to seek the riches of the sea. For the first three hundred years after discovery, they were frontiers of extraction rather than settlement. Like mining and foresting frontiers, they went through cycles of boom and bust, population and depopulation. Fortunes were lost as quickly as they were made; these latter-day hunter-gatherers came and went almost as rapidly as the creatures that were their prey.[49]

Europeans exploring the northern latitudes of the New World were certain that they had discovered a kind of lost paradise, not on land but at sea. Short growing seasons and poor soils made the coast itself somewhat unwelcoming to agriculturalists, but there was no doubt in English minds that they had discovered a watery abundance unknown on their side of the Atlantic. They scarcely seemed to notice the previous impact of Native Americans on the land or the sea, in part because when they finally settled the coast in the early seventeenth century local populations had been dying off for some time, making both land and sea appear empty and untouched, pristine nature ready to yield up its riches to its new masters.[50]

When Europeans explored the coasts, they viewed them through commercial eyes. They saw the great trees as mast wood, the animal life as furs, and fish as the most valuable of all the commodities to be found there. When Captain John Smith surveyed the northern latitudes in 1614, he pointed out that the Dutch had gained greater wealth "by the contemptible trade in fish" than the Spanish had mined in Spain. "But this is their Myne," he wrote; "and the Sea the source of those silvered streames of all their vertue." Smith's vision at that point was more that of the hunter than of the gardener, the modern-day forager rather than the farmer. He admitted he had no knowledge of the interior, but "even the very edges do naturally afford us such plenty, as no ship need return empty." The native fishing villages he saw encouraged him to urge settlement in New England, where, unlike Newfoundland, it would be possible to fish all the year, where those "fishing before your doors, may every night sleep quietly a shore with good cheare and what fires you will, or when you please with your wives and families." Here was a second Eden, built on the conquest of nature and requiring hard work, but promising a much easier life than in England. "If a man works but three days in seaven, he may get more than hee can spend, unlesse he will be excessive." Smith's instinct was much more that of the affluent forager than that of the yeoman farmer.[51]

Virtually every voyager compared the diminishing stocks and size of fish in European waters to what appeared to be the vast abundance found in the Americas. It began with the reports of Cabot from Newfoundland, now lost, which circulated far and wide: "They assert that the sea there is swarming with fish, which can be taken not with the net, but in baskets let down with a stone, so that it sinks in the water." The cod were superabundant, but so too were the whales, which were so numerous as to interfere with navigation. "The abundance of Sea-Fish are almost beyond beleeving, and sure I should scarce have belieeved it except I had scene it with mine owne eyes," one Englishman reported. It was said by one observer that the runs of fish up streams were so great that he could walk across them without getting his feet wet. This utilitarian perspective had not changed much when Captains George Vancouver and James Cook surveyed the west coast at the end of the eighteenth century. They too thought they had discovered a commercial bonanza of fish and timber.[52]

In fact, there was nothing pristine about this environment, which had already seen hundreds of years of exploitation by native peoples. Recently, evidence has come to light of human-induced global warming and increase in CO_2 levels due to the cutting and burning of tropical forests prior to 1540. Europeans ignored evidence of this past history and, despite physical evidence of native cultivation, came to regard the New World as pure, untouched wilderness, treating the indigenous peoples as "nature's children," in need, like the land itself, of civilizing. Not having had the opportunity to witness the semiagrarian hunter-gatherers at full strength before they were cut down by European diseases, Europeans had no idea what efficient cultivators and predators they had been. Had they examined the massive shell middens to be found on both the east and west coasts, they would have seen that the lowest levels contained much larger shells than the most recent layers, evidence of the predation that had already reduced the sizes of oysters, clams, and mussels over time.[53]

Even though they took advantage of the mosaic of open fields and woodlands that native burning practices had created, New Englanders came to believe that they had encountered a virgin forest untouched by man. They made themselves superheroes in their own story of taming the wilderness that the Indians had let go to waste. There is no evidence that the "savages," as they were called, were conscious conservationists, but their low numbers had limited their impact. And the fact that they regarded themselves as being spiritually related to fish and animals may also have restricted their take to some degree. But because the prior history of their ecological crises was never recorded, it seemed to the European newcomers that the aboriginals were passive and the environment they inhabited was timeless, a convenient myth that seemed to legitimate European claims to the right to cultivate the land and civilize its inhabitants in the name of their Christian God, the great gardener.[54]

Native Americans on the west coast had been fishing inshore waters for four thousand years before Europeans arrived. While they still migrated seasonally both along the coast and to prime fishing sites on salmon rivers, most operated out of permanent settlements. One historian calls their fishing and gathering skills "frighteningly efficient," but these were never deployed for commercial purposes. The take was also limited by certain taboos and rituals and a fundamental "respect for the fish that sustained life," a notion they shared not only with the natives of the east coast but also with European fishers.[55]

When Europeans arrived on the west coast in the early nineteenth century, they again brought disease and depopulation. By 1850 the indigenous population was reduced to less than 6 percent of its precontact levels, resulting in a rebound in fish stocks that left Europeans with the impression that the native fishers were natural conservators who had no impact on their environment. The abundance of salmon and shellfish prompted the mistaken notion that they had encountered a bountiful Eden, encouraging them to commercialize and ultimately despoil it.[56]

Had they been more observant, Europeans would have detected the ecological effects of the native practice of forest burning, which had created rich edge environments but also had contributed to the silting of streams. More difficult to detect were the effects of the Pacific trade in otter pelts, which may well have resulted in the devastation of local sea otter populations, thereby multiplying the sea urchin populations, which, in turn, degraded marine habitats near shore. Still, Native Americans were few in number and spread over large territories where they might exhaust one local resource but could always move on to another. These hunter-gatherers also resorted to birth control by various means, including abortion, and never taxed the ecotone to its limit.

A Transcoastal Atlantic Culture

During the early modern period, the northern latitudes of Europe and America were attached to one another by their coasts. The seaboard cultures of the Dutch, English, and French were successfully exported to the New World, where they often had more in common with one another than with residents of their hinterlands. By the eighteenth century, they constituted a necklace of loosely connected coastal and island enclaves that stretched around the rim of a great inland sea. They had by then a kind of common culture, a lingua franca, similar lifestyles, diets, even housing. The sea was not only their prime lifeline but also the source of the commodity that initially contributed most to prosperity in the northern latitudes. Farther south, the slave trade and sugar production would provide another source of wealth, but for the first century or more, northern Europeans showed more interest in navigational rights to certain waterways and sea tenures than in territorial possession as such. Europeans operated on Hugo Grotius's notion that the ocean "can be neither seized nor inclosed: nay, which rather possesses the earth than is by it possessed." Nevertheless, they recognized the concept of local use rights, a notion shared among coastal peoples worldwide. When fishermen from different regions found themselves contesting for the same resources, it was not the rights of private property but custom to which they appealed.[57]

The common feature of all these strand cultures was maritime transhumance, the constant movement of communities pursuing their prey in the manner that hunter-gatherers had done for millennia. Native Americans in New England were mobile, moving seasonally, sometimes several times in a year. Their wood-framed houses were covered with grass mats or bark so they could be taken down and transported by water. It was said that they lived lightly and that "they love not to bee cumbereed with many utensilles." In Maine, they visited islands in the summer and stayed close to the sea even in colder months. It was only when they became more deeply involved with the European fur trade that they spent more time inland during the winter, when snow made animal tracking easier. Sixteenth-century European fishermen on the northern coast followed a similar pattern. They too saw themselves as sojourners, following seasonal routes rather than establishing permanent roots. To them, land was something to be used as a staging area, not to be claimed as property, an attitude that still prevails in Newfoundland.[58]

Their housing was often, like that of the aboriginals, prefabricated, constructed in such a way as to be easily transported by water or across the winter ice. In the Newfoundland outport village of Tilting, this practice, called "launching," is still common. In Maine as well, moving houses was a common practice. During the Revolutionary War, Tories escaping from Castine, Maine, brought their houses with them to St. Andrews, New Brunswick, where they still line the harbor. Houses on Cape Cod were also moved and recycled. Robert Finch found that the residents thought of their "houses less as family seats, founded for the ages, than as temporary shelters, like the borrowed shells of hermit crabs, to be shifted about and exchanged, in location and function, as the need arose."[59]

"God performed no miracle on New England soil. He gave the sea," writes Samuel Eliot Morison. The Separatist colonists who arrived in 1620 were mainly inland people, farmers and craftsmen, ill equipped to deal with the land and with no skill whatsoever in harvesting the sea. The *Mayflower*'s passengers were no mariners. Their passage to America was a nightmare, and they had no desire to go to sea again, but as Daniel Vickers puts it, "they became by necessity a maritime people." As none of them had maritime skills, they traded with the natives for fish. They managed to survive the "starving years" with the help of the indigenous people, but even when they began to harvest a surplus of corn, they discovered that they had no cash crop to pay for imports of necessities from the home country. Still needing a viable commodity, the next step was to invite

FIGURE 20. Schoolhouse being barged on the Vinalhaven, Maine, waterfront. Courtesy of the Vinalhaven Historical Society.

non-Separatist Dorset fishermen, who had previous experience in migratory fisheries, to settle on the rocky shores at Marblehead. The fishery was not only physically but culturally distinct from the inland farming communities. It was said that "sailors and fishermen are in general averse to engage in any occupation upon the land. They prefer to linger upon the shore, and draw a precarious subsistence from the ocean. A sailor, when away from the water, is like a fish out of his proper element. The mountain and the forest have no charm for him." Those who settled what was to become known as Boston in the 1630s had dreamed of a pastoral existence but were forced by the unyielding nature of the land to turn to the sea, ultimately staking their fortune on fishing and coastal trading.[60]

The fishers brought over from seaboard England were not Separatists but Church of England men, regarded by the Puritans as a "wicked and drunken crue," called by John Winthrop a "trouble-some people." In time, this fishing population would settle down, but never in the manner of their interior neighbors. Especially the men continued to be seasonally migratory, ranging "down east" to the coast of Maine and the Maritimes in the summers. In Massachusetts and Maine they squatted in places that were of no use to the farmers, their property rights tenuous, regarding the immediate hinterland as a commons where all were free to gather wood. They were more interested in sea than land tenures, roaming the coasts and islands, frequently moving house and setting up fishing berths in summer months, leaving in the fall to sell their catch to English and New England merchants, clearing their debts before winter set in. Initially they tended to spread out along the shore, each with a landing and a small boat. Deep-water ports and fishing villages came only later, for most of their voyages were by small craft rather than deep-sea vessels. This was still a protomaritime existence, played out alongshore, not by crossing the ocean.[61]

Coastal communities all around the North Atlantic rim were relatively poor, with weaker family and community ties, culturally distinct from their inland neighbors. For the most part, fishers were young single men, who, according to Cotton Mather, spoke "the Pagan Language of a Good Fortune," articulating, as did fishermen everywhere, the "Luck of Fish." The men rarely fished their whole lives but eventually settled down, married, had children, and sent their own sons to sea. In the later seventeenth and eighteenth centuries, Maine and Massachusetts coastal people often had small "saltwater" farms, rarely large enough to produce a lifelong living. They turned to cottage industry, but "seafaring was the primary antidote to youthful unemployment."[62]

It would not be until the eighteenth and nineteenth centuries that the fishery became a career. Until then, coastal people continued to have one boot on the land and the other in the boat, which perpetuated the difference between the coast and a hinterland that by the end of the eighteenth century was already entering into a protoindustrial phase, a transition to a new age when young people, female as well as male, would go off to seek their fortunes in towns and cities. Still, the sea remained for many coastal Americans, as well as Europeans, the real frontier, one of the reasons that Alexis de Tocqueville wrote of Americans in the 1830s: "I cannot help believing that one day they will be the foremost naval power on the globe. They are born to rule seas, as the Romans were to conquer the world."[63]

For three centuries, the rimlands of the North Atlantic were shaped more by the sea than by the land. Coasts belonged to the water, were named for what lay just offshore: thus Cape Cod and Maine's Bar Harbor. Before the shore was explored from land, it was known only from the sea and by what existed in the sea. The first explorers were much more interested in discovering what lay hidden beneath its surfaces and upriver than they were in charting inland territories. Today, the situation is more often the reverse, with land defining sea, yet there are still places where little has changed over the centuries. Even after the crofters of the Scottish Isle of Harris turned exclusively to landed pursuits during the course of the nineteenth century, they continued to talk of going "in" when setting out for sea and "out" when returning to land. In Newfoundland outports, the orientation is still water. Cardinal points mean little when everything is oriented either "up the bay" or "down the harbor." There life on land is an extension of that at sea. Locals speak of "climbing aboard" their cars and "hauling in" to a parking place. Visiting neighbors is called "cruising," and as we have already seen, moving houses is referred to as a "launching." While it is now common everywhere to call porches decks, only in Newfoundland are they still called "bridges."[64]

It is not only coastal geography that differs but also coastal temporality. It should not surprise us that in Newfoundland, as in Maine and other coastal places, time is "not linear but diastolic, pulled by centripetal and centrifugal currents. Like the year, all things go out from and return to this one place." It is no wonder that historians have had trouble coming to grips with places that do not fit neatly into their linear narratives. It was at the coast that T. S. Eliot recorded a time, "not our time . . . a time older than the time of chronometers . . ." We ignore coastal peoples' understandings of time and place to our own peril. Like the tides and currents that are known to sweep away unwary landlubbers, the hidden flows of coastal history need to be understood if we are to learn to live as sustainably as earlier generations did.[65]

It has been said that "old salts and johnnies-come-lately speak differently of the sea; those who know it best feel no need to speak of it at all." Most of the writing about the coasts comes from the pens of landlubbers, but despite this, it is possible to fathom how those who inhabit the edge of the sea think about it. In Maine they are "more prone to believe in fate than destiny and to concentrate [their] attentions on the cycles of life rather than on the ever-changing." Those who have learned to live *with* as opposed to just *on* coasts know that it is folly to believe that they are wholly in control of their own destiny. They are not fatalists, but they are respectful of tides and currents that set the tempo and scale of their world. In this respect, they are still like ancient foragers, more gamekeepers than the gardeners who regard it as their destiny to transform nature. Historians, whose business it is to tell dramatic stories of linear change, also believe in destiny, one of the reasons they have been slow to grant to nature, and to coasts and coastal people, a place in their narratives. As a result, they have failed to tell an important part of the human story.[66]

4 · SETTLING THE SHORES

It is a cold thing a map, humorless and dull, born of calipers and a draughtsman's board. That coastline there, that ragged scrawl of scarlet ink, shows neither sand nor sea nor rock; it speaks to no mariner ...
BERYL MARKHAM[1]

Coastlines are not found in nature; they are products of human initiative, first imagined, then discovered, named, and, ultimately, surveyed and settled. Since I am a historian, my task is to tell the story not of a physical object but of a cultural process, one by which our modern understanding of coasts was brought into being. The word, derived from the Latin *costa*, originally meant the side of something: of beef, of the human body, of any piece of land or water. It took on its modern meaning only toward the end of the eighteenth century, becoming for the first time "the coast," not just the side of something else but a place in its own right. It was also then that the word *coastline* entered into our vocabulary, giving form to the world where land and sea met, creating something quite different from the coasts of earlier eras.[2]

Our ancestors did not make as sharp a distinction between land and water as we now do. They preferred to see the planet as *terraqueous*, a term used frequently in the seventeenth century. Until quite recently, shores resisted mental and physical fixity. Mariners had always approached them with great trepidation, knowing them to be far more unpredictable and treacherous than the sea itself. It was said of the coasts of Nova Scotia, now regarded as some of the most beautiful sights in the world, that they were repulsive to the earliest visitors, places "from which the eye turns with painful dissatisfaction." But no less repulsive were the coastal dwellers themselves, who until the nineteenth century were regarded by inlanders as barbarians, notorious for their "adultery, polygamy, incest, drunkenness . . ." According to the biblical geography that prevailed until then, God had ravaged the once-smooth earth in retribution for humankind's sins, setting sea against land and reducing coasts to "nothing but ruins." The rocky shores that we now see as natural bulwarks, as our first line of defense, were then viewed as points of vulnerability, potent sources of disease and death. And people associated with coasts were considered as savage as the sea itself, to be avoided whenever possible. Even today, there is something different about coasts. According to Shauna McCabe: "Like all waterlands, the coastline is a 'terra infirma,' equally limen and boundary, neither land nor sea, at once fragile and resilient, equally symbolic of death and regeneration, of isolation and intimacy."[3]

Unsettled Coasts

With the exception of Spain, no early modern European imperial power was interested in possessing a continuous coastline, and even the Spanish effort fell far short of that ambition. Instead, the Dutch, English, and French established shore or riverine enclaves, entrepôts from which they could conduct trade. They settled disparate and disconnected places— islands, protected bays, broad rivers, anywhere that was easily accessible by water. As seaborne mercantile empires, they had little interest in the land as such. When the English began to settle New Jersey in the seventeenth century, they completely ignored the beaches that came ultimately to define the state and make its real estate some of the most valuable in the world.[4]

Territory was of interest to the Dutch, English, and French only insofar as it gave access to water, and to the commodities—timber, furs, fish— that had drawn them to the New World in the first place. In the sixteenth century, they camped on the shores but established no permanent settlements. Of Maine it has been said that "the mainland was an afterthought, something to put an edge on." Making that edge was an extended and contested process, one that Thoreau thought as late as the mid-nineteenth century had scarcely begun, and that is not finished even today. At first only a very few points along the coast, namely deep harbors and river mouths, were visited and charted. The rest was ignored. The coasts of North America were indeed *terra infirma*, a threshold providing access but resisting occupation. No territorial imperative like that operating in New Spain was as yet at work in North America. The new arrivals turned their backs on the hinterlands to face the sea and remained much more closely connected to Europe than to inland America. Only after the settlers won their independence and began the process of nation-building did they become a continental rather than a seaboard civilization.[5]

Until the late eighteenth century it was an aqueous imperative that prevailed. In an age of waterborne transportation, no place without access to water, riverine or oceanic, stood any chance of survival. As Adam Smith knew well, both trade and production were wholly dependent on water. Not only did it bring raw materials and goods on which trade depended, but it was the source of the power that turned the millstones and mechanical devices that drove protoindustrial development. Before industry turned to steam power, it was waterbound. The Dutch found what they were looking for on the broad estuary of the Hudson. The French, a great riverine people, made the most of interior waterways, while the first British settlements were often on islands. The initial settlements in North America all turned their backs on the hinterlands. England's American colonies have been described as "fragmentary, shallow in continental impact," much more closely connected to the mother country than to one another, more like islands than mainlands.[6]

The idea of a shore as a continuous, linear border between land and sea did not arrive until the nation-building efforts of a newly independent territorial state, based on a new kind of capitalism that was less based on trade than on agrarian and industrial production, had begun. Then, for the first time, coasts were reimagined as continuous, the edges of something greater, namely continents. The notion of continents did not arise until the discovery of the Americas, and it was not until the nineteenth century that the political and economic center of gravity shifted from coasts to interiors. Until then, the land bordering a coast or a port was known as a hinterland and was presumed to belong to it rather than to the continent as such.[7]

The idea of the continent and the notion of the "coastline" emerged simultaneously. Coasts were initially mapped from the sea, there being no easy way to approach them from land. And sea charts reflected the interests not of landlubbers but of mariners seeking safe harbors and protected landings. They depicted the shore that lay between as featureless. For the sailor it was no-man's-land, uncharted and therefore dangerous, something to steer clear of. As all coastal pilots knew, "the safest distance between points is rarely a straight line." The mariner's path heeded currents, winds, and underwater features that were found on no map and known only by locals, who were depended on to pilot foreign ships approaching unknown shores.[8]

"Landscapes without place names are disorienting," writes Paul Shepard, and those "without categorical forms, awful." James Hamilton-Paterson agrees that the way to tame a threatening landscape is to subject it to the control of language. Giving waters names helped still the fears of ancient mariners. Europe gradually overcame the terror of the encircling chaos that the ancients called Oceanus by naming and charting near-shore seas. They named these after the lands they bordered—the Sea of France, the Sea of Spain—but it was a very long time before the body of water we call the Atlantic was finally named, followed by the Pacific. And even after that was done, each of these oceans remained a vast unknown, something to be gotten across rather than a destination in its own right.[9]

The next step was naming the most dangerous part of the sea, that which approaches land. Of course the shores of North America had never been nameless, but Europeans set about replacing the descriptive Native American names—Far Away Island, Burned Place—with terms more familiar and less disorienting, but initially still leaving the straight shore unmarked. When coastal traffic increased in the eighteenth century, naming accelerated. As Horace Beck points out: "Rocks cannot be named until they are found, the usual way of finding them—for naming purposes—was to run a vessel upon them." Mishaps produced colorful usages on Maine's coast. A ledge off Monhegan Island was called Cold Arse, while a reef near Great Cranberry Island was initially called Bunker's Whore for a woman who had drowned rowing out to board Captain Bunker's ship. Later, in a concession to Victorian sensibilities, it became Bunker's Ledge, while Cold Arse was renamed Ragged Island.[10]

In the wake of the cartographers came the artists and, later still, the photographers who would freeze in time the fluid features of the coast. Initially artists worked aboard ships, looking back toward the land, framing the anchorage and waterfront in conformity with European conventions of harbor painting. Places of destination and protection were thereby rendered less frightening. Selected ports were domesticated long before the terrors of the rest of the coast were exorcised. Only toward the end of the eighteenth century did artists begin to make cliffs and rocky shores their subjects, and it was even later that they faced the open sea to attempt to capture its limitless power and glory.[11]

Bringing the Coast into Line

For most of human history, the shore has been, as described by Paul Carter, "obstinately discontinuous, abysmal, anti-rational, impossible to fix." It belonged to the sea and thus was considered beyond human control. Humanity had taken advantage of its natural features for millennia, but only a very small proportion of the coast offered safe harbor, espe-

FIGURE 21. Representation of the effects of the Lisbon earthquake and tsunami of 1755, published in 1756. Courtesy of the Kozak Collecton, NISEE Earthquake Engineering Online Archive, University of California, Berkeley.

cially to larger sailing ships. The great Lisbon earthquake of 1755 shocked Europe into a realization of just how vulnerable even its greatest seaports could be. The destruction wrought by the ensuing tsunami, amplified as it was by the structure of the Lisbon harbor, was as great as that of the quake itself.[12]

The *Mayflower* found no mooring on the Massachusetts shore and had to anchor off Plymouth and keep its passengers onboard until the Pilgrims could build a habitable site. They left no record of having stepping ashore on the rock that later generations would fetishize as a place of origins in American history. In fact, they were forced to build a pier over the rock so that they could dock there. Rivers proved no more hospitable, and English penetration of the interior was stopped at the fall line where rapids halted upstream progress. The French got around river rapids by portaging, but the English used heavier craft that could not move until they learned to build canals and employ locks. This did not happen until the late eighteenth century, when attitudes toward nature itself began to change and the idea of engineering the shore, fixing it for utilitarian purposes, began to prevail.[13]

The ability to "outwit nature, bringing it into line," had long been a dream of educated European town planners who had been thinking about providing easier access to the sea for cities like Bordeaux. In the late eighteenth and early nineteenth centuries that dream began to be realized by means of surveying and mapping, drawing lines where none had previously existed, creating a wholly new "neutralized edge" consistent with landlubbers' Cartesian logic. This was the first effort to shape the shore according to rational design, and from that point onward the capitalist economy and the nation-state have become ever more insistent on remaking the shore to suit their purposes, an effort at odds with nature and in defiance of the previous history of coasts and coastal dwellers. By the end of the nineteenth century, this epochal mental and material conquest was largely complete. The sea had been domesticated and "its dangerous edges [reduced] to a quantifiable set of co-ordinates." Not only had the coast been wholly transformed, but its original population had been largely displaced. The result was the disappearance, "real and figurative, of Coastal Man, *Homo littoralis*."[14]

Today when most of us approach a shore, we have in mind a line dividing land and water. But as Tim Ingold reminds us, straight lines do not exist in nature. In reality, coasts are fractal, broken, and fragmented. Coastlines are convenient fictions, "a virtual icon of modernity, an index of the triumph of rational, purposeful design over the vicissitudes of the material world." For ecologists like Rachel Carson, "always the edge of the sea remains an elusive and indefinable boundary," but this is a truth lost on those of us who have grown up in a world so thoroughly bridged, tunneled, and geometricized that, in William Bunting's words, "the lay of the land has never counted for less than it does today." As Bunting points out, the same can be said for the lay of the sea, which even in port cities is "fenced off by highways, and largely forgotten."[15]

The coast was once navigated by touch and feel, by listening for the sounds of surf breaking on unseen ledges or smelling the land. Beginning in the eighteenth century, sight began to displace the other primary senses when what Martin Jay has called the "scopic regime of modernity" pushed to the fore. In contrast to other ways of knowing the world, sight distances the observer from the observed. Our visual culture, which relies so heavily on cartography for way finding, has conditioned us to see lines in nature where none exist. Because of their tidal nature, seacoasts are notoriously difficult to delineate and measure. Ecologists tell us that they should be treated as broad zones where land and water are inseparable, but we insist on seeing them from a Cartesian perspective that imposes binaries.[16]

Of course, there are still those who still know the lay of the sea as well as that of the land and resist any simplistic division between the two. There are still coastal dwellers who depend on the sea for their livelihood and for whom the shore is a place of touch, smell, and sound as well as sight. They are to be found on every coast, though in diminishing numbers. For most of us, the sea is the great unknown. It appears in the media only when there is a disaster. Big-city newspapers have not carried the shipping news since the 1960s, and except in hurricane season, weather maps rarely display what is going on at sea. In the words of Alan Sekula, "the metropolitan gaze no longer falls on the waterfront, and a cognitive blankness follows." Paul Theroux, a resident Cape Codder, has observed that "the stranger who walks or drives to the shore . . . always sees divisions," while "the local does not distinguish between land and water, and keeps going, actually or mentally seeing shoals and eddies and sunken ships and rocks that are exposed only at low tide—not barriers but features."[17]

The coast in the mind of the local person is much closer to that which still prevailed until the eighteenth century, a water world where the distinction between land and sea was blurred, often a "marsh realm [which] is neither landscape nor seascape." But the stranger embodying the modern perspective, experiencing the coasts as boundary, stands on the shore and, seeing only the surface of the sea, remains ignorant of the hidden features that can be known only through direct experience and local knowledge. She or he is likely to overlook what connects land and sea, for, ignorant of the old vocabulary of such places—*guzzle, creek, gutter, bore, wrack*—landlubbers cannot name and therefore are not likely to understand what lies between them and the open ocean. Like the road map that has brought them to the sea, strangers register all that lies off-shore as blank space, a wild blue yonder.[18]

Making the Modern Coast

Settling the coasts was much more than a matter of populating them. It also meant fixing them on maps and engineering their features to suit the purposes of the state and the economy. What was once the edge of the sea, defined by the reach of water, became the seaside, a feature of land. What had been a threshold open in both directions became an ever firmer border. Every year governments around the world spend billions trying to "fix" their coasts, make them conform to the lines they have drawn in the sand. They build seawalls, groins, and jetties, dredge mountains of sand, and haul still more to replace what has been washed away. In the name of coastal protection, they destroy estuaries and wetlands, actually desta-bilizing shores by encouraging devastating erosion and flooding by sea surges. As contemporary coastal science has shown, it would be hard to imagine a more counterproductive activity carried out in the name of protecting the nature of our shores.

The settling of the coasts of North America began in earnest in the eighteenth century and reached an apogee in the later nineteenth cen-tury, when continental interiors were explored and populated for the first time. Settling was much more than the material process of making fishing villages permanent, creating seaports with fixed harbors, building light-houses and fortifications. There was also the mental process of reconcep-tualizing the relationship between human beings and nature as well as between land and sea. The desire to settle the shape of the shore once and for all was at least as important as settling people along the littorals.

From the mariner's point of view, the coast is the most dangerous part of the sea, and what was called for centuries the "straight shore" is the most terrifying of all. As we have seen, early mariners navigated from harbor to harbor, estuary to estuary, avoiding it. What in today's real es-tate market is the most attractive of properties—the beach—was consid-ered *terra nullis*, a void to be avoided. Harbors and estuaries were first mapped from the decks of ships, for the convenience of mariners. Until the eighteenth century, charts reflected their perspective, emphasizing harbors and estuaries, barely limning the straight shore. The continuous coast was plotted for a different constituency, namely landlubbers. The surveying of coasts was an Enlightenment project driven by the territorial imperative of pinning down property lines and fixing the boundaries of the emerging interior nation-states. Before there can be a space, there must be a boundary. Coastlines were products of the political imperatives of nation-states busily consolidating themselves.

Earlier kingdoms had been content to organize their centers, leaving their coasts and inland borders ragged. Old boundaries were "intended less to define a region and establish an effective relationship to the outside world than to isolate and protect something within it." Coastal peoples had not heeded lines. According to Michael Pearson, "the littoral formed a frontier that is not there to separate and enclose, but which rather finds its meaning in permeability." *Homo littoralis* moved with ease and by necessity across and along a zone that encompassed both land and water. Preindustrial coastlines have been described as zones of transfer and transmission, as seams rather than separations. They were open frontiers that faced both landward and seaward, facilitating rather than inhibiting movement of both human and animal species.[19]

Coasts were borderlands long before they were borders. They were neutral ground where traders from different countries might meet on equal terms. In short, they brought peoples together rather than separating them. In the early modern period, shores were not the first line of defense, for kingdoms preferred to stand their ground well inland. The idea of the fortified coast was perfected only in the nineteenth century, when the United States' coastal fortification became the country's largest peacetime military expenditure. Britain's great age of coastal defense began during the Napoleonic Wars and resulted in the building of over a hundred Martello towers. When Bonaparte's nephew Napoleon III spooked the British into another round of building in the 1860s, the towers, which were vulnerable to the new rifled artillery, became known as Palmerston's Follies. The twenty-five that still stand offer no real protection but are preserved as part of Britain's coastal heritage.[20]

Birth of the Seaport

In our current era of massive waterfront redevelopment, when every city with access to water exploits this as a commercial and residential bonanza, it is difficult to believe that there was once a time when cities turned their backs to the sea, distancing themselves as much as possible from what was regarded as its dangerous, degrading qualities. As far as northern Europe was concerned, a reconciliation between the city and the sea was not achieved until the expansion of overseas trade in the early modern

period. It was then that Amsterdam organized itself around its waterways and the waterfront became a center of social life for Parisians and
Londoners. During the same period, urban planners imagined bringing
the sea to the city or the city to the sea, even though the age-old antago-
nism between civic order and maritime chaos never really went away, especially along the Atlantic seaboard. Legends of drowned cities haunted
European imaginations. Plato's fictional Atlantis was thought to exist first
in the Mediterranean and then in the Atlantic, and local legends, like
the myth of the sunken Kingdom of Lyonesse, lying somewhere between
Cornwall and the Isles of Scilly, also played upon the fears of those living
along the shores. Like Atlantis, Lyonesse was a cautionary tale of a people
condemned by their own corruption. Anyone living near a coast knew
of villages and towns that had been badly damaged by storms, and some,
like Dunwich, that had disappeared almost entirely. The association of
the sea with death and destruction remained fixed in Western minds until the late eighteenth century, when the lure of the sea finally outweighed
its repulsion. The sea and the city came together late, and from the start
this was an unstable compound that did not survive the twentieth century. Today the port-city no longer exists; in the era of the container ship,
the port and the city are once again separate entities.[21]

The birth of the seaport was the product of the same commercial forces
that settled coasts in the early modern period. Although there had been
man-made ports in the ancient world, it had become common to rely on
natural harbors and riverbanks. Landings and temporary trading posts
left little record of their existence. In northern Europe, stone piers and
jetties were very rare; docks became common only in the eighteenth century. Visitors to today's Sigtuna, once Sweden's busiest inland entrepôt but
now the smallest place in Sweden still designated a city, have a difficult
time imagining its past glories. Only the existence of nearby Arlanda International Airport has saved it from total depopulation. There are thousands of once flourishing ports where nothing at all now exists. They were
little more than beaches or clefts in cliffs where freight could be dropped
to the decks of waiting boats. On the California coast, there are dozens
of what were once called "dog hole ports," harbors just big enough, it was
said, for a dog to turn around in. Most of these have disappeared without
a trace, without even a name to recall their prior existence.[22]

In northern Europe, ports gradually moved toward the coasts, becoming more like cities in their own right and distancing themselves from
their interior counterparts. There was a proliferation of small ports in
the eighteenth century, only to be displaced by a few large harbors by the

FIGURE 22. Dog Hole Port on the coast of northern California. Courtesy of the Library of Congress.

end of the next century. In the New World, both Native Americans and Europeans preferred "landings" as trading posts, keeping their permanent communities at one remove from the sea, a sign of the respect that all coastal peoples had for the destructive power of the ocean and the fear of those who might arrive unexpectedly by way of it. Indigenous peoples preferred to canoe out to European ships, trading with them on the water rather than risk having them land. For the most part, ship captains were happy enough with this arrangement, for they were better protected on their armed vessels or on fortified islands.[23]

In North America, cities appeared first on the coast rather than in the interior. All colonial major North American cities were initially seaports, created for the purpose of exchange and only later developing civic and religious institutions comparable to their commercial prowess. In contrast to New Spain, the center of North American urban life was not the town square or the plaza but the harbor, toward which all the major private and public buildings faced, and which functioned like "large outdoor rooms" to which all the streets led and all attention was directed. From the very beginning, residents of these towns reached out to embrace the water, building piers and wharves. Initially, American saltwater towns were not so much extensions of land as extensions of water. Only later did territorial imperatives cause the filling in of bays and harbors, a move initially resisted by Bostonians on the grounds that it obstructed an aqueous "highway greater than any ever laid out and constructed by City or County Commissioner . . . laid out and constructed by the Great Creator himself."[24]

On both sides of the Atlantic, the first seaports were not so much *of* the coast as *on* the coasts. Many were located on actual islands, others on islandlike peninsulas. All were detached from the lands around them. Seaports like Boston had very shallow hinterlands, and some none at all. The French port on Cape Breton Island, the French fortress at Louisbourg, had little connection with the rocky mainland shore or the forbidding forest that lay inland. "The true hinterland of Louisbourg," writes John McNeill, "and the source of its wealth, lay offshore." In the early modern period, seaports were far more attached to other ports than to their own hinterlands, for they were by nature *entrepôts*, a world derived from the French word for "warehouse." Ports were originally conceived of as trading posts where commercial goods could be imported and exported by water without payment of import duties.[25]

Dutch New Amsterdam was just such a trading post, producing nothing of its own for export. It would be a long time before its English successor, New York, developed a relationship with the land itself. This was also true of the early French sites at Saint Croix and Port Royale. The Puritans who settled Boston in 1630 had not intended it to be a port, but when their dream of a pastoral economy failed inland, they turned back to the sea to make money from fishing and coastal trading. All these early ports were nodes in complicated networks where profits were made on trading goods rather than importing or exporting things from the mainland as such. Had they existed only to do business with the thinly populated and initially unproductive hinterlands, they would never have been viable in the first place.[26]

As entrepôts, seaports were destinations in their own right. Ultimately, however, they became transit points for their back countries. In time, warehouses were replaced with factories as they added production to their commercial functions. Ports became less like offshore islands and became more connected to mainlands, first through canals, then with roads, and ultimately by railways. By the middle of the nineteenth century, they no longer belonged to the sea but had become transit points between it and the interior. New York boomed when it became connected to the Midwest by the Erie Canal in the 1820s. Boston, with no similar landward water connections, found itself at a disadvantage until rescued by the railway.[27]

The Making of Waterfronts

Initially, mariners took advantage of natural features, but it was not long before the residents of ports began "improving" their access to water, building wharves and extending piers to replace the old shallow-water landings. In London, the enormous expansion of coastal trade in the eighteenth century so overcrowded the Thames that the city engaged in a frenzy of dock building. Ever larger ships demanded changes that soon replaced the old ecotone with a new kind of edge, described by the newly invented term *waterfront*, which marked a much sharper divide between land and water. But these feats of engineering interfered with the natural scouring function of estuarial tides and river flows, leading to silting and the necessity of dredging harbors. Embanking the Thames closed off its old flood plains and led to repeated flooding of the city. In Japan, the deepening of harbors and straightening of channels had the effect of increasing the velocity and mass of storm surges, which, in turn, required a new term, *tsunami* or "harbor wave," to differentiate them from the ways seas had behaved when they came ashore in meandering rivers and coastal wetlands.[28]

And even as ports extended their piers seaward, they became more closely attached to their hinterlands, ultimately bifurcated between residents who made their living by the sea and those who were engaged in purely terrestrial pursuits. They became less like islands and more continental, whether by bridging or by tunneling. With the construction of the Brooklyn Bridge in 1883, Manhattan lost its islandness. It was said that "the continent is spanned and one may visit, dryshod and without the use of ferry boats, every city from the Atlantic to the Golden Gate." By that time, with the exception of their waterfronts, port cities had become an integral part of mainlands, the hard edge of the continent.[29]

To be sure, small ports, which far outnumbered deep-water harbors until the nineteenth century, remained ecotonal, connecting land and sea. In its early days, Salem had not one waterfront but many, because like so many other settlements on the Massachusetts coast, it was surrounded by water. People went everywhere by boat, and all the streets led directly

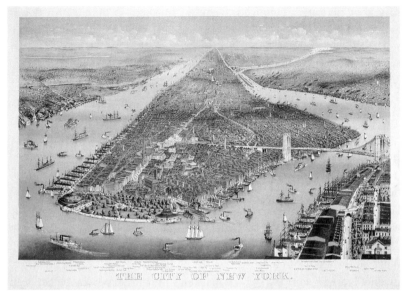

FIGURE 23. *Bird's Eye View of Manhattan,* Currier & Ives, 1884. Courtesy of Corbis.

to the water. Merchants, who often accompanied their ships to sea, lived as close to the water as possible. Everywhere farming and fishing were still joined, and few made the sea a lifetime career. Only in the larger ports of Europe and North America did anything like a full-time seaman or fisherman exist, and even there the notion of "maritime" meant to border the sea rather than to belong fully to it. Those who fished did so seasonally or went to sea for a few years during their youth, and thus were not a breed apart but quite indistinguishable from other members of the coastal populations all around the Atlantic rim.[30]

Initially, the inhabitants of places like Boston, Philadelphia, and New Orleans sent their sons to sea to learn the merchant trade. The most competent of them became ship captains and globetrotting merchants in their own right. Seagoing was initially more a phase of life than an indicator of class position. But by the mid-nineteenth century, both fishing and seagoing became lifetimes of labor. Class divisions appeared on the waterfront, and by the later nineteenth century there existed everywhere a "deep-sea proletariat," recruited increasingly from foreign rather than home ports. It was at this point that cities began to turn their backs on their waterfronts. What had been a center of sociability and civic pride came to be seen as a foreign presence, a danger zone that, like the sea itself, should be kept at a safe distance. The old ecotonal coastal life was now torn asunder as the line between sea and land was ever more deeply etched around the Atlantic. Like New Yorkers and Londoners, Parisians turned away working waterfronts and those who labored there. The urban bourgeoisie now preferred the artificial ponds and fountains to the river that ran through the city.[31]

By the middle of the nineteenth century the respectable classes were retreating from the docks, and cities like New York were turning in on themselves. Members of the merchant class, which had profited so much from seaborne commerce, had ceased to go to sea themselves except to sail their yachts during leisure hours. It was about this time that wharves became places of Sunday recreation. As one Bostonian observed: "Our wharves . . . were in every truth water parks for the people, and contained no end of object lessons. On pleasant Sundays whole families resorted thither. On holidays and special gala occasions, they were immensely attractive." But respectable folk avoided the waterfront on weekdays, for this had become a distinct zone, a betwixt-and-between world that, like the liminal shores of old, was inhabited by strange creatures, this time of a human kind. It was where the "new, colorful, changing, and alien is found." There concentrated foreigners, immigrants, and those pursuing a host of illegal activities: smuggling, pilfering, drug trading, and human trafficking. For respectable citizens, the waterfront became a no-go zone, a "frightening hotbed of marginality," the haunt of addicts, homosexuals, prostitutes. Bourgeois males enjoyed the privilege of slumming at the urban edge of the sea, but no respectable woman could feel comfortable there, except to board a ferry or transatlantic liner.[32]

The great era of the proletarianized waterfront, roughly 1850–1950, was distinguished by a unique environment greatly affected by the pollution generated by urban populations used to thinking of the sea as a great sink into which everything could be emptied. Seaports quickly lost their soft edges as dredging and landfilling destroyed the life-giving wetlands. When Henry Hudson first surveyed what was to become New York's harbor, he described it as an Eden, brimming with fish and shellfish, including the greatest oyster beds in the world, capable of filtering all the water in the surrounding bays in but a few days' time. Like all coastal people, the seventeenth-century Dutch reaped this bounty and made it commercially profitable. Until the twentieth century, the city dined on the harvest from its own shores. "The oyster was New Yorkers' link with the sea and it was eventually lost," however. Today, almost all that is served on the half-shell in Manhattan is flown in from around the world.[33]

After the middle of the nineteenth century, great cities became cultur-ally, if not physically, landlocked. Water worlds that had once been fa-miliar were now known less through firsthand experience than through literature and art. But it was also at this time that inlanders became fas-cinated by the sea as never before, discovering it anew but from a wholly different angle, no longer through work but at leisure. As noted earlier, in the 1850s New Yorkers, most of whom no longer had any connection with the sea, were flocking to the waterfront on Sunday afternoons. "Al-most all men . . . , some time or other, cherish very nearly the same feel-ings toward the ocean with me," wrote Herman Melville. He was clearly astonished by what he witnessed on the Manhattan waterfront: "Posted like silent sentinels all around the town, stand thousands upon thou-sands of mortal men fixed in ocean reveries. Some leaning against the piles; some seated upon the pier-heads; some looking over the bulwarks of ships from China; some high aloft in the rigging, as if striving to get a still better seaward peep. But these are all landsmen; of weekdays pent up in lath and plaster—tied to counters, nailed to benches, clinched to desks. How then is this? Are the green fields gone? What do they here?"[34]

Melville's question still cries out for an answer. He thought it an an-cient impulse, the same that had caused Narcissus to become so enam-ored of his own reflection in water that he plunged in and drowned. For him, the oceans offered "the image of an ungraspable phantom of life." T. S. Eliot believed the sea hinted of "earlier and other creation," a view shared by Henry David Thoreau, Rachel Carson, and all those who would agree with Melville that "meditation and water are wedded forever."[35]

The Half Life of the Fishing Village

Those involved with the sea on a day-to-day basis had no time for water gazing. That activity did not arrive in the fishing village until the twen-tieth century, when working waterfronts were displaced by marinas. With a few exceptions, they had become places where "aspects of fishing are displayed and performed, yet where fish are no longer locally caught or sold." The stereotype of the fishing village, with its well-appointed cottages, tidy waterfront, accommodating inhabitants, bears false witness to the fishing communities of the past. We insist on assigning to fishing villages a contrived antiquity, attributing to their inhabitants, whom we are accustomed to calling "fisherfolk," a largely spurious genealogy. This is yet another way that we have settled the coast, in this case through illusions generated in retrospect.[36]

There were very few permanent fishing villages before the early modern period, and it would not be until the eighteenth century that they became at all common. Only when fishing became a commercial enterprise did anything like fishing communities emerge, and even then, these remained "communities in flux," following the fish, their fortunes ebbing and flowing like the unpredictable movements of prey on which they depended. The life of the small fishing community was normally short, and by the middle of the nineteenth century, they were eclipsed by ever larger ports, when fishing became a full-time, largely proletarian deep-sea occupation.[37]

Even as villages formed in convenient harbors along the coast, their inhabitants kept their distance from the sea itself, facing their cottages landward wherever possible. The first to occupy the beach and build residences facing the sea were upper- and middle-class inlanders convinced of the therapeutic quality of sea air and water. Lured beginning in the mid-eighteenth century from interior health spas by extravagant promises of miracle cures, English invalids and hypochondriacs began flocking to places like Scarborough, Brighton, and Margate, where they entered and exited the sea by means of newly invented bathing machines and spent endless hours beachcombing and sightseeing, activities wholly alien to the local population, who, as Jane Austen observed, avoided the water except when making a living from it. For them "the sea is not only invisible—even its sound and smell shut off in all but the worst of weathers. Sea views are only for urban folk, who never experience its menace. The true sailor prefers to be landlocked rather than face the ocean."[38]

The reality of the fishing village runs counter to all the stereotypes that have been so carefully invested in it over the past two centuries. As it turns out, it is not at all a survival of some archaic form of life. Quite the contrary, it was a thoroughly modern phenomenon, the product of the great economic transformations of the modern era, first the agricultural and then the industrial revolutions, which initially set in motion vast movements of people from the interior to the coasts. Uprooted peasants and small holders who had lost their place on the land turned to fishing out of necessity, often as a last resort, from the sixteenth century onward. This pattern was repeated when New World settlers, finding they could not wrest a living from the land, turned out of desperation to the sea. As Samuel Eliot Morison put it so memorably: "God performed no miracle on the New England soil. He gave the sea. Stark necessity made seamen of would-be planters. . . . Massachusetts went to sea, then, not out of choice, but of necessity."[39]

Working people were not so much drawn to the sea as driven to it. It was events in the interior as much as those at sea that accounted for the settling of the shores. In Scotland, the great landlords whose properties extended to the coasts were busy creating "fish-touns" in the eighteenth century by forcing their tenants to go to earn their rents from the sea. Autonomous fishing villages did not emerge there until the early nineteenth century, and they remained poor and dependent on fish merchants. During the nineteenth and twentieth centuries, fishing populations were increasingly confined to harbors, pushed off the beaches by the latest migrants from the interior, summer vacationers. Today, they are even losing their place in the harbors, driven inland by rising property values and zoning laws.[40]

From the earliest times, fishing villages were products of commercial markets, inland or overseas, and as such were vulnerable to the fluctuations of supply and demand. They were highly unstable and prone to failure, and their populations were transient, ready to move on or go back to farming when conditions dictated. In the eighteenth and early nineteenth centuries, they lacked familial or communal continuity. Their reputation for inbreeding came much later, for, by no means a "breed apart," they were like earlier coastal peoples who moved back and forth across the tide line over a lifetime, mixing farming and fishing: jacks of all trades whose distinguishing feature was their adaptability rather than exclusivity. In the early nineteenth century, Maine's coastal people were among the most traveled and cosmopolitan people on earth. "In the old days, a good part of the best men here knew a hundred ports and something of the way people lived in them," noted Captain Littlepage, one of Sarah Orne Jewett's fictional characters. They were also one of the most up-to-date segments of the American population, scorning everything old in favor of the new. In Europe as well, mariners were harbingers of new trends in dress and speech. When they had accumulated a modest amount of wealth, they built new houses and furnished them in urban styles. Their parlors were filled with exotic items—parrots, ostrich eggs, corals—and they ate off imported china. Even their tombstones were new.[41]

The notion of "fisherfolk," like the stereotype of the peasant, was the product of late-eighteenth-century Rousseauist romanticism, which launched a quest for people, both inside and outside Europe, untainted by civilization. Just as geologists turned to eroded sea cliffs for fossil evidence of deep time, antiquarians scoured coasts and islands for what they believed to be ancestors who could put them in touch with their own remote pasts. In the process, the eighteenth-century images of the pirate and the wrecker were replaced by those of the heroic lifeboat crew and lighthouse keeper. The image of Jack Tar, associated in the eighteenth-century England with rowdiness and radicalism, was wholly domesticated by the mid-nineteenth century, sailors having become icons of patriotic Britishness.[42]

In the wake of the loss of colonies abroad, Britain turned to settling its own coasts for political as well as economic reasons. In 1786, the British Fisheries Society had been formed for the purpose of creating model fishing villages where the poverty of unemployed sailors and dispossessed small holders could be alleviated. Most of these—Tobermory, Ullapool, Lochbay, and Pulteneytown—were located in Scotland, where clearances had cut thousands adrift from the land. Each provided facilities for fishing but also adequate land to supplement that part-time occupation. At Lochbay, access to land undermined the fishery when the inhabitants all turned to farming, but in the most successful of the communities, Pulteneytown, located in what is now the town of Wick, an ecotonal economy lasted from 1803 to 1893, with as many as seven thousand residents during the fishing season.[43]

The British sailor, once the cause of so much anxiety, was rapidly becoming an object of nostalgia, stereotyped in art and photographed in archaic settings that had little to do with his actual working circumstances. In the new United States, the process of folklorization took longer to develop, but by the 1880s the image of the "old salt" had been similarly constructed, ultimately disguising all traces of the proletarianization that prevailed everywhere fishing was the poor person's only alternative. As John Stilgoe has put it: "By 1910 the coastal people had become specimens or characters, something they remain—in the popular imagination at least—to this day."[44]

The idealized peasant and fishing villages were both products of the fertile imaginations of artists and writers, outsiders who seized upon certain landscapes as representing a way of life they could no longer find in modern urban centers. In England, the country village became the essence of Englishness, while in Scotland it was the fishing port that came to represent a certain kind of authentic Scottishness. In the Canadian Maritimes and New England, fishing communities also became bearers of regional, even national, heritage. This process culminated in the 1920s and 1930s, when the global economy became unhinged. It seemed to many who knew coastal people only from summer visits to the coasts and islands that they were more rooted, of purer stock than urban people. Although fishermen constituted a smaller portion of Nova Scotia's Cape

Breton working population than either miners or farmers, they came to be an icon of all that was worth preserving there. The same was true among Nantucketers and the outport populations of Newfoundland.[45]

Ironically, it was in the wake of the collapse of the fishing industry that the fishing village came to exercise such a hold on the modern imagination. Gloucester, one of the few seaports that refused to die a quiet death, never attained the iconic status of nearby Rockport, whose abandoned wharves and rotting schooners made it a magnet for artists. In the wake of the collapse of its whaling industry in the mid-nineteenth century, Nantucket's business elite searched desperately for new uses of its abandoned wharves and decaying housing stock. It turned out that history was a commodity that could reinvigorate the tourist and real estate markets. By the turn of the twentieth century the local tourist industry had managed to hide the unsavory history of whaling behind the quaint facades of refurbished colonial houses, convincing tourists that "history stopped nearly a half century ago."[46]

Coasts, like islands, were now represented as places where time stood still. When the American painter Marsden Hartley went looking for a secular version of eternity, he believed he found it on the east coast of Nova Scotia. Coastal peoples were imagined to be survivors from an earlier time, and admirable for it. Despite their migratory tendencies, they were categorized as "natives," taking on the characteristics of the place where land and water meet. In France, coastal peoples were exoticized, imagined as primitives, likened to Tahitians and Australian aboriginals. But they were no longer considered savages, for even as coasts shed their reputation for danger, their residents were reimagined as quaint fisherfolk, harmless characters. By the end of the nineteenth century it was not uncommon to find French tourists playing fishermen in the same way that Americans played Indians, as a way of shedding the restraints of civilization and getting in touch with their archaic selves. Painted and photographed but rarely really known by the tourists under whose gaze they now fell, coastal peoples, like fishing villages, became increasingly stereotyped, conforming to the homogenizing conventions of the tourist trade. In Rockport, the artists' favorite village, much had changed, but care was taken that one fish house located on Bradley Wharf be kept just the same for the benefit of genre painters. When what became known as "Motif Number 1" was destroyed by a blizzard in 1976, it was quickly rebuilt, an immutable icon not just of Rockport but of every fishing village on the New England shore.[47]

FIGURE 24. Painters' icon, Motif Number 1, Rockport, Massachusetts. Courtesy of Wikipedia.

Nova Scotia's Peggy's Cove, probably the most painted and photo-graphed place on America's east coast, was brought to Canada's atten-tion in 1944 by the writings of J. F. B. Livesey, an Englishman born on the Isle of Wight, who found there "a little pulsing human cosmos set in an uneasy sea." But it was the artist-writer William E. deGarthe, who began summering at the cove in the 1930s and moved there permanently in 1955, who did most to realize Livesey's pastoral vision. DeGarthe was a coastal Finn of Swedish background who had migrated to Canada in 1926. Trained as a painter, he dedicated his life to finding what he called "the most beautiful place on earth." This he located on the edge of St. Margaret's Bay in a cluster of houses still without electricity or indoor plumbing, though within an easy drive of Nova Scotia's major city, Hal-ifax. Deeply nostalgic about the "passing era of the sea," deGarthe be-friended the dwindling population of local fishermen and began trans-forming the place through his paintings and a pamphlet, *This Is Peggy's Cove.* The name of the cove had derived from the bay of which it was a

FIGURE 25. Waterfront at Peggy's Cove, Nova Scotia. Courtesy of Wikipedia.

part, but deGarthe invented a fictitious Peggy, a shipwrecked woman who supposedly gave her name to the cove when she married one of her local rescuers. Locals were convinced that deGarthe "made it up," saying "he had to, no one else ever heard of it." Yet they did not object too much, because by the 1950s tourism had replaced fishing as their major source of income. DeGarthe became the impresario of the village's fame and fortune until his death in 1983.[48]

The emergence of Peggy's Cove and its counterparts around the Atlantic was the end product of a long process of cultural colonization, which by the late nineteenth century had wholly erased the earlier vision of coasts as ugly and forbidding. That Livesey and deGarthe could imagine the coastal people who had been barely hanging onto their precarious existence as more stable than their inland neighbors was a feat of their highly active imaginations. "The island of calm, a friendly haven from the confusion of the world," was what Livesey wrote about a place that was in fact experiencing economic collapse and rapid loss of population. Today few boats ever leave the harbor, but the pristine image of the fishing village is maintained by regulations from the 1960s that guarantee that

Peggy's Cove will not change visually, whatever may happen to the fishing itself.[49]

Life now imitates art, even at the expense of life itself. From Scotland to Newfoundland, fishing villages survive, even thrive, in the absence of fishing. The coastal district of Buckie lives off the tourist trade, its motto "Our Future Lies in Our Past." Many fishing settlements have disappeared, but others reinvented themselves as aestheticized, sanitized versions of something that had never really existed. As Jan Goss has observed: "The maritime landscape is attractive only in the past or at a distance . . . for its 'grittiness' close-up is inconvenient to middle class consumption."[50]

The images of fishermen conjured up by artists and writers beginning in the early nineteenth century bore little resemblance to those who worked the shore. We have few realistic depictions of maritime labor, especially of the women who were an integral part of that economy. There were even fewer creditable figures in seascapes than in landscapes. The ship, the object of merchant pride, was most often foregrounded. Life on the high seas inspired artists and writers, but inshore fishing and coastal shipping failed to fuel their imaginations. Earlier, those exploring the coast from the sea had overlooked it for what lay inland. "To the earlier articulate observer," writes Ian McKay, "the coastline was ugly and uninteresting and the fisherfolk primitive, pitiable outcasts from the 'march of progress.' Rockbound coastlines and grizzled fisherfolk were not seen as uplifting symbols of Nova Scotia." But later the coasts and the remnants of the population who inhabited them were transformed into bulwarks of a society that had, in the eyes of those like Livesey and deGarthe, been undermined by a century of industrialization and urbanization. What Jean-Didier Urbain has described as a century-long process of "desavaging" coastal people worked miracles. The people who had been described as wild as the coasts themselves were now portrayed by Bernard DeVoto as the "People of Granite," Maine Yankees of unshakable character who could weather any of modernity's storms, including the Great Depression. When the American artist Marsden Hartley went to Nova Scotia in 1935, he, like Livesey and deGarthe, was looking for "bedrock in a shifting world."[51]

Land's End

For Rachel Carson, "the boundary between sea and land is the most fleeting and transitory feature of the earth." For millennia, it had also been the most dangerous. As late as the early nineteenth century Britain was losing about one thousand ships a year, most of them wrecked near shore, many in ports themselves. The creation of permanent harbors and embankments that made tidal ports more alluring also made them more treacherous by reducing natural scouring, narrowing channels, and raising tide levels. These threats to coastal prosperity launched the first great sustained effort to understand the sea, which focused first on tides and only later turned to deep-sea oceanography.[52]

By the end of the nineteenth century, shores that had once been terra incognita became among the earth's best-known features. Shipwreck near shore became rare, and the coast lost its association with danger to become a place of pleasure. No longer borderlands or frontiers, seacoasts were declared by Lord Curzon "the most uncompromising, the least alterable and most effective" of all boundaries precisely because they appeared to be so natural. In the course of less than a century, the process of discovering, surveying, and naming had the effect of naturalizing the shore, fossilizing it in the minds of inlanders. Coasts were emptied of their original historical significance to become places where history began or ended, no longer where it was made.[53]

In 1835 it was still possible for Alexis de Tocqueville to imagine a maritime future for America. But by the end of the century the nation thought of itself, as did most of the great European powers to which it compared itself, as a continental nation. Both geography and history had been seized by what Denis Cosgrove has called the "territorializing vision," which assumed that nations are by nature bounded, centered, terrestrial units. The landings at Jamestown and Plymouth had become America's mythic origins. The rocky shores that mariners had once feared foundering upon were now the venerated foundations of a national shrine. Plymouth Rock, of which there is no record in the initial Pilgrim records, and which, in fact, had been removed from the shore by 1774, had become an icon of origins. Returned to its original setting in 1859, by the end of the century it had become a national tourist attraction.[54]

By then history had taken a landward turn, no longer moving offshore or, as they say in New England, "Down East," but resolutely from east to west. There was a time early in the nineteenth century when Americans had imagined moving on into the Pacific to fulfill their destiny, but the sea frontiers were closed and Jefferson's "empire of liberty" would halt at the west coast rather than proceed immediately to Hawaii and beyond. Jonathan Raban has observed that "people who live on continents get into the habit of regarding the ocean as journey's end, the full stop at the end of the trek. When North Americans reached the Pacific, there was nothing to do except build the end-of-the-world state of California."⁵⁵

A measure of the hegemony of the prevailing territorializing vision was the number of "land's ends" that began to loom on the coasts of Europe and America. The best known, located on the south westernmost promontory of Cornwall, was named as early as the fourteenth century Landesynde, meaning "End of the Mainland." Other land's ends, such as Spain's Cape Finisterre and France's Finistere, are also westerly locations. So too are the land's ends in California, one in the Baja, the other at Presidio Point just to the west of San Francisco.⁵⁶

By the early twentieth century, the west coast had become America's final frontier. It was fitting that the Panama-Pacific International Exhibition was hosted by San Francisco in 1915. For it, James Earle Fraser sculpted in plaster an exhausted Indian warrior slumped on his horse, a symbol of the final defeat of Indians by advancing white civilization. *End of the Trail* was a hugely popular image, and Fraser planned to have it bronzed and placed facing west on Presidio Point, high above the Pacific. The First World War intervened, however. All metal was requisitioned for the war effort, and Fraser's intentions were thwarted. Nevertheless, the promontory just south of the Golden Gate retains its significance as the end of road, if not the end of the Indian race, for many Americans.

The westward orientation was deeply embedded in European culture. The Celts looked west to the sea for their land of the dead; the Romans located their deceased heroes on isles in the western sea; and Christianity, whose sacred sites were originally located in Eastern holy lands, came to expect the Second Coming of Christ to be located in the west, where not only land but time was seen as terminating. In the minds of believers, salvation moved from east to west, taking the end time with it. The west came to be associated with death but also with resurrection. In Christian thought, endings have always been inseparable from new beginnings. John Wesley, who visited England's Land's End in 1743, found the coast there an "awful sight" but anticipated that, according to the biblical geography of the day, its ugliness, a result of original sin, would "melt away when God ariseth in judgment."⁵⁷

Once prominent landfalls for mariners, land's ends did not take on meaning for inlanders until the nineteenth century, when coasts finally became accessible by land. When Richard Ayton and the illustrator William Daniell initiated their exploration of what they called the "unaccountably neglected" coast of England in 1813, they had planned to go by sea but found it too dangerous and decided instead to do their "sailing

FIGURE 26. Land's End, Cornwall. Courtesy of Library of Congress.

by horseback," initiating an appetite for coast-wise travel that has only grown over time. While it is not entirely clear why they chose to begin their journey at Land's End, it is certain that the place already had a special meaning to the crowds who "gaze at it, scratch their names upon a sod, and then depart, with that fulness of satisfaction which a man ought to feel, who is conscious that he has done all that can be done." Ayton and Daniell followed "the customary observance of going to the extreme edge of the point" before proceeding around the coast in a clockwise manner.[58]

It could be that they were witnesses to the survival of some ancient ritual, for, as W. H. Hudson noted a hundred years later, the "ancient association of the place remains, and if a visit is rightly timed, they may invest it a sublimity and fascination not its own." But if there was any Celtic or Christian meaning attached to Cornwall's Land's End, it was soon to be displaced by romantic associations that were of a vastly different, and wholly modern, origin. When Ayton and Danielle began their journey, the coast was largely terra incognita to all but the locals. On the coasts of England only fashionable spas had previously attracted visitors. The rest of the coast was regarded so unhealthy and dangerous that only light-houses and watchtowers existed there. These intrepid travelers were true explorers of the unknown, keen to "illustrate the grandeur of its natural scenery, the manners and employment of people, and modes of life, in its wildest parts." Up to this time, it was precisely the wildness that had been avoided. Now this became the coast's greatest attraction. The very *terra nullus* that had once repelled now attracted, leaving plenty of room for visitors to invest it with their wildest imaginings.[59]

In the course of the nineteenth century, Cornwall's Land's End became one of the best-known places in Britain, visited by tens of thousands who came by road and rail to observe what had by then become a tradition of going to the very edge. Those who witnessed the ritual likened it to a pilgrimage. Wilkie Collins compared Land's End to Jerusalem but detected in the pilgrims no obvious religious motive. W. H. Hudson described the destination in wholly secular terms, as "the great and final object of a journey to the westernmost county in England, its Ultima Thule." For him Land's End was "a name that strikes us most in childhood when we learnt our geography; which fills the minds of imaginative people with visions of barrenness and solitude and dreams of some lonely promontory, the place where the last man in England will be found waiting for death at the end of the world."[60]

By the late nineteenth century Land's End had become a prime destination for day-trippers, some of whom came from as far away as the colonies to stand, if only for a few moments, facing west on this shabby promontory before reboarding the trains for Manchester and London. "I've always wanted to see Land's End, and it's the same with all of us," Hudson reports one working man saying; "we've come to see it and nothing else." Many were old men fulfilling a promise, nurtured since childhood, to visit before they died. Once done, they had no reason to linger or return. For the wealthy few there was a hotel overlooking the sea, but for most their visit lasted only a few minutes.[61]

Locals expressed astonishment at such behavior. Those who lived nearby knew it to be a dangerous, forbidding place. "I've never seen it and never want to see it," one Cornishman told Hudson. Whatever local meaning it might have had was now lost. The place belonged instead to the imagined space of the nation, which in the course of the nineteenth century came to be defined by its coasts from south to north as well as from east to west. Hudson called Land's End a "national possession," an inalienable part of the national anatomy. In an era when certain landscapes were enshrined by schoolroom maps and postage stamps and featured for the first time in national anthems, coasts became icons of national identity and security.[62]

Coasts played an increasingly prominent role in the emergence of a coherent national geography. In 1832 it was still possible for Daniel Webster to stand in the halls of the US Congress and declare: "What can we ever hope to do with the western coast, a coast of three thousand miles, rockbound, and cheerless, Mr. President. I will never vote one cent from the public treasury to place the west coast one inch nearer to Boston than it is now." By the end of the nineteenth century, however, coasts had come to define America. Nations without access to the sea felt their inferiority. They compensated for this by maintaining navies, most of them operating only on rivers or lakes. Bolivia, which lost access to the Pacific in the so-called War of the Pacific in the late nineteenth century, still has the largest of these. Its duties are at present confined to patrolling Lake Titicaca, but it remains of great symbolic importance to Bolivians, whose longstanding hopes of returning to the sea were given a lift in 2010 by access agreements with Peru.[63]

The phrase "coast to coast" was first used to describe the United States in the 1850s. When Katherine Lee Bates composed "America the Beautiful" in 1893, she had just ascended Pike's Peak, from which "all the wonder of American seemed displayed there in sea-like expanse." The glorious "amber waves of grain" evoked the bounty of oceans, but Bates's vision extended only from "sea to shining sea," for by then the United States identified itself not as a maritime but as a continental nation. In 1879 a Cornishman by the name of Robert Carlyle pushed a wheelbarrow from Land's End to John O'Groats in the far north of Scotland. Since then, retracing his route has become something of a patriotic observance. Connecting the edges was a demonstration of individual prowess but also a tribute to national unity. "End to enders" who walk, cycle, or drive the route compete among themselves for speed records, but the journey is also a kind of national pilgrimage and, like its religious counterparts, a source of collective identity for those who undertake it. Shores have come to provide a cohesion that interiors could not. As Paul Theroux was to discover when he later replicated the circumabulation of Ayton and Daniell, "Britain was its coast." No other country has become so identified with its coasts as this island nation, but everywhere around the Atlantic rim what had previously been alien territory is now embraced as a source of national pride and pleasure.[64]

By the end of the nineteenth century, coasts had taken on an entirely new appearance. Once having a fluid geography populated by transient edge species, coasts had become spatially and temporally fossilized. There movement paused and time seemed to stand still. The old coast now lay in ruins, overlain by what John Cheever has described as "a second coast and port of gift and antique shops, restaurants, tearooms, and bars where people drank their gin by candlelight, surrounded by ploughs, fish nets, barnacle lights and other relics of an arduous and orderly way of life of which they knew nothing." Today the decor of the second coast is more likely to be manufactured than antique. John McKinney speaks of the boutiquing of California's coast, which has gone so far that "visitors are unable to reach the waterfront, unable to see the shores for the stores." Even the "beach glass" sold in gift shops comes not from the shore but from inland factories. The surrealism of the second coast is more and more obvious, the product of inlanders' imaginations, sustained by their needs and desires. They have taken possession of the reliquary of the first coast and used it to legitimate their mythical geographies and historical fictions.[65]

5 · THE SECOND DISCOVERY
OF THE SEA

The sea is one of the most "universal" symbols in literature; it is certainly the most protean. JONATHAN RABAN[1]

The oceans have been discovered twice over. In the first Age of Discovery, seas were explored and charted as a means to reach distant lands, but little attention was paid to the waters themselves. It has been said that "the deep sea made hardly an impression. . . . Even ocean-going explorers were more land than ocean oriented; they used the sea merely as a highway to get to the next landfall." This was a discovery more *by* sea than *of* the sea. Early modern science knew much more about the heavens than about the oceans, and more attention was paid to extracting the wealth of the seas, namely fish, than to the waters themselves. All that lay beneath the surface—the Deep—was thought to be an unfathomable abyss, impenetrable and unknowable, a dark dead zone that trapped all that sank below the surface, never revealing its secrets. Until the nineteenth century, notes James Hamilton-Paterson, our understanding of the sea was "literally superficial, . . . a navigable surface, obviously, above the abyss."[2]

The second discovery of the sea, beginning in the nineteenth century, produced a vast expansion of knowledge of the sea itself, now as a three-dimensional living thing with a history and geography all its own. Modern times accomplished what no other era had even attempted: the discovery of the deep sea. At the same time it brought about another discovery, this one as much literary and artistic as scientific, a metaphorical rather than physical reconnaissance that has had equal, if not greater, consequences for popular culture in the modern era.

Since ancient times, the oceans had been considered utterly alien to humankind. One went to sea out of necessity rather than desire. The voyage was a "necessary evil, a crossing of that which separates and estranges," writes W. H. Auden. It was fate, not choice, that took Odysseus offshore. During the entire voyage it was *nostos*, homecoming, not the sea, that was at the forefront of his consciousness. For medieval Christians, the sea was comparable to the desert that had inspired the first generation of churchmen. St. Brendan launched his boat upon its vast emptiness in the hope of finding God there. His voyage was that of a *peregrinato*, an ordeal meant as a test of faith under the most adverse conditions.[3]

Erasmus warned that it was "folly to trust in the sea," and John Donne wrote in 1619 that "the sea is no place of habitation, but a passage to our habitations." That was the way William Bradford understood the *Mayflower*'s ordeal. For him the voyage was a "sea of troubles," but it is significant that he reserves the description "hideous and desolate wilderness" for the *land* that was the Pilgrims' destination. For these Christians, the voyage was an encounter not with nature but with the supernatural. The voyage to America was itself an act of faith in obedience to divine providence rather than an act of free will that later, more secular observers would have it be.[4]

The sea was not only dangerous but ugly, unworthy of artistic or literary treatment. For Shakespeare the sea was a backdrop rather than a principal subject. Early modern sea fiction and painting were surprisingly impoverished when it came to oceans themselves. The focus then was almost entirely on ships and the skills of the men who manned them, with the sea itself almost an afterthought. In the sea novels of the sixteenth and seventeenth centuries, interest dwelled, as it did in marine painting, on the details of the mariner's craft. After 1750, interest in the toilers of the sea diminished greatly and the English novel became landlocked, "territorialized" as it were. When sea fiction revived in the nineteenth century, it was concerned more with the psyches than with the work of men at sea.[5]

The sea as such began to loom large only when land had finally been conquered. It took almost until the twentieth century for all the continents to be fully explored and settled. Until then the territories behind the coasts were referred to as hinterlands and associated with backwardness. By the twentieth century, the positions of coasts and interiors had been reversed. The latter, now described as the "heartland," had become the center of economic and political gravity. The first phase of capitalist development had been commercial and maritime; the second was agricultural and industrial, and thoroughly terrestrial. When the great age of sail gave way to the era of steam in the second half of the nineteenth century, the seas retreated and the continents opened up. Destiny now belonged to land rather than to water for the first time in centuries. The new industrial age was based not just on trade in commodities but on their manufacture, and this gave the advantage to large landmasses with populations capable of scaling up to mass production and consumption.

No country could afford to be a hinterland, as the future now belonged to the heartlands that the geographer Halford J. Mackinder in 1904 called the future pivots of world history.[6]

But even as nations turned away from the sea as a place of work and power, they returned to it, as never before, as a place of re-creation, both physical and spiritual. In the nineteenth century the sea itself, as opposed to ships and mariners, began to enter art and literature in wholly unprecedented, modern ways. In what Margaret Cohen has called the "sublimation of the sea," it was given a new cultural status, a higher aesthetic power. The ocean became a fountain of images and metaphors—the shipwreck being only the most prominent—that have continued to dominate Western culture to the present day. Even as the numbers of those who went to sea for a living diminished dramatically, more and more people began describing their life as a voyage. As one student of this extraordinary turn of events has put it, those who "who live on land nevertheless prefer, in their imagination, to represent their overall condition in the world in terms of a sea voyage." At the same time, qualities once associated with land, notably wilderness, moved offshore. Pristine nature, by then in short supply in industrialized heartlands, found refuge in the oceans, while the mystery once associated with terra incognita relocated to the deeps. Simultaneously, the sublime, previously associated with mountains and forests, came to be associated with whitewater.[7]

The Sea as Acquired Taste

It was in the wake of the great maritime era of the late eighteenth and early nineteenth centuries that the sea first became a part of mainstream mainland culture. Then, for the first time, the American and European middle classes took on what Henry David Thoreau called a "marine tint." To some young men like Richard Henry Dana, sailing before the mast was a rite of passage. A passion for yachting developed on both sides of the Atlantic; and water sports became hugely popular. In the course of the next half-century, millions of Dana's countrymen, who had originally arrived by sea, would return to it imaginatively, and some physically. Beginning in the mid-nineteenth century there were those, often men of evangelical persuasion, who took up sailing not to go somewhere but to recapture some sense of manly independence and moral compass they could no longer find in their everyday landed existence. Jonathan Raban observes that "the small boat voyagers were rarely out of sight of a society they were trying to call to order, and they used the sea to prove some-

thing to the land." Yet most of those who returned to the sea went no farther than the shore. Still today, most of us acquire our marine tint not on
water but at the beach.[8]

But even those who never crossed the tide line embraced maritime
figures of speech and made the sea a metaphor for life lived on land. They
fell in love with the toy boat and the sailor suit, began to colonize the
shore for fun as well as health, and filled their urban and suburban parlors with aquariums and seascapes. As one historian has put it: "During
the nineteenth century, the ocean entered the minds, homes, dreams, and
conversations of ordinary people." It did so through the art of seascape,
through adventure literature, and in a much more mundane way: collections of tropical fish, seashells, corals, and scrimshaw. "Often it seems
the more people become urbanized," writes James Hamilton-Paterson,
"the more they want about them talismans of nature on their walls, their
shelves, and their keyrings."[9]

In the nineteenth century, people began to come back to the sea in
search for a quality they felt to be missing in the new industrial environment, something they called wilderness. The desire for an experience
of untamed nature originated in the eighteenth century among a small
group of European aesthetes for whom the awesome power of the sea, as
witnessed from the safety of land, was a powerful emotional and mental
stimulant. The terror and awe that religious folk had previously associated with the supernatural were now relocated to nature itself. In 1712 Joseph Addison wrote of the "agreeable horrour" evoked by tempests: "Of
all objects that I have ever seen, there is none which affects imagination
so much as the sea or ocean. . . . A troubled ocean, to a man who sails
upon it, is, I think, the biggest object that he can see in motion. . . . Such
an object naturally raises in my thoughts the idea of an Almighty Being, and convinces me of his existence as much as a metaphysical demonstration." In France, Denis Diderot was drawn to the shore for similar
reasons, while the Englishman Edmund Burke also preferred the sea to
the land as a tonic for mind and soul. No one knew this better than Jules
Verne, who wrote: "The human mind delights in grand visions of supernatural beings. And the sea is the very best medium, the only environment in which such giants—compared to which land animals, such as
the elephant and the rhinoceros, are like dwarfs—can be produced and
developed."[10]

The romantic imagination of the early nineteenth century, initially focused on the sublimity of mountains, eventually turned to the wild shore,
a place previously avoided by all but those who made their living there.

FIGURE 27. Winslow Homer's representation of the coastal sublime at Prouts Neck, *Driftwood*, 1909. Photograph copyright Museum of Fine Arts, Boston.

If in earlier periods the surge of the sea was expected to evoke images of the biblical flood, of death and destruction, now, in a more secular age, the same waters promised bodily and spiritual resurrection. The coasts of Britain and France were by then lined with spas offering the blessings of seawater, at first only for the elites, but by the mid-nineteenth century for the middle classes as well. In the twentieth century the masses followed them to the most modern of all pleasuring places, the beach.

Direct physical experience of the sea had been replaced by an imaginative familiarity no less vivid and compelling. Up to the eighteenth century, the sea itself was largely invisible, of interest more for the fish it contained and the lands it connected than for itself, rarely appearing in the foreground of either art or literature until the romantic movement of the eighteenth and nineteenth centuries made it a fit subject for both.

But once that turning point was reached, the sea rapidly became embedded in popular culture. Soon imaginative representations of it were giving shape to new nautical realities. Furthermore, the sea became the stage on which the human condition could be acted out in the most melodramatic fashion. Dreams and nightmares that had previously been projected on terrestrial landscapes now became invested in seascapes. Even as the oceans became for the first time objects of science, the sea was undergoing a new round of mythologization.[11]

Eventually science would get its sea legs, but oceanography was the last-born of the new disciplines, and even now only a very small part of the ocean deeps, at most 5 percent, are known in any detail. Popular notions of the oceans are still products more of films and novels than of research. The sea remains, as it was in the Bible, the ultimate other, but now a natural rather than a supernatural phenomenon. As in the first discovery of the sea, imagination charted the way that explorers would follow. Science would take its lead from writers like Jules Verne and Herman Melville, who were the first to move offshore to explore not just the nature of the sea but human nature.[12]

Once marginal to Western culture, the sea has now gravitated to the center of its collective consciousness, a master metaphor of all human conduct. Raban has called the sea the most protean of all symbols because it is "not a verifiable object . . . it is, rather, the supremely liquid and volatile element, shaping itself newly for every water and every generation." During the nineteenth century the sea took up an entirely new position in the mythical geography of Western culture. What Joseph Conrad referred to as the "imperishable sea" became a refuge for hopes and fears that could no longer be accommodated inland.[13]

Even as most Americans and Europeans became less physically connected to the oceans, they became more intimate with them mentally and imaginatively. Water had always had sacramental powers, but now for the first time the sea offered a kind of secular redemption. It became a symbol of eternity, a comfort to those who, having lost their faith in divine dispensation of everlasting life, came to see in its apparently timeless flows evidence of nature's immortality and of life everlasting. There, at the place where land and water meet, time and history held no sway. Land became associated with limits, with beginnings and endings, but the sea came to represent bountifulness, an apparently endlessly renewable resource, a wholly new frontier to be explored and exploited. For Joseph Conrad, who despised what had happened to land in the industrial age, the sea was the only viable alternative. Only in our own time has the myth of the boundless sea been challenged by the evident results of pollution and the unsustainable pillaging of the world's waters; yet even so, the idea of the everlasting sea endures in popular culture.[14]

New Horizons

The second discovery of the sea was the accomplishment of inlanders like Henry David Thoreau and Rachel Carson rather than mariners, writers whose practical experience of the oceans was limited but whose imaginations were unbounded. They came down to the sea to discover not what lay beyond but that which lay within themselves. In earlier generations the awe-inspiring dimension had been the vertical, especially the heavens above. Now the water gazer replaced the stargazer, as the horizontal took on new meaning and horizons themselves became frontiers of the imagination, especially to those artists who flocked to the shore for the first time. At first it was the wild nature of the sea that drew them, but they soon discovered its temporal as well as spatial depth. On land, industrial change seemed to be sweeping aside the past, but the sea, now increasingly referred to as "eternal" or "imperishable," appeared primordial, an repository of that which had disappeared on land. Jules Verne argued that because it never changes, "why should the sea, in its unknown depths, not have conserved some of those giant specimens of life of another age?" And the people of the sea, mariners and fisherfolk, who had previously been beneath the notice of artists and poets, were suddenly also of interest as vestiges of the old and the enduring. The seascape, once a minor artistic genre, became a major one in the course of the nineteenth century, bringing images of marine life into the parlors of those who had never been near a coast, much less at sea.[15]

In England, where there was little interior wilderness left, the "wild" sea lured romantics early on. In America, where there seemed a vast abundance of untamed lands, it took longer for the quest for sublime experiences to become focused on the ocean. In the course of the nineteenth century, however, as land ceased to convey personal and national grandeur, the boundlessness of the sea became ever more appealing. Its "horizontal immensity," combined with its perpetual motion and mysterious deeps, had immense appeal on both sides of the Atlantic. The sea became a mirror that landlubbers would use to reflect on their own condition. Rapidly industrializing societies, and especially the men of those societies, would use it to measure themselves, to test their fitness and manliness in a world that no longer presented sufficient challenges.[16]

Even as actual involvement with the sea diminished, its symbolic and metaphorical presence increased. Hans Blumenberg tells us that in an era when ships of state were threatened by revolution, the shipwreck metaphor loomed larger than ever. In the Victorian era the English masses also belatedly discovered themselves as a maritime people. The occupation of the common sailor, previously avoided as something akin to slavery, was now glorified as honorable and heroic. While an identification with soil became foundational to nineteenth-century nationalism in France and Germany, in Britain it was the sea that roused strong patriotic passions. Robert Louis Stevenson observed that "if an Englishman wishes such a [patriotic] feeling, it must be about the sea. . . . The sea is our approach and bulwark; it has been the scene of our greatest triumphs and dangers; and we are used in lyrical strains to claim it as our own." In the Victorian era, the English would create a pantheon of naval heroes and endow Jack Tar with a nobility that no earlier generation of sailors had enjoyed.[17]

It was then that the sea came to be considered "the natural home of the Englishman," the birthright of the nation, an invitation to and a justification for imperial expansion. The islandness of Britain, previously seen as a disadvantage, came to be a "wise dispensation of Providence," both a protection from foreign invasion and a means of access to the wider world. "We have a fine sea," declared Charles Dickens, "wholesome to all people; profitable for the body, profitable for the mind." Although the era of great voyages was well past, the sea offered the English a retrospective vision of themselves as a heroic nation in a way their tenuous terrestrial domains could never do. In America as well, there developed what was "essentially a coastal, sea-consciousness culture with a developing literary tradition anchored in romantic impulses."[18]

But the sea also operated on a more personal level, as metaphor for life itself. In an era when everything seemed to be in a state of becoming, the sea represented metaphorically the flow of life. "Here," wrote J. G. Francis of the seaside, "better, we think, than in any inland scenery, man can muse and meditate." The flood tide was a reminder of childhood and youth, the ebb tide of old age, while the horizon "tells a steadfast future, an immutable eternity." Now that all was seen in terms of change, of evolution, nautical metaphors were to be found everywhere in art as well as literature. Traditionally, the favorite image of the life course had been the "Ages of Man," a rising and falling staircase on which each stage of life from birth to death was represented as static. Prior to the nineteenth century, the journey of life had been represented terrestrially as a road or path, but in 1842 the American artist Thomas Cole produced four paintings called

Voyage of Life that quickly became the most popular representation of the life course. In it, figures of childhood, youth, manhood, and old age are shown aboard a boat going down a river that will ultimately lead to the sea, representing death.[19]

Now the notion of the voyage took on a whole new significance. It was the voyage itself, not the destination, that gave life meaning. What had previously been associated with fate, undertaken only out of necessity, now became the ambition of every young man. Sea was associated with growth, land with stagnation. Once the last resort of the poor, going to sea came for the first time to be seen as an ennobling activity. In both England and North America the voyage became for a certain elite a virtual rite of passage, distinguishing them not only from the landlocked common man but also, perhaps even more important, from all women. Paradoxically, even as the sea came to be reimagined as maternal and the ship as female, seafaring became even more exclusively male than it had been in earlier centuries. In a complete reversal of the ancients' understanding of *nostos*, it was the sea that was now home. For men, going to sea brought out the fullness of masculinity; for women, in the "proximity of the mothering sea, feminine instincts blossom." As the sea came to be seen as the womb of all life, the shore became the nursery, increasingly identified with childhood as more and more middle-class Victorians traveled as families to vacation there. Before the beach was sexualized it was domesticated, a realm belonging to mothers and children, which men remembered nostalgically as a lost paradise of childhood that repeatedly lured them back in adulthood.[20]

The same generation that established the deep time of evolutionary theory was equally invested in the ocean deeps. Mysteries once thought to exist inland now moved offshore. The sea became the new wilderness and the new frontier, the next horizon of human aspirations, taking on the burden of fulfilling hopes and dreams once invested in landed frontiers. The capacity of humankind's imagination to outpace its powers of observation meant that even as the second era of discovery plumbed the seas in ever greater depth, the oceans became the latest location for mythical geography, which, as Mircea Eliade reminds us, is the only geography man could never do without.[21]

How the Sea Became Wild

The sea had long been associated with wildness, but not the kind that attracted the romantic generation. *Wilderness* is one of those mutant words, constantly changing in meaning and application. Once associated with places unfit for human habitation, it was identified with desolate lands, especially deserts and impenetrable forests, before it was attached to the sea itself. It became a place to experience the depth of feeling that was so prized among generations of European and American romantics. In the course of the nineteenth century, wilderness ceased to be something feared and avoided to become a place to be enjoyed and protected.

In many cultures the sea is strongly associated with the supernatural. It is frequently the location of the dead, of immortals. This was true in China and pagan Europe. Christianity defined the sea as the realm of Satan but reserved ultimate control for God. In biblical geography the waters obey his will, remaining mysterious and unpredictable. It was not until the eighteenth century that it was possible to contemplate that oceans might be subject to laws of nature, and even later before these laws were spelled out by modern oceanography. Until then, humans felt at home only on land. Monsters were still featured as illustrations on sea charts long after they had disappeared from maps of the interior. Fears had always been projected to the margins of the known world, and as the continents became better known, the oceans became the repository of dangers that no longer could be imagined on land. There lurked great white whales and killer sharks, whose purchase on popular culture would grow over time, first in literature and later in films. The deeps continued to keep their secrets much longer than even the remotest parts of earth, giving much greater play to the imagination. Fears and fantasies were greater the farther one got from the shore, "a resonant reference for people who did not work at sea or live along the coast."[22]

As civilization encroached on lands around the world, the pristine had no place to go but to sea. By the end of the nineteenth century—and still today—it was assumed that, of all the places on this planet, the oceans have been the least affected by humankind. Frequent references to "the eternal sea" make it seem that its waters remain beyond the reach of time, an illusion that has contributed to the oceans' absence from serious historical treatment, even by environmental historians. Wilderness appealed most to city dwellers who looked to find in it the sources of personal and social inspiration they felt slipping away from them in capitalist industrial society. Sensing a loss of connection with nature, Europeans and Americans looked about for spaces where its purest forms might be found and protected. Mountains, forests, and deserts were the first to be designated and preserved as wilderness. The sea was the last to be protected, largely because it seemed so boundless as never to be endangered.

As the continents were fully explored, landed frontiers became scarce. Only the United States and Canada had room for wilderness, but by the late nineteenth century North Americans were also looking to the deep sea as "a great void, idealized as outside society, a wild space of nature that was antithetical to the social places on land that could be planned, controlled, and developed."[23]

Among the first to discover the sea as a new frontier were Native Americans like Maine's Wabanaki people, who had initially been pushed back from the coast by European settlers and then displaced from their interior hunting and gathering grounds by the expansion of white farming and logging. As salmon rivers became blocked by dams built by logging companies, the Wabanaki had no choice but to return to the coast to fish. And there they discovered new commercial opportunities opened up by coastal tourism.[24]

Wabanaki coastal numbers increased in direct proportion to the rise of white summer visitors. Beginning in the mid-nineteenth century, they were again camping on the shores that for hundreds of years had been the hunting and gathering grounds of their ancestors, but this time exploiting subsistence skills for commercial profits. Harvesting sweetgrass, they created a viable basket-making trade. They returned to seal hunting for the purpose of making moccasins, while hunting porpoises, previously a minor subsistence activity, became a major commercial enterprise, providing lighthouses and mechanized agriculture with an invaluable source of high-grade lighting and lubricating oil. In effect, the Native American was "profiting by the very machinery that had driven him and his game from the woods." Increasingly limited by game laws, Maine Indians had turned to the sea as their last wilderness. It has been said that "when the woods became pastures, when the salmon rivers spun saws, [they] went to the sea where there were no fences, axes, or plows."[25]

It was this same moment that Henry David Thoreau was discovering the sea as wilderness. He did so as a result of two visits to Cape Cod, the first in 1849, the second in 1855, and published his experiences in the 1860s, writing that "the ocean is a wilderness reaching round the world, wilder than a Bengal jungle and full of monsters." The metaphor stuck, as did his notion of the sea as boundless and pristine, standing outside history. The sea as wilderness was not something that Thoreau learned from the maritime folk he met when sojourning on the Cape, for such a concept was utterly alien to them. He did not take to the water at any point; all his observations were from the shore, making him America's pioneer beachcomber. But he believed the edge of the sea opened up a whole new

FIGURE 28. Shoreside view of Indian encampment at Bar Harbor, Maine, 1881. Photo by Kilburn Bothers. Courtesy of the Abbe Museum, Bar Harbor.

world, a new frontier of spiritual growth. The oceans had become for him a bigger, more inspiring version of Walden Pond. For Thoreau as well as for the Wabanaki, the sea was a place of no fences.[26]

The sea had always been associated with danger and death, but now the shipwreck became the master metaphor for human disaster until it was replaced by the passenger plane crash much nearer our own times. There had been an abundance of shipwrecks throughout history, but they had never taken on so much symbolic import, not just for seafarers but for inlanders. Before the nineteenth century, wrecks had been too common to be made much of by coastal people, but they had a great impact on inlanders. As he traveled toward the Cape in 1849, Thoreau was detoured to the shore, drawn by a handbill announcing: "Death! One hundred and forty-nine lives lost at Cohasset." The brig *St. John*, an immigrant ship from Galway, had wrecked, attracting vast numbers of Boston Irish to the shore. Even as the bereaved collected their relatives' bodies, the locals went about their work of picking up seaweed "as if there had never been any wreck in the world." This was not for any lack of sympathy but reflected a different, older maritime sensibility that accepted death at sea as inevitable. The idea of shipwreck had a different meaning when sinkings were part of the natural order of things, something that should not give pause to the work of those whose fate was to die as well as live by the sea.[27]

Shipwrecks had been so frequent in earlier centuries as to be unremarkable. The sites of some three million wrecks have been identified by modern archaeologists, and more no doubt exist worldwide. In the nineteenth century, more and better lighthouses, together with the development of steam power, reduced the number of wrecks significantly. But it was precisely in the era when ships were not supposed to founder that the horror of the event was magnified for landsmen, for whom it came to signify humans' helplessness in the face of the sea's overwhelming power. In a story by Washington Irving, an encounter with a drifting wreck rouses thoughts of utter oblivion. In the nineteenth century, shipwreck became the symbol of the power of nature and the hopelessness of human efforts to control one's own fate on either land or sea.[28]

In nineteenth-century literature, the sea became the prime locus of danger and adventure, the ultimate rite of passage for inland boys yearning to affirm their manhood. In England the sea was considered the "only untamed wilderness, where man might still be small and alone in the vastness of Creation. . . . To go to sea was to escape from the city and the machine," as Raban notes. In earlier eras, mountains and forests had served a similar purpose, and they still did for northwest coast Native American populations, who had always turned inland on their vision quests. But for European Americans, who were in the process of exorcising all traces of wildness from the land, only the oceans offered the degree of challenge that was guaranteed to bring out the heroic in the class of gentlemen to which Thoreau himself belonged. Late nineteenth-century middle-class men felt themselves to have inherited a much diminished world, emptied of the wild things necessary to the maintenance of their virility. "I cannot but feel as if I lived in a tamed, and as it were, emasculated country," Thoreau wrote in 1855. The taste for the marine, acquired from the safety of the shore, was his salvation.[29]

Nothing was more emasculating than the highly feminized Victorian domestic world. and it was no accident that virility came to be associated

FIGURE 29. *Tumblehome*, photograph by Peter Ralston. Courtesy of the artist.

with the only space from which by the mid-nineteenth century women were systematically excluded, namely the sea. In earlier centuries, women had been very much a part of the coastal world, involved in virtually every aspect of trading and fishing. With the advent of steam, however, they were increasingly confined to onshore activities, or, when allowed on boats, relegated to the passive role of passenger. Although the sea was most frequently represented as female and womblike, it had come to be seen as the exclusive domain of men. Women's prior involvement with the marine world was forgotten as the sea came to perform yet another metaphorical service by reinforcing, indeed intensifying, gender differences in ways that the land was no longer capable of doing.[30]

In its new role as wilderness, the sea offered an escape from time, from history itself. With the rise of the territorial nation-state, land became ever more intensively historicized, obscuring the role of the sea. National histories now began and ended at the shore, while the notion of the eternal became ever more firmly attached to oceans, as if to remove them from the corrupting march of time that seemed so relentless on land. Timelessness was something that Thoreau came looking for on his visits to Cape Cod, and he found it at the shore: "We do not associate the idea of antiquity with the ocean, nor wonder how it looked a thousand years ago, as we are of the land, for it was equally wild and unfathomable always." As such, the sea was immune from the losses suffered constantly by land. It was immortal.[31]

Thoreau found something spiritually uplifting and regenerative about the sea. Several years before the Cape Cod rambles, while living briefly on Staten Island, he had written that "the fittest locality for human dwelling was on the edge of the land, where there the constant lesson and impression of the sea might sink deep into the life and character of the landsman, perhaps impart a marine tint to his imagination." A descendant of a Massachusetts seacoast merchant family, Thoreau had always felt a connection with the sea. "It is a noble word, that *mariner*. . . . There should be more of what it signifies in each of us. . . . Perhaps we should be equally mariners and terreners, and even our Green Mountains need some of the sea-green to be mixed with them." It seems that Thoreau was not quite the landsman he is so often made out to be, but neither was he a mariner in the way his ancestors had been. He was instead a progenitor of a new breed of edge species, turning his face to the sea while still firmly rooted on land. He was the first of what Emily Dickinson called "shore-based watergazers." Soon he would be joined by others, including Walt Whitman, who wrote of the beach as a place that suggested "contact, junction, the solid marrying the liquid—that curious, luring something."[32]

Those who derived their livings from the sea rarely expressed any emotion toward it other than fatalism. They spent their leisure time with their backs to the sea, dismissing those engaged in "chasing the shore" as odd, even demented. Intoxication with the sea was not part of the old maritime culture. Ralph Waldo Emerson called the "sea-life an acquired taste, like that for tomatoes and olives." What Thoreau referred to as the marine tint was something cultivated by landlubbers. Emily Dickinson's poem "Exultation is the going" makes clear that the love of the sea had inland origins:

> Exultation is the going
> Of an inland soul to sea,
> Past the houses—past the headlands—
> Into deep Eternity—
> Bred as we, among the mountains,
> Can the sailor understand
> The divine intoxication
> Of first leagues out from land?[33]

For H. G. Wells there "is no romance about the sea in a small sailing ship as I saw it. The romance is in the mind of the landsman dreamer."[34]

The Therapeutic Shore

Europeans and Americans were drawn to the sea even as fewer and fewer of them crossed the tide line. The coast first appealed for its wild, sublime features, but in the end it was not the rocky but the sandy shore, what today we call the beach, that became its most alluring feature. The beach was an invention of the modern age, a wholly new landscape culturally as well as physically. *The Oxford English Dictionary* tells us that the dialect word *beach* originally meant a certain kind of stone that the English call "shingle" or "cobble." It took some time before it became the name for a unique kind of place. Shingle and cobble beaches are more common in Europe, while sand beaches are frequent in the Americas and Australia, but what all have in common is the way they are created and altered by the movement of water. Rivers carry stone to the sea, where it is ground ever finer and carried alongshore. More than other parts of the coast, beaches are nourished by movement. It has been said that "a beach is a place where sand stops to rest a moment before resuming its journey to somewhere else." When rivers dry up and coastal currents are retarded, beaches die and disappear.[35]

Because beaches are alive and ever-changing, they are hard to define and even harder to pin down. No wonder our ancestors had no name or affection for them. They feared their fickle nature and made little effort to control them. Today, when we invest so much effort to stabilize beaches through beach nourishment and other measures, they continue to elude our control. And so we talk of shifting sands and the dangers of building on sand. Of all coastal features, apart from wetlands, beaches are the most fluid of all landscapes, the ultimate *terrae infirma*. Today beaches around the world are also among the most artificial of all places. Sand, principally white sand, has become the universal standard for beaches even where it is wholly unnatural and has to be imported. What was once a worthless substance is now a priceless symbol. Many beaches are now wholly human-made, some of them even located indoors, away from the sea and from nature itself.[36]

This is an astonishing turnabout, for when Europeans and Americans first settled the coasts, they largely ignored, indeed avoided, what are today's most coveted stretches of shore. When first approached from the sea, the beach was used for landing but not for settlement. Its featureless barrenness was not only inhospitable but repulsive. It was long associated with disease and death, and it would be a very long time before the beach's hellish reputation was replaced by its current designation as earthly paradise. And even now fear still haunts the beach, erupting in periodic panics about shark attacks and ongoing concerns with water pollution and skin cancer.[37]

It was centuries before the beach became a destination rather than a transit point between land and sea. Before the nineteenth century, it was the easiest place to land shallow draft boats. Our ancestors had long "beached" their vessels before they ever thought of beaching themselves. Even those who made their living from the sea avoided the strand, building their dwellings inland and facing them away from the sea. For a very long time, visitors could find little that pleased them about the shore. As late as 1903, a Swedish traveler on that country's west coast noted that, "throughout the whole journey, not a single beautiful place was seen."[38]

When English elites began in the early eighteenth century to abandon inland spas for resorts located on the coast, they were not seeking warm water and sandy beaches. It was the relief of pain, rather than search for pleasure, that motivated the first surge to the sea. The ill and the convalescent were drawn by the reputedly superior medicinal qualities of cold sea water. And the treatments they encountered there were, by our standards, more hellish than heavenly. They came not to swim but to bathe, and they were assisted in that activity by so-called bathing machines, cabins on wheels that transported them across the beach and into the water, where, with the assistance of hired attendants, women and men alike dipped into the sea as part of their mental and physical cures, which also included drinking sea water, considered at the time medicinal. Before railways reached the New Jersey shore, the journey there was described as "more penance than joy . . . the pilgrimage was as wearing as that of the Muhammadans to Mecca." Later, when England's elites began to look south to the Mediterranean for their cures, they went in winter, for it was not until the twentieth century that the sun replaced cold water as elixir of health and vitality.[39]

Not any shore would do as a spa. English beaches were initially chosen for their flat, firm surfaces which gave easy access to bathing machines, which bogged down in soft sand. By today's standards the preferred strands were ugly and uncomfortable. They were more associated with invalids than athletes, with diseased rather than healthy bodies. Swimming skills did not become widespread until the twentieth century. Wading and dipping prevailed on the Jersey shore, one of the reasons

FIGURE 30. Bathing machines. *Terror of the Sea*, Thomas Rowlandson, ca. 1800. Permission of the Thanet District Council.

that shallow waters were preferred beach locations. While nude bathing was tolerated until the mid-nineteenth century, the chosen means of approaching the sea remained the bathing machine, which not only provided a measure of safety but hid the body, a service particularly valued by women. But by the end of the nineteenth century salt water was losing its therapeutic reputation, and growing numbers of people were coming down to the sea for the pure pleasure of swimming, a form of exercise that had become increasingly popular. New bathing costumes for both men and women resolved the issue of privacy and made the bathing machines obsolete. They would be parked at the edge of the sand as changing rooms for the new beachgoers. Eventually they would evolve into sea-facing beach huts and then into beach houses. By then the beach itself had become the destination.[40]

But before the beach was a place to swim or sun, it was a place to walk, ride, and, ultimately, to explore. The English coast was discovered intellectually and spiritually long before it was explored sensually. Geologists found in sea cliffs the fossilized "archives of the Earth." Initially, the natural wonders found at the edge of the sea confirmed rather than weakened arguments for divine design. In time, fossils would date the beginning of life far earlier than biblical accounts had suggested, but for most of the nineteenth century religion was still at home on the beach. The shore was a prime destination for not only time travelers but also amateur botanists and zoologists, who, in an era before the professionalization of science, included many women. They and their children could be found exploring rock pools and dipping for specimens, which would find their way into the domestic aquarium, which was all the rage in middle-class America and Europe in the mid-nineteenth century. And then there was the more general passion for beachcombing, which accounts for the collections of shells, beach stones, and sea glass that cluttered Victorian nurseries and parlors. In the long run this intensive collecting had dire results. Edmund Gosse remembered the shore as a treasure trove in the 1850s. He regretted that by the end of the century "all that is over and done with. The ring of living beauty drawn about our shores was a very thin and fragile one. It had existed all these centuries solely in consequence of the indifference, the blissful ignorance of man. . . . No one will see again on the shore of England what I saw in my early childhood."[41]

The first instinct of Europeans and Americans, given the long-standing fear of the sea, was to push it back by extending the land as far as possible. By the mid-nineteenth century, the hotels and villas that had previously been built back from the shore and facing away from it were being moved closer, creating for the first time a visible, stable seafront in many spa and resort towns. What had once been a porous boundary between land and sea was now becoming an impenetrable border, complete with sea walls and purpose-built promenades. In the eighteenth century, when people did not yet spend as much time *on* the beach as *at* the beach, the sand and shingle was still an alien, anxiety-filled liminal space between land and sea, between civilization and nature. As late as the 1870s, visitors to Atlantic City were complaining about the sand that drifted everywhere. The boardwalk was created to keep nature literally at bay. The same aversion to seaside wilderness explains the enormous number of piers and boardwalks that were built in the later nineteenth century. In Britain alone more than sixty piers were built between 1850 and 1900. Early pleasure piers were essentially extensions of land and carried visitors over rather than onto the beach itself, protecting them from its unsavory sights and smells while giving them a safe vantage point to look both to sea and back to land. They also made certain that too much beach sand and wrack would not be tracked into the shore hotels and villas that now lined the shorefront.[42]

FIGURE 31. *Pegwell Bay in Kent, A Memory from October 5, 1858.* Courtesy of Wikimedia Commons.

At a time when the beach itself was not yet a place from which to see or be seen, piers and promenades served that function. They allowed visitors to "cheat nature," coming as close to the sea as possible without abandoning any of the trappings of dress and decorum that constituted the Victorian middle-class claim to respectability. As an added bonus, the new infrastructure prevented mixing with those people who for so long had occupied the beaches, namely local fishers and gatherers; the newly forming shoreline was also a class line, a social border no less clearly delineated and defended than the coast itself. At first, visitors had simply tried to avoid "the riffraff" by segregating themselves spatially from the beach, keeping it literally as well as figuratively below them. But in time, the lure of the sea and the beach itself became too powerful. By the end of the nineteenth century the old occupants of the strand had to be cleared out, made to disappear like other "natives" when urban elites decided to set aside mountains and forests for their own aesthetic or recreational purposes.[43]

FIGURE 32. Black-
pool, England, photo
by Elliott Erwitt. Per-
mission of Magnum.

Shore dwellers were removed just as the highlands and other places had
been previously cleared. But as the foreshore had always been regarded as
commons, this, the last of the great enclosure movements, met with stiff
resistance by resident coastal dwellers, particularly the fishers and gatherers who had been accustomed to beaching their boats in the most desirable spots and storing gear and curing fish within sight and smell of
genteel bathers. As in the case of fenland drainages earlier, the struggle
between the last souls of the edge and the latest newcomers was already
intense during the early nineteenth century, but over time the hunters
and gatherers lost their places and were pushed to nearby harbors, later
to be dispossessed once again when inlanders began to covet and buy up
shorefront property.

Jean-Didier Urbain calls this process the "desavaging" of the beach, an "aesthetic conquest of the shore by the vacation ideology," resulting in the disappearance, "real and figurative, of Coastal Man, Homo littoralis." An 1858 guide to Hastings reassured visitors that "the beach has been vastly improved by the removal of the quaint-looking old fishing huts, that formerly so much obstructed the sea view." French fishermen and shellfish gatherers defended their right of access until the end of the nineteenth century, but they too were finally banished to local ports. In the twentieth century, coastal people were expelled from all but the most undesirable parts of the beach; ultimately, and equally significant, all memory of *Homo littoralis*'s presence was erased.[44]

The Potential of Emptiness

The beach was created ex nihilo, providing neither the sense of place nor the sense of history associated with other vacation destinations, like the country village. The beach thus began as a nonplace, a void, and it has remained so ever since. From the start its emptiness, its artificial desertification, has been part of its appeal. Developers have always looked for empty places for locating spas and resorts. From the start, they were competing for limited coastal space, which became ever harder to find. Nature itself proved the first enemy of the booming resort business on both sides of the Atlantic. Where wetlands and rocky shores stood in the way of beachfront expansion, they were simply filled in or leveled.[45]

In the course of the nineteenth century, the beach was denatured even as it was reconstructed as the purest expression of nature. The natural flora and fauna were eradicated and replaced by sterile sands or shingle. In Britain today there are virtually no untouched beaches, and in North America there are very few except where these have been deliberately preserved. The sensibilities of inlanders demanded that beaches be cleared of the unsightly and the smelly. In the nineteenth century, beaches were littered with flotsam and jetsam. Wrecks attracted crowds, and hulks were left to rot into the sands. But now that beaches were identified with life rather than death, these memento mori were no longer tolerated, and the organic life that once attracted hunters and gatherers is no longer allowed to gather there either. Today, beaches are cleared and cleaned by mechanical means. Their sand is rarely a product of the natural action of the sea but is dredged or trucked in.

Yet this desertification is the modern beach's major attraction. It has been said that "the purest form of potentiality is emptiness itself." Holy men once populated deserts for their spiritual promise. Later, deserted islands attracted hermits and pilgrims. Today, though, a beach's emptiness is more likely to evoke sensual than spiritual potentiality. There we can vacate all the cares and responsibilities associated with our ordinary lives, hence the term *vacation*. In earlier periods, a vacation meant an involuntary suspension or loss of work. It was only toward the end of the nineteenth century that it took on more positive connotations.[46]

In seamen's jargon, "to be on the beach" once meant to be unemployed and destitute. But the beach is no longer associated with the down and out. While beaches are a favorite destination for families with children, they are also associated with the exotic and erotic. Beaches convey status; they also confer sexual and other kinds of identities. Beaches have been used to enforce racial and sexual segregation, but in the case of nude and homosexual beaches, they can be seen as empowering. Populated by body builders and sun worshipers, these are places where we shed, if only for a time, our conventions and find new selves. As a limen, the edge of the sea has always suggested the potentiality of shape-changing and was in earlier times the haunt of creatures part-animal, part-human, the mermaid and the selkie. These have disappeared, but change is still associated with shifting sands as with no other terrestrial environment. Water remains a dramatic medium of religious conversion, and the shore is still the scene of baptisms, but the beach has also become the place for a raft of new secular rites, especially those associated with family.[47]

The beach is what Marc Auge defines as a nonplace, something to pass through, not to dwell in. Nonplaces get little attention from geographers, and few beaches have their own historians. The beach suggests beginnings and endings but offers no narrative, for the beach has no history and beachgoers have no connection with earlier *Homo littoralis*. Instead it presents itself as a point of eternal return that promises never to change— a place where nothing ever happens. As Urbain puts it, beaches have forgotten their history. Redevelopment has expunged most traces of the prior life of coastal peoples. Even those fishing villages that remain are disconnected from the past, mere simulacra of working lives now extinguished. The appeal of the beach lies in the fact that it excludes all that is "workful." Its true relation to nature and history must always be concealed, for it functions in modern culture as a primary place of getting away, of oblivion and forgetting.[48]

The shore that emerged in the nineteenth century initially presented itself as wild nature but was quickly tamed, acquiring its own protocols and etiquette, which would ultimately become so universal that beaches

FIGURE 33. Mixed group of watergazers, photo by Elliott Erwitt. Permission of Magnum.

began to resemble one another. The beach has, like all modern nonplaces, lost touch with locality. Once its original inhabitants had been cleared and its past erased, it was ready for reconstruction as a separate world, belonging to neither land nor sea, with its own spaces, its own architecture, its own temporalities. From the early nineteenth century onward, the old health spas were transformed into pleasure palaces, high-end amusement parks that, initially patronized by the upper classes, were soon overrun by the urban bourgeoisie. By the middle of the nineteenth century, working-class day-trippers were pouring in from industrial towns. At first they came as boarders, renting spare rooms from fishermen's wives. Better-off excursionists stayed in newly built hotels. Seeking to ensure their status, the rich began to either move elsewhere or privatize the shore, erecting their own grand beach houses. The middle classes emulated them on a smaller scale, and by the 1930s there were whole towns of modest bungalows crowding the shores of both Europe and North America. After the Second World War, the automobile revolution brought caravan parks. For the first time, working people had sufficient vacation time to join the surge to the sea, and by then it seemed that "the seaside belonged to everyone." Once mostly seasonal homes, by the 1970s and 1980s beach communities were becoming seaside suburbs, populated year round by retirees who had decided to turn summer places into permanent residences. Now they are also bedroom communities, with workers who once commuted from the city to the seaside for their holidays commuting daily from the shore to work.[49]

The Beach as Cultic Site

What had begun as an excursion would ultimately evolve into what we now know as the family vacation. In resorts like Rome's Lido, Philadelphia's Cape May, and London's Brighton, all just a short train journey away from the cities, mothers and children established themselves at the summer shore and fathers joined them on weekends. Early in the nineteenth century the beach had become identified with the nuclear family. It came to be associated with childhood, and as children became the temporal and spatial pivots around which family life revolved, it took on a special meaning as the one place where "adults play at becoming children." This was particularly important for men, who in everyday existence had become strangers to their own children, and for whom the beach was a reconnection not only to their little ones but also to their own childhood, now remembered through the rosy lens of nostalgia.[50]

Already in the late nineteenth century families began to return year after year to the same beach resorts, ultimately investing in seashore property that could be passed on from generation to generation. What had once been a touristic trip took on all the trappings of a secular pilgrimage. With the enshrinement of the beach as the ideal vacation spot, life there took on an increasingly ritualized quality. No longer a place of status display, the beach served as a performance space for sentimental rites of family solidarity. As Urbain describes it, the beach had become "a cultic site and a 'prayer rug' for the performance of a ritual." For most of the week, it was the realm of women and children, but on the weekends families were able to reconstitute themselves and live up to their idealized version of themselves. Among all the other family occasions that had arisen in the course of the last century or so, the seaside vacation required the largest investment, even as it offered the greatest rewards. In the course of the late twentieth century, beaches replaced mountains and country villages as the preferred destination of Europeans and North Americans.[51]

As a refuge from the speed of modern life, nothing could compete with the beach. Time stopped at the edge of the sand. The beach had become the world's favorite place for doing nothing. It was a nonplace, and nothing was supposed to happen there. Suspended between past and future, it is a place

FIGURE 34. Beach health class at Ocean City, New Jersey, in the 1920s. Courtesy of Library of Congress.

for dreaming as opposed to doing. All reminders of work had long since been banished. By the 1970s the most common reason Angelenos give for coming to their Pacific beaches was that they were not only the most carefree but also the safest of all public spaces. "The sand is like a sanctuary to me," reported one young woman. "Once I'm there I relax and mellow out." Until recently, even vigorous physical activity was kept at bay. As we have already seen, swimming came late to the beach. Surfing arrived only in the 1960s and was well regulated in most beach areas. Extreme sports, such as hang gliding and wind surfing, had to find homes elsewhere on the coast, in places previously considered more sublime than pleasurable.[52]

While the beach is a wholly modern invention, it was quickly invested with a degree of nostalgia rarely attached to other topographies. Fond memories bring adults back to the sands of their childhoods, but like the millions of photos that record modern life at the beach, memory freezes time and obscures the real history of such places. A century ago, those fortunate enough to buy up abandoned fishermen's houses began doing so. Now it is more common to build new houses as close to the shore as possible. In the 1970s and 1980s, 80 percent of all construction in the United States took place in coastal areas, often right on the beach. Once the least populated parts of this country, the coasts are now the most densely populated. In Europe there has been similar movement toward the sea. There, where land is much scarcer, the shores of Belgium, Spain, and Italy have become like an megalopolis. In both Europe and North America coasts have come to define inlands to a degree unknown in the past. Each year in the 1970s, twelve to eighteen million people visited the main Los Angeles public beaches, which were only three miles in length and constituted just 353 acres. By then these sands had not just come to define the immediate coast, but had become the dream spaces for a huge urban area.[53]

Water Gazing

The beach has become the modern era's favorite place for daydreaming. In earlier periods, mountains and forests gave free rein to the imagination, but in the twenty-first century it is the sea that "pulls the mind outward and away." Hindus in India placed their shrines at the edge of the sea, which is to them "land's end, the brink of terrestrial life, where the devout and the reflective might gaze out over the void, the 'black water' of early Sanskrit literature." They wade out ankle deep fully clothed, dipping in the water but rarely swimming. We have seen how in pre-Christian Europe the shore was treated as a portal to other worlds and was made the site of rituals and burials. Christians were less likely to place their churches at the edge of the sea, for their imaginations were drawn upward rather than outward. In the Middle Ages, when life was physically quite circumscribed, the world seemed to open only vertically, and the imagination was directed to the heavens above rather than the worlds beyond.[54]

In the Age of Discovery, the world became for the first time "broad in surface, but low in ceiling." The horizontal dimension became all-important, and frontiers, both sea and land, took on unprecedented symbolic as well as material significance. With the closing of land frontiers in the later nineteenth century, however, sea frontiers took on new meaning. They became ever more important for defining and defending national identities. In the late nineteenth century, the English became convinced that "the liberty of England was preserved in brine—the brine being the

English Channel . . . the 'silver streak' that separates happy England from continental strife."[55]

With the closing of the interior frontier, it was left to the seashore to give unobstructed access to the horizon. The Victorian bourgeoisie were the first to discover the way the horizon provided a "space into which imagination and inner vision may travel." In the twentieth century, the shore became the preferred dream space for the masses. It is "always in principle open—to new content, new structure, and new possibilities." Yi-Fu Tuan argues that the modern seashore is unique among modern landscapes in offering simultaneous refuge and escape, security and open horizons. In a world that leaves little room for imagination, we yearn for a "beyond that is, by its very nature, unreachable in fact and in representation."[56]

The quest for horizons has become ever more personal. It is foundational to modern tourism, but we no longer have to travel great distances to find new horizons. In earlier times it was necessary to cross beaches to find new possibilities. Today we need only come down to the shore. The minds of millions travel far even as their bodies remain stationary on the beach. And like the Hindus of India, they are more likely to wade than swim. When he hiked the coasts of Britain in the 1980s, Paul Theroux was intrigued by the people he found in all weathers spending endless hours peering out to sea. "The British seemed to me a people forever standing on a crumbling coast and scanning the horizon." He decided that it was "the poor person's way of going abroad—standing at the seaside and staring at the ocean. I believed that these people were fantasizing that they were over there on the waiting horizon, at sea. . . . I seldom saw anyone with his back toward the sea (it was the rarest posture on the coast). Most people looked seaward with anxious, hopeful faces, as if they had just left their native land."[57]

But it was not just a British eccentricity. W. G. Sebald describes Germans who might be mistaken for fishermen: "I do not believe that these men sit by the sea all day and all night so as not to miss the time the whiting pass, the flounder rise or the cod come into the shallower waters, as they claim. They just want to be in a place where they have the world behind them, and before them nothing but emptiness. The fact is that today it is almost impossible to catch anything fishing from the beach."[58]

Herman Melville had already taken note of how Manhattanites were drawn to the water's edge in the mid-nineteenth century. "But look! Here come the crowds, pacing straight for the water, and seeming bound for a dive. Strange! Nothing will content them but the extremest limit of land;

loitering under the shady lee of yonder ware houses will not suffice. No, they must get just as nigh to the water as they possibly can without falling in. . . . Inlanders all, they come from lanes and alleys, streets and avenues—north, east, south, and west. Yet here they unite. Yes, as everyone knows, meditation and water are wedded for even." For Matthew Arnold, Dover Beach was redolent with loss: "it brought into his mind the turbid ebb and flow of human misery." Today, water gazing has many purposes but is so common as to be unremarkable. It is evident in every part of the Western world, especially on coasts that face west, where "sundowning" is a nightly ritual.[59]

Earlier, the most prized seascapes invariably included ships and other marine activity, paying tribute to those who made their livings from the sea. But by our own time working people have vanished from paintings and photographs, just as they had disappeared from the beach itself. Beginning in the nineteenth century, the eye ceased to dwell on the harbor or the near shore and was increasingly directed to the sea's horizon. In our own times "the sea is to be gazed at and even celebrated," writes Philip Steinberg, "but as an actual place of production and transportation it is largely hidden." It is the ocean's emptiness that is now the focus. As Michael Taussig has observed, the sea is no longer a place to be inhabited but a place to be contemplated.[60]

And now everyone wants an unobstructed view, and the beach, having been cleared of distracting people and things, is the perfect place to obtain that. In Sweden the "very emptiness and simplicity of the landscape made room for finding oneself, entering into a trance like or meditative state of mind." Houses with a sea view had already begun to fetch a premium in the late nineteenth century. The old fishermen's cottages, which faced away from the sea, were rotated or rebuilt to fit the new cultural requirements. In our own times, little else seems to matter but the view. It has become "priceless."[61]

While attracted to the sea's purity and otherness, today's seaside tourists are less likely to engage with or venture on it. As John Stilgoe observes, "the wildness, the openness, the naturalness attracts tourists, but nowadays's tourists want to *watch*, not do." In the wake of the nineteenth-century passion for seascapes, the sea itself became scenic. Cleared and cleansed sands no longer offer much of the picturesque, and now that the smell and feel of the old fisheries are gone, there is not much in the way of sensory experience apart from the optical. Earlier, romantics had preferred the rocky shore as a fearsome place to experience the sublime, but today we seek gently sloping beaches protected by shark nets and lifeguards. That has become the perfect place "to dream, far from nature's turmoil and turbulence, and far from everyday historical, social, and cultural realities." Disconnected from both the sea and the land, these are the only spaces where one can turn one's back on the world, on history itself. Unlike the hinterlands, beaches rarely contain memorials. Even the wrecks that once littered shores are now cleared away promptly, leaving no reminder of tragic events that might drive down tourism or spoil a vacationer's reverie. The shipwreck, like so much about the sea, has become purely metaphorical.[62]

When Paul Theroux walked the British coast in the 1980s, he sensed loss not just of nature but of history. Everything had been eroded—cliffs, fishing, ports—including the beaches themselves.[63] By then Brits were pulling back from the beach, preferring to lounge about hotel pools that offered "a much better-managed version of the beach, nice water temperature, no sand between the toes, close to the hotel bar." Elsewhere, people were even turning inland to new indoor beaches that originated in Japan and have now spread around the world. But the image of the beach remains powerful and the ahistorical nostalgia surrounding it undiminished. Margaret Drabble, who spent her childhood on the insalubrious Lincolnshire coast, where she remembers swimming in sewage, now prefers not to return there, not because of the pollution but "for fear that it is already ruined, a paradise lost." Beaches are among the most transient of all landscapes, but their association with the paradisiacal stubbornly resists all change. Frozen in time in billions of photographs, the seaside is where we consign our precious dreams and our most frightening nightmares.[64]

6 · COASTAL DREAMS AND NIGHTMARES

Civilization, we expect, will end on the beach.

FELIPE FERNANDEZ-ARMESTO[1]

There was a time when only those who lived at the coast could be called coastal, but today people living hundreds of miles from the sea identify with coasts, stage seafood festivals, and bask, even surf, on indoor beaches. More and more people are living on coasts, and it seems that virtually everyone identifies with them. Perhaps this is because, as John Murray reminds us, "every person born in this world has a coast, an edge, a boundary, a transitional zone between themselves and the world." People who have never been to New Jersey are familiar with "the Shore." California's icon is the beach, while Maine would like everyone to think of it as the Lobster Coast. Nova Scotia advertises itself as "Canada's Ocean Playground." When hurricanes and oil spills strike, whole nations rally to the defense of coasts.[2]

This may not have been true a hundred years ago, but today shores not only define states and nations but connect them regionally, even globally. The beaches on which Europeans once erected defenses against one another now form one continuous shore from the Baltic to the Mediterranean. All parts of Europe now claim the sea as a common heritage, a source of common identity. After the Second World War, the North Atlantic rim came to be seen as defining Western civilization. Although it was created to oppose a continental superpower, the Soviet Union, the North Atlantic Treaty Organization chose to define itself oceanically. And now the peoples of the Pacific Rim also see themselves as having more in common with one another than they do with the inhabitants of their various hinterlands.[3]

Coasts have taken on enormous symbolic potency. Paradoxically, they are modernity's primary place of dreams but also of its nightmares. It is at the edge of the sea that we imagine both the birth of new worlds and the death of old ones. Everywhere, people are coming back to the sea, bringing with them their greatest hopes and worst fears, lured by visions of fantasy islands and Edenic beaches, but also haunted by the old demons of wind, water, and fire. On what California like to call their Coast of Dreams, the city council of Santa Barbara debates whether to paint a bright blue line on its streets indicating the extent of future sea rise. Environmentalists favor the idea as a consciousness-raising device, but homeowners, fearful that it will devalue their property, mount a ferocious opposition. The same city is also all too aware of the fact that it belongs to what is called the "fire coast," where homes are lost to wildfires on a regular basis. Coasts are simultaneously the most desirable and the most vulnerable of habitats. Encroachments on places never suited to permanent habitation have contributed directly to beach erosion and ocean pollution but also to devastating blazes. Coastal Californians live in what Mike Davis calls an "ecology of fear," an environment largely of their own making. And as if real threats were not sufficient, we have managed to conjure up a whole new set of sea monsters, given birth well inland by writers like Peter Benchley, the creator of *Jaws*.[4]

When Steven Spielberg released his film version of *Jaws* in the summer of 1975, the *New York Times* reported that "anglers and bathers who never really took time to look carefully at the water before are doing so now, and often anything remotely resembling a shark is identified as one." Later that fall, two neurologists wrote to the *New England Journal of Medicine* about what they called "the *Jaws* neurosis." This had been detected in a seventeen-year-old Midwestern girl who, after seeing the film, experienced five bouts of terror, fully aware that "the risks of shark attacks in western Kansas were indeed remote." The original story in the *Times* was perceptive when it noted that "[the] mad monster . . . in *Jaws* comes from the depths of inner-space—the sea as well as man's nightmares."[5]

Just how far coastal fantasies and fears reach is one measure of the expanded notion of coast. On one hand, there is the tendency for land to incorporate sea, to treat it like itself, as territory that can be parceled, leased, and owned. In effect, the sea has become *continentalized*. The term *continental* was not used until the late eighteenth century, but by the 1890s it was being deployed to describe near-shore islands. The term *continental shelf* was used from the 1950s onward and institutionalized by the United Nations Convention of the Law of the Sea in 1982. In earlier centuries, state sovereignty extended only three miles from shore. By the 1970s it had extended to twelve miles, and with the international mandating of Exclusive Economic Zones in 1982, states could claim the economic resources two hundred miles to sea.[6]

The discovery of offshore oil and gas, as well as the profits to be made

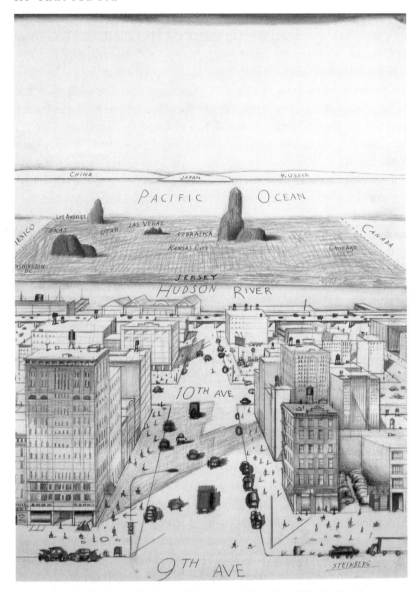

FIGURE 35. Saul Steinberg, *View from 9th Avenue*, 1976. Copyright of The Saul Steinberg Foundation / Artist Rights Society (ARS), New York.

from sand and mineral mining, have concentrated strategic thinking on near-shore waters. The United States Navy published *Forward . . . from the Sea* in 1994, refocusing attention from its traditional blue-water domain to brown-water warfare. Its author, Rear Admiral Paul Gaffney, argues that because half of the world's population lives within fifty miles of the sea, future conflicts are likely to involve coasts, particularly coastal cities. In 1999, the navy planned to stage urban warfare exercises in Monterey and Alameda, California. Protests against their landing in environmentally sensitive areas caused the exercises to be cut back, but the idea of littoral warfare remains high on the agenda.[7]

On the land's side, the coastline has increasingly given way to the notion of the coastal zone, which can extend hundreds of miles into the interior. It sometimes seems as if Britain is nothing but its coasts. The Brits say that "as islanders we are drawn to the edge; it is where we sense most strongly the essence of our floating landmass." But the same is also true of continental nations, where coasts seem to loom ever larger. By the 1970s it seemed that the United States was becoming its coasts, its interior reduced to something to fly over or pass through. Saul Steinberg's 1976 cartoon "A View of the World from 9th Avenue" made visual this mental map.[8]

Coastal has ceased to be a single geographical location and has become a free-floating symbol to be appropriated for a host of commercial and social purposes not necessarily having anything to do with the place where land and water meet. The magazine *Coastal Living* has a large inland readership, more interested in the lifestyle it portrays than in the conditions of the coasts themselves. As coasts take up increasing mental space both inland and offshore, the actual experience of coastal environments is marginalized. In the wake of the twentieth-century collapse of coastal fishing and shipping economies, tourism and recreational activity have colonized the shores as never before. As work has been replaced by consumption in the day-to-day lives of those who live on the shore, the continuities of coastal life, going back millennia, have been ruptured and the coast has become a place with no memory of itself, without a geography or a history on which to construct a sustainable future. Even as we become more coastal in one sense, we are becoming less in others.[9]

Lost Coasts

In the modern era, a sense of loss has become all pervasive. It is in part a product of the violent, even catastrophic nature of contemporary history, which has seen whole groups and even nations decimated. Both a personal and a collective sense of loss are easily projected onto places, especially if these places never really existed. The lost continent of Atlantis, a fiction created by Plato as a cautionary tale for the Greeks, did not have any real purchase on the popular imagination until the nineteenth century, when it was revived by the American populist Ignatius Donnelly in a best-selling publication in 1882 as a warning to his contemporaries. From that point onward, Atlantis has been the subject of hundreds of books and numerous films. Its appeal has been matched only by that of the lost continent of Lemuria, which began to obsess the Tamil people of South Asia in a period when their existence was threatened. The appeal of the "lost" has only increased over time.[10]

Given the history of coasts, it is easy to understand why loss has been projected onto them. Mariners are familiar with the phenomenon of looming, an optical illusion that can make coasts appear and disappear. Coastal fog has this effect, but so too does history, which has seen coasts come and go with a rapidity matched by few other topographical features. The northern coast of California, bordering on Humboldt County, is now known as "the Lost Coast." Its only deepwater harbor, Humboldt Bay, was missed entirely by early European explorers. Charted by an American working for the Russian-American Fur Company in 1806, it went unvisited by whites until surveyed by an inland expedition in 1849. From that point onward, the booming redwood timber industry made it one of the busiest shores on the west coast. But a coastal highway was not completed until the 1920s, and when the timber industry declined, this coast became again one of the most isolated parts of North America. The name Lost Coast was an invention of the postwar tourist industry, capitalizing on a universal desire to discover untouched places. In an era when lost continents, lost tribes, and lost civilizations occupy such a large place in the popular imagination, this spectacular part of the California coast remains lost but not forgotten.[11]

For most of the twentieth century, coasts around the world were afflicted by losses not necessarily of their own making. They were and still are threatened by changes in the fishing industry, which already in the late nineteenth century was becoming a deep-sea enterprise, detached from particular coasts. Long before there were runaway factories and offshore banking, fishing had become globalized in the relentless search for larger fish stocks and cheaper maritime labor. The same was true of shipping; it too gradually ceased to be a localized coasting operation.

In the nineteenth and early twentieth centuries, coasts had been defined by their seaports, their working waterfronts. Today, cities by the sea are no longer seaports, for ports have moved elsewhere along the coast or upriver. With the advent of the container ship in the 1950s, sea traffic originated and terminated in specially built facilities that had no resi-

FIGURE 36. Rare instance of contemporary coexistence of working waterfront and bathing beach, Beer, Devon, England. Courtesy of Wikimedia Commons.

dential populations to speak of. The old waterfronts lost their functions and by the 1960s were being transformed into residential or recreational areas. In the process, coasts became best known for their marinas and beaches.[12]

Beginning with the age of steam and becoming ever more apparent in the recent era of global positioning systems, the sea has become more like land. "Factories became mobile, ship-like, as ships became increasingly indistinguishable from trucks and trains. . . . This historical change reverses the 'classical' relationship between the fixity of land and the fluidity of the sea." Ships now depart and arrive like clockwork on their transoceanic routes, largely unaffected by tide or wind. The old seaports like Miami and Stockholm are visited by cruise liners, but apart from recreational boats, coastal traffic has largely vanished in both Europe and North America. Coasts are less attached linearly to themselves than they are to distant shores. It can now be said that Vancouver and Seattle are more *on* the Pacific than they are *in* North America.[13]

The world has been losing one kind of coast and gaining another, one much less connected to its natural environment, the ecotone that sustained coastal people for millennia. The new coast is a product not of nature but of design. It is an anthropogenetic coast, engineered to the specifications of both the inland populations who now colonize the shore and the deep-sea fishing and shipping industries, which operate according to the same temporal and spatial specifications as their more terrestrial counterparts. As activity at sea becomes ever more like that on land, the coast itself is subject to what Callum Roberts has called the "coastal squeeze," which threatens all the species of coast life, including the human. It would sometimes seem that the coast has been reduced to a line of sand, a shadow of its former self, alienated from its own history and geography.

Footloose Fisheries

The coasting world of the North Atlantic and North Pacific reached its peak in the middle of the nineteenth century and has been in decline ever since. The ancient nexus between land and sea, farming and fishing, is now severed. Much fishing activity continues to be focused on the rich waters of the continental shelves but is now conducted in a wholly different manner, by a labor force more often recruited inland or abroad than on the coast itself. Both capital and labor are migratory, detached from local communities, concentrated in ever larger ports, becoming cogs in the great wheel of globalized enterprise.[14]

Fishing boats were steam powered by the 1860s and steel hulled by the 1880s, and their size and range increased rapidly, enabling them to employ trawling techniques that had been impossible in the age of sail. Bottom trawling had been practiced since the Middle Ages, but the catch was minuscule compared to that of steam trawling, which began in near-shore waters in the 1880s and then moved ever farther offshore as it scraped clean huge stretches of the continental shelf, turning them into unproductive deserts, devoid of life. Mark Kurlansky has called trawling "the fishing equivalent of strip mining," only in this case the devastation at sea preceded that visited on land. In the wake of declining inshore catches, trawlers and boats equipped with miles of driftnet moved ever farther offshore. By the twentieth century fishermen were spending increased time at sea on ships that combined harvesting with processing.

Each tethered to land only at one the few large ports capable of handling the vast volume of their catches, by the 1960s they had become "factory" ships, mechanical marvels that were capable of sweeping whole stretches of the ocean clean. Pioneered by the British, this industrial-scale fishing was perfected by the Soviet Union and Japan. In the scramble to exploit the seven seas, all the world factory fleets benefited from enormous state subsidies. Local fishermen using smaller boats, especially those of underdeveloped nations, were driven from their own waters. In Somalia displaced fishermen have now turned to piracy, taking their revenge on passing ships from wealthy nations.[15]

Expansion of the range of fisheries had happened before, of course, beginning in the fifteenth century. What was new this time was the demand for fresh fish, based on an entirely new relationship between land and sea. Large interior markets for fresh fish were not possible before the age of steam, which not only allowed refrigerated ships to deliver their catch in a timely manner but also provided railways that could deliver a fresh product well inland. Rail connections privileged a few large ports over small coastal harbors, which had served only local markets; the ultimate result was the demise of thousands of small communities that for centuries had mixed farming and fishing. Some survived by focusing on a specific species, like lobsters, but most coastal fishers have found it difficult to complete with the more highly capitalized fleets working out of larger ports. These huge factory ships and the internationally recruited crews that man them operate on the seas, but they are no longer a part of a distinctly maritime culture.

From the mid-nineteenth century onward, fishing ceased to be a seasonal occupation practiced largely by young single men anticipating their future as farmers or craftsmen. Increasingly it became lifelong proletarian labor, carried out by workers recruited largely from the inland poor or foreign migrants. Class divisions, which had been rare in earlier coastal communities, now became pronounced. Gender differences, blurred in earlier periods when women played many important roles in inshore fishing, likewise intensified: as boats grew larger and voyages longer, fishing became thoroughly masculinized. Women continued to work, but only onshore in the processing end of the business.[16]

Over the course of the nineteenth century, maritime work became ever more segregated. We have seen how the waterfront hived off from the rest of port cities, each of which now had its own "sailor town," exotic to the life of the rest of the city. Fishers had never before been a breed apart, but now they were confined to their own district, connected more to other

FIGURE 37. German factory ship, *Kiel NC105*, 2008. Courtesy of Wikipedia.

ports than to the hinterlands. Sailor towns were a cosmopolitan space in, but not of, the territorial nation, associated with foreign elements, crime, and prostitution. They were avoided by law-abiding citizens, subject to discrimination and repression by the state itself.

Fishing had always been a matter of boom and bust going back at least to the Middle Ages, but the long history of ecological collapse and species extinction was either forgotten or ignored when the bounty of the sea was rediscovered in the nineteenth century. It was not uncommon for the sea to be described as an "inexhaustible mine of wealth," a mantra for those who saw it as the last great frontier, the earth's one unspoiled Eden. On America's west coast, native salmon fisheries had been "frighteningly efficient" before the arrival of Europeans and Americans, but relatively small numbers of fishers and the lack of a commercial market meant that stocks had never been fished beyond the replacement level. When whites arrived on the west coast, they brought diseases that devastated the native fishers, producing a rebound in the salmon runs that inspired euphoric visions of abundance among the newcomers. Immigrant fishermen from all over the world—Chinese, Sicilians, Portuguese, Chileans—arrived in the wake of the California Gold Rush. After fishing out the Sacramento River system in the 1860s, they moved north to the mouth of the Columbia River, where an industrial-scale canning industry was established. In time those stocks were also depleted, leading to motorized offshore fishing in the early twentieth century.[17]

In this new era of highly capitalized deep-sea fishing, the oceans represented a new frontier, and seaports were the frontier towns that appeared wherever new technologies opened up a natural resource to profitable extraction. Mining was a favorite metaphor for industrial fishing. And fishing ports shared the fate of mining settlements insofar as they became ghost towns as soon as the mother lode was exhausted. In the course of the late nineteenth and early twentieth centuries, fishing fleets followed the fish from one place to another in an expanded marine transhumance that made a mockery of the notion of fishing as a stable, rooted occupation. The vision of the quaint fishing village haunted the ruins of coasts that were rapidly depopulated and proletarianized, where generational continuity was increasingly rare and many of the old families had already sold their waterfront properties and moved inland. Beginning in the 1960s, US coasts were repopulated, but the harbors were now likely to be filled with pleasure craft, their residents more interested in consuming fish than catching them. Gloucester, Massachusetts, which resisted this trend, had difficulty maintaining a working waterfront as it increasingly became a suburb of Boston. In the early twenty-first century, it seemed that "all the coastlines of the world will house nothing but tourism and yachting."[18]

The global fishery is now floundering despite lavish government support and protection. Some coastal fishing with small boats, aimed at local markets, continues, and here and there fishermen have established a counterpart to the farmers' market, offering catch that is fresh and local to complete with the products of factory fishing and mass distribution. In places like Port Clyde, Maine, the connection between land and sea is being slowly, painfully reconstructed. A new dream of sustainability is emerging, but it is too early to tell whether it will endure.

Vanishing Seaports

The relationship between the city and the sea, like that between civilization and nature, has never been a settled one. We have seen how in the nineteenth century the waterfront emerged as a buffer between city residents and the water. For the industrial seaport, "water was its life blood, not its soul." As cities became more landlocked mentally if not physically, the waterfront became alien territory; and in the twentieth century it was as if it did not even exist for most Bostonians, Londoners, and Parisians. By then they had turned elsewhere for fresh air and water. It was said of New Yorkers that they had "lost all connections with the sea, almost forgotten the sea is there." Even Norwegians, once most maritime of all peoples, have turned away from their waterfronts. It has been said that today wheels have replaced keels in most Norwegian ports.[19]

City dwellers had once flocked to waterfronts in their idle hours. Now, cut off by rail yards and highways, those who could afford to turned to nearby shores for recreation. New York had its Coney Island and London its Brighton and Margate. The growth of seaside resorts was fed by urbanites wishing to escape the heat, dirt, and noise of industrializing cities. They pioneered new forms of recreation, including the amusement park, and created a plethora of new seaside styles, sports, and architecture. In the meantime, the old urban wharfs rotted and waterfronts became wastelands. Not until the 1970s did American and European cities turn back to the sea, this time to construct an entirely new relationship with it.

"Technology made and then broke the traditional waterfront," notes Peter Hall. Its fate was sealed when the Suez crisis of 1956 disrupted oil transport from the Middle East to Europe, forcing commerce to turn to the supertanker, which could not be accommodated at the old docks. In the same decade an American, Malcolm McLean, invented the modern container ship, which also required wholly new port facilities capable of handling high volume and fast turnaround. Old ports could not provide adequate access to rail and highways. Manhattan's finger-pier system lost out to New Jersey's Port Elizabeth across the Hudson; Oakland displaced its Bay neighbor San Francisco; and Rotterdam became the gateway to Europe. The old ships had spend half of their time docked, but container ships, working according to precise schedules, reduced time in port to less than 20 percent of the voyage. Labor-intensive port costs had amounted to between 60 and 75 percent of all shipping outlays, but now, as mechanized cranes replaced stevedore labor, profits soared. The container ship became known as the "longshoreman's coffin." The new ships carried smaller, less well paid crews. Like fishing, shipping had become a footloose industry, operating with vessels built and registered in foreign ports, avoiding taxes and regulations by flying so-called flags of convenience and internationalizing their crews.[20]

What Alan Sekula has called "runaway ships" no longer had a fixed home. By the 1960s the port was a way station in a continuous voyage, a placeless place, invisible and forgotten. With turnaround time reduced

FIGURE 38. The *Peking*, historic ship docked at South Street Seaport Maritime Museum, New York. Courtesy of Wikimedia Commons.

to virtually nothing, crews were confined to the ship and the old sailor towns vanished. A ship had become, as Michel Foucault put it, "a floating piece of space, a place without a place, that exists for itself." This was equally true of the cruise ships that replaced oceanic passenger liners in the same period. Carrying over six thousand passengers and crew, these mega-vessels required new ports, like that at Miami. A self-contained world with its own shops and restaurants, the ship itself became the destination. In a ship designed to make passengers forget they are even at sea, the "passenger's attention is actually diverted away from the sea, to the vessel and the pleasures it promises." Like the contemporary waterfront, it is on but not of the sea.[21]

The waterfront once had its own distinctive culture, but when ships no longer docked and the piers began to rot, neglect quickly became desolation. Unused railway yards became the home of the homeless. By the

1960s, the harbor was the place where New Yorkers dumped not only their refuse but also the least fortunate of their neighbors.

But it was precisely at this moment that waterfronts around the world began what Hans Mayer has called a "spectacular resurrection." In a few short years, derelict waterfronts were being bought up by developers. Railways and highways that had separated cities from their waters were razed and rotting piers demolished. In a textbook case of creative destruction, the world's waterfronts died and were reborn, all in a remarkably short period.[22]

The newly evacuated spaces were quickly put to mixed use: partly residential, partly commercial, partly recreational. Boston's Long Wharf led the way; Baltimore soon followed; then came London, Rotterdam, Singapore, Sydney, San Francisco. In an era of increased globalization, cities borrowed from one another. Waterfront development became formulaic in the same way that resort development had been. Building as closely as possible to the water, development pushed landfilling to its limits. Adjoining wetlands were sacrificed, and the last natural features of the old harbors were engineered out of existence. All around the world, the day of the anthropogenic coast had arrived.[23]

Anthropogenic Coasts

From the 1970s onward city people came back to the sea, but in a manner that had no precedent in the previous history of seaports. Today's waterfront residents have no occupational connection to water. Apart from ferry services, the gentrified waterfront is no longer a transit point. Only a few places allow access to the water itself, and these are largely private marinas. Phillip Lopate notes how "Manhattan is almost pathologically averse to letting you wander to the river's edge and get close enough to touch the water." The new harbor residents are largely upper or middle class, people who in earlier decades had turned their backs on the inner city to seek a better life in the suburbs. Not only are they more affluent than the maritime and industrial working classes they replaced, but they are likely to be both older and younger. Suburbs had become the place to bring up families. Waterfront development caters to single adults, who find this place to be a "new frontier," a place of heterogeneous lifestyles. The waterfront had always been a nonconformist's paradise, but now it is no longer associated with danger, crime, and toil, but with the pursuit of the good life as defined by consumption.[24]

FIGURE 39. Container ships in San Francisco Bay. Courtesy of Wikipedia.

Like the beach, the waterfront was first cleansed of its indigenous population and then colonized by inlanders. Once a place of work, it is now
largely a place of consumption, of "shopping instead of shipping," as Ann
Buttenwieser puts it, and festival space from which to view fireworks and
tall ships. Those who gather at the water's edge are spectators rather than
participants. Like those who populate the modern beach, they are not
there to go to sea but to look. The waterfront is no longer a place but a
landscape. Like the beach, the new urban waterfront is a nonplace, cut
off not only from its natural environment but from its own history. It has
been said that "the only thing New Yorkers ignore more than nature is
history."[25]

Initially, the redevelopment of harbors, like that of beaches, constituted
a colossal act of forgetting. Then, beginning in the 1960s, developers discovered the commercial value of maritime history as a lure to tourists and
began to add historical restoration to their agenda, even though, in the
wake of the utter devastation of the old ports, there is actually very little to
restore. Instead, they invented their own versions of the past—San Francisco's Fisherman's Wharf, New York's South Street Seaport, the London

Docklands—designed to capture their share of maritime tourism. Today, what passes for historic waterfronts has little to do with the past. For the most part, these places are commercial rather than marine enterprises, a kind of urban shopping mall. "How can New York, having strangled to death its port (whatever the valid reasons for doing so), turn around and ask us to celebrate that once-mighty engine of commerce, in the most sterile and manicured of surroundings, frequented mainly by tourists?" asks Lopate. The waterfront has now become wholly the edge of land. It has ceased to be a point of contact or of transit. It is no longer an eco-tone where environments connect with, challenge, and reinvigorate one another. No longer part of the larger coastal zone, the seaport is not a unique place inhabited by a distinctive population. In fact, it is questionable whether seaports can be called coastal in anything but location.[26]

Never have shores been so rich in property values and so impoverished in what had once made them the first home of humankind. What Henry David Thoreau believed to be the threshold of the last wilderness has become perhaps the least natural place on earth. It is said of Britain's coast that virtually none of it is any longer pristine. This is particularly true of beaches, which in the Western world are virtually all man-made to some extent. The quest for the pristine in farther reaches of the globe has only increased the amount of beach engineering there. Fully half of New Jersey's shore is now armored. Its beach protection programs, involving groins, jetties, and sea walls, go back to the 1920s, and "newjersification" is now practiced (and protested) everywhere in the world. But nowhere is coastal engineering more evident than in Japan, where 65 percent of the shores are now covered with concrete.[27]

Natural coasts are, Paul Carter warns us, "obstinately discontinuous, abysmal, anti-rational, impossible to fix," and efforts to stabilize them have had just the opposite effect of what was intended. Beaches, like the creatures that inhabit them, are mobile. Sands are constantly moving, shifting on, off, and alongshore in response to changes in both land and sea. They are replenished by sediments washing down from the interior. The great barrier islands of America's Atlantic and Gulf coasts have been moving for centuries. Of Hatteras, North Carolina, it has been said: "This island is nothing fixed. It has transience, shiftiness, built into its very existence." In the 1980s, Hatteras "houses well back from the beach [were] sold on the basis of 'Ocean Front Property by the Turn of the Century.' Even erosion can turn a buck." It is only when barrier islands are fixed in place that they are breached and eroded. Prevented from moving, they literally die, shrinking in size and viability. When rivers are dammed or diverted and currents and tides no longer replenish shores by pushing sediments toward the coast, disasters follow. Governments attempt to renew beaches by pumping sand, but it is well known that "restored" beaches are twice as likely to erode as those that are left alone.[28]

The reason we continue to "fix" coasts only to destroy them is not hard to fathom. We have allowed people to build right up to the edge of the sea, creating property that for coastal communities in economic decline is the principal tax base. As one Florida consultant put it, "we had to protect the golden goose." Newcomers to the coast believe that "all land [is] permanent and all borders fixed." As we have seen, this process was begun by wealthy Europeans and Americans in the nineteenth century with the building of spas, bathing places, and, ultimately, seaside estates. Samuel Eliot Morison could write in 1921 that "factory cities and yachting centers have now replaced fishing villages; Italian gardens and palaces blot out even the memory of rugged seashore farms."[29]

Middle-class tourism sustained the growth of resorts in the first half of the twentieth century, but it was after the Second World War that the real surge to the shore began. From the 1960s onward, shore communities not only grew in size but became ever more like suburbs. They attracted retirees, many of whom had summered or wintered there before settling permanently. Working people who had previously commuted from city to shore now reversed direction by making over seasonal dwellings into year-round residences. This was particularly true on coasts near large cities, but the process could also be seen in Maine, where fishing villages were fast becoming more like suburbs. At the turn of the twenty-first century, millions were abandoning the suburban crabgrass frontiers for those of the seafront, bringing with them a mindset that placed the highest value on property and privacy. Developers responded to this surge by building recklessly ever closer to the sea, a practice that contributed mightily to damage incurred during storms, large and small. Government-guaranteed property insurance encouraged rebuilding even on the most vulnerable sites. The goose that laid the golden egg would not be allowed to die, even as natural features of the coast were laid waste by engineering projects that increased coastal erosion.[30]

Today, more than a half of all shoreline activity is devoted to tourism and recreation. Farming, fishing, and shipping are now confined to a very small part of the total coastline. Maine's working waterfronts occupy but 20 of a total coastline of 5,300 miles. What had once been a fluid frontier, the edge of the world's greatest commons, is now a heavily patrolled border that discourages entry from both land and sea. With wetlands drained and shores seawalled, what had been a soft edge has become a hard, impenetrable one. In the United States, 83 percent of the eastern coasts and 60 percent of western shores are privately owned. The public still has a time-honored right to access the shore below the highest tide line, but its access to tide flats is severely restricted. When awareness of just how little coastal access was left began to dawn in the 1970s, groups pressured and sued property owners to secure easements that would allow access to beaches. On Nantucket, the One Big Beach movement has been active since 2004, but with only limited success. In other places privatization seemed to be winning the day. In Destin, Florida, for example, property owners have even opposed beach nourishment projects in an effort to maintain what they regard as their sovereign right to privacy. They would rather have no beach at all than share it with strangers. Before its beachfront boom in the 1970s, Destin was a decaying fishing community. Now it is a prime tourist destination, replete with luxury malls, golf courses, amusement parks, and a 4.5-billion-dollar tax base. Its developers christened it "the world's luckiest fishing village," though no fishing, apart from sport fishing, goes on there.[31]

All around the world, coastal villages are now the focus of a kind of nostalgia that had no precedent in earlier centuries. What once repelled the urban visitor now attracts millions. The fishing village has replaced the peasant village as the idealized version of the way life should be. Such towns seem to stop time and make the past accessible in ways that big cities and sprawling suburbs cannot. Their isolation and small scale offer an illusion of refuge, a home in an otherwise heartless world. Around the North Atlantic rim—in Scotland, New England, Brittany, Nova Scotia, the English Channel, and Maine—so-called heritage trails snake their way along coasts, depositing us at one quaintified village after another.

Nostalgia—derived from the Greek word for homecoming, nostos—was first noted in the seventeenth century as a serious medical condition among some Swiss mercenary soldiers, so overwhelmed by homesickness as to be unfit for duty. Its transformation from physical illness to psychological condition, associated with longing more for a past than for place, came only in the nineteenth century. Today nostalgia is a pervasive feature of modern societies, a foundation of the antiques and heritage industries, a motive force in everything from historic preservation to family reunions. We can't seem to get enough of the past, or rather of an idealized version of the past that bears little resemblance to historical reality. Though it is no longer treated as a serious malady, nostalgia does have serious consequences for those places and people toward which it is directed.

We have already seen how the fishing village came under nostalgia's spell. In Scotland, the Fishing Heritage Trail directs tourists mainly to places where fishing no longer exists because it generally assumed by tourism experts that "the maritime landscape is attractive only in the past or at a distance . . . for its 'grittiness' close-up is inconvenient to middle class consumption." In Gloucester, where the fishery is dying, visitors follow a red line around the harbor to spots where it used to be. Where fishing survives, the conflict between newcomers and residents continues. When developers wanted to introduce cobbled streets in the little Scottish port of Pittenweem, the remaining fishermen objected on the grounds that cobblestones were slippery and would make their work dangerous. But perhaps the greatest danger is nostalgia itself. In the twentieth century positive stereotypes replaced negative ones but left village inhabitants feeling, as one Newfoundlander put, as if they were "on a reservation," more like museum exhibits than real people. As tourism replaced fishing as the single largest source of coastal income and employment, many coastal people reluctantly adopted the identity assigned to them. They became resigned to ordinances that privileged the scenic over the functional, dictating the colors they could paint their houses and the amount of gear they could store in their side yards. As marinas take over working waterfronts, many Maine fishermen have become commuters. No longer able to afford waterfront property, they have themselves become strangers, subject to the same sense of loss as outsiders.[32]

But the sense of loss experienced by locals should not be confused with the nostalgia brought to the coast by inlanders. Fisherfolk are far less likely to idealize the past, to want to freeze it in place. For them the past is a living presence, something to build on, or as the members of the Heritage Society in Buckie, Scotland, put it: "We're still here. Let us tell you how we lived." Newcomers arrive seeking a refuge from what they know to be the deficits of progress. They cast a jaundiced eye on the future, something that the underemployed people of Buckie cannot afford to do. For the latter heritage is not a commodity but something they draw on to glean lessons for the future. Their motto, "Our Future Lies in Our Past," expresses their determination not to let their village become a maritime theme park. "We're not particularly interested in tourism," they say, "we're interested in preserving the community."[33]

At Port Clyde, a "postcard-perfect" village on Maine's St. George peninsula, a place associated with three generations of the artistic Wyeth family, the community seemed on its way to losing its entire fleet. Realizing that they could be "the last fishermen in Port Clyde," ground fishermen there responded in the spirit of the people of Buckie. The Midcoast Fishermen's Cooperative founded Port Clyde Fresh Catch, a community-supported fishery modeled on community-sponsored agriculture. With the support of the Wyeths and Maine's Island Institute, the cooperative has opened a way to the future based on past practices of selling directly to local customers.[34]

Heaven and Hell at the Shore

For much of the nineteenth and early twentieth century, coasts seemed to be on the way to exorcising the fears that had for so long been associated with them. Paradise seemed finally to have established itself on the beach. The geography of utopia moved decisively from the interiors to the shore, and offshore to islands, which John Fowles declared were the "original alternative societies." But even as coasts were cleared of shipwrecks, they were still shadowed by a new set of imagined threats. Winslow Homer's 1899 painting *The Gulf Stream* provided an unforgettable image—a black sailor cast away on a demasted, rudderless boat surrounded by a sea of sharks—that seemed to capture the human condition in "the face of a remote deity and overwhelming nature."[35]

The shark had not loomed large as a predator until the end of the eighteenth century but became ever more threatening over the next hundred years. A shark attack was commemorated in a 1778 painting by John Singleton Copley, commissioned by an Englishman named Brook Watson who had lost a leg as a boy in Havana Harbor. Romantic paintings like Gericault's *Raft of the Medusa* popularized the theme, but it was Homer's canvas, first shown in 1900 in Boston, that riveted attention. As Peter H. Wood has pointed out, the connection between blacks and sharks would not have been lost on Americans or Europeans. J. M. W. Turner's *Slave Ship (Slaves Throwing Overboard the Dead and Dying, Typhoon Coming On)* (1840) had exposed slavers' practice of disposing of dead and dying Africans in the Middle Passage of the Atlantic slave trade. Wood estimates that as many as 800,000 Africans may have become "shark bait," and "sharks may have altered their feeding and migration patterns to take advantage of this windfall." This would account for the aggressive swarming of sharks in tropical waters that Homer depicts. Fishermen in temperate zones had been taking sharks for hundreds of years without observing

FIGURE 40. *The Gulf Stream* by Winslow Homer, 1899. Courtesy of Wikimedia.

any such behavior. Indeed, prior to the exhibiting of Homer's painting the popular image of sharks was one of timidity and passivity.[36]

From that point onward, the myth of the Man Eater migrated beyond the tropics to every part of the oceans, so that the shark replaced the whale as the world's greatest sea monster. As the whaling industry went into momentary decline in the second half of the nineteenth century, contacts with whales diminished, while encounters with sharks increased as sea bathing became popular in both North America and Europe. For the first time, humans were invading the sharks' element, and a new kind of shark bait appeared. Though few in number, attacks began to be reported with some regularity. In the early twentieth century the image of the shark shifted dramatically from passive prey to vicious predator.

Our image of sharks comes down to us not from old maritime cultures, which were averse to swimming and approached sharks with the respect that hunters usually give their prey, but rather from the fear generated by an urban-industrial society that has largely lost its connection with the sea. Events in the long, hot summer of 1916 would transform shark-human relations in North America. Intense heat, together with a polio epidemic, lured thousands to the beaches, and in less than two weeks, four men were killed in the waters off the New Jersey shore. These deaths produced the first modern shark panic, which threatened the tourist industry and drew the attention of President Woodrow Wilson, a former New Jersey governor, resulting in the greatest federally funded animal hunt in history. In subsequent years, while commercial interests wished to consign the whole episode to oblivion, the legend of the "Jersey Man-Eater" would not go away. It returned with a vengeance in 1975, when the film *Jaws* came to the screen; and it has refused to go away despite every effort to educate the public.[37]

Feeling personally responsible for the wanton killing of sharks that followed in the wake of *Jaws*, Peter Benchley subsequently wrote books to set the record straight. Richard Ellis has observed that "man fears what he does not understand, and of all the large creatures with which he shares the planet, man probably knows least about sharks." While the myth of the man-eater has been massively undermined by recent scientific studies and the slaughter has slowed, this has not affected public culture. For those who seek a close encounter with wildness, there is still no substitute for a face-to-face encounter with a great white shark. Since the 1960s, swimming with sharks has become a commercially successful wilderness adventure, and what Ellis calls "shark people" continue to heed the call of the wild in an era when wolves and bears have become off limits as protected species.[38]

In the meantime, the whale, once the archetypal sea monster, had become the darling of conservationists. Whales appear only four times in the Bible, and not as creatures of nature but as instruments of God's will. In the Middle Ages, whales loomed larger than sharks in the bestiaries of the sea. The Norse began to hunt them on a commercial basis in the ninth century, but it was Basque whalers who first pursued them beyond the coasts of Europe into the North Atlantic. During the monumental expansion of commercial whaling in the eighteenth and early nineteenth centuries, the animal attained its most menacing dimensions, playing the villain to the heroic seafarers of the day. Fear entered the consciousness of landsmen through a plethora of romantic accounts of whaling by Sir Walter Scott, James Fenimore Cooper, and a host of lesser writers. None of them had any firsthand knowledge of whales, apart from the dead ones washed up on nearby shores. They drew instead on accounts by whalers, who projected onto the prey their own aggressiveness, even calling the normally passive gray whale populations of Baja California "devil fish." As whaling intensified, so did violence between men and whales. When attacked, whales were known to ram and sink not only smaller whaling boats but the ships that launched them. Of all the new maritime novelists,

FIGURE 41. Killer whales perform at Sea World, Orlando, Florida. Courtesy of Wikipedia.

only Herman Melville had any real experience at sea, but he too drew on tales of other sailors, including those aboard the *Essex*, which went down in Pacific waters when struck by a huge sperm whale in 1820. Melville was also drawing on accounts of the infamous Mocha Dick, a white bull first spotted off Mocha Island near the Chilean coast in 1810 and responsible for several assaults when harpooned over the next two decades.[39]

But by the time Melville published his great novel in 1851, whaling was on the verge of decline. The petroleum revolution was a decade away, and the romance had gone out of whaling. The whale oil industry had all the characteristics of onshore capitalism, employing a natural resource by means of a largely proletarianized workforce. Melville's book received devastating reviews, one calling its author "maniacal—mad as a march hare—mewing, gibbering, screaming, like an invincible Bedlamite." It was not until the market for whale oil had collapsed and the industry's sanguinary realities faded from memory that it was possible to see *Moby-Dick* as the literary masterpiece it was. That only happened in the 1920s, and it was not until the film version of the 1950s, and the global renewal of whaling itself, that the massive mammal loomed large again in popular imagination. The whale returned not as the leviathan of old, the terror of the high seas, but as a model endangered species. Its killer qualities transferred to the shark, whales were transformed into headliners for marine theme parks like Sea World. Commercial whale watching began in the 1970s and paved the way in 1982 for a worldwide moratorium on commercial whaling. It is now accepted that whales attack only when on the defensive, when protecting themselves and their young. In our own time, whales are "icons that represent everything that is mysterious, wonderful, and life-giving in the ocean." Humans have established a kind of totemic kinship with marine mammals that they have not extended to fish as such. Whales' monstrosity turns out to have been the product of our ignorance rather than their nature, something we are now beginning to see is also true of sharks.[40]

From Ramparts to Ruins

It is as if worlds have been turned inside out, with edges displacing centers. That which had been the ramparts of continents, their first line of defense, has become their greatest point of vulnerability. In the late nineteenth century, Lord Curzon could declare coasts "the most uncompromising, the least alterable and most effective" of all natural frontiers. By then the science of coastal fortification was perfected. It had never occurred to Winston Churchill's ancestors that England should be defended from its beaches, but he made his famous rhetorical stand there in 1940 because by the twentieth century coasts were considered the thick skin of the body politic, even after airpower had made them useless as barriers to bombardment. The militarization of coasts reached its high point during the Second World War, when certain landscapes—the white cliffs of Dover, Hitler's Atlantic Wall, California's Marin Headlands—became the symbolic ramparts of mid-twentieth-century warfare.[41]

D-Day showed the folly of this strategy, but it would be a long time before coastal fortification was abandoned. During the Cold War, both the United States and the Soviet Union remained strangely fixated on shoreline defenses. The latter made the coasts of its Baltic client states off limits to tourists, while the Marin Headlands overlooking the Golden Gate became a sequestered Nike missile base. In time, however, the significance of coastal defense diminished. Even England's vaunted insularity has been in remission since the completion of its Chunnel link with the European continent in 1994. Today, abandoned bunkers and silos have joined Martello towers and lighthouses as major tourist attractions. In an age of airpower, coast guards everywhere are more concerned with drug smugglers, terrorists, and illegal immigrants than with the threat of armed invasion. Fortifications along coasts now lie in ruins, but their

FIGURE 42. Coastal guard in World War II England. Courtesy of Library of Congress.

abandonment has left one unanticipated legacy. As Tom Killion points out, because former military reservations are among the few parts of the coasts in metropolitan areas "unsullied by the sterile nightmare of urban sprawl, that fine edge remains where earth meets the sea."[42]

In a few decades, a landscape that was once considered a rampart has become one of the most compromised and vulnerable of all natural features. Once regarded as our best defense against all enemies, human and natural, it is now the coast that needs defending. Only two hundred years ago, coasts belonged more to sea than land and could be approached only by water. Apart from ports, shores were sparsely inhabited, often only by the lighthouses built both to guide ships to safe harbors and to warn them away from dangerous ledges. Lighthouses saved many lives, but today the lighthouses themselves are threatened. Shipwreck is now a rarity, but the coasts are strewn with the ruins of lighthouses that have toppled from eroded cliffs or have been abandoned due to coastal flooding. Today the beacons that once saved many lives are in the need of saving. Previously symbols of humans' ability to stand up to the powers of nature, lighthouses now raise questions about human vulnerability not just for mariners but also for inlanders. In South Carolina, an organization called Save the Light has taken custody of the Morris Island lighthouse, just off Folly Beach outside Charleston. The light here was built in 1876 some 1,600 feet behind the tide line. Today, due to erosion and the retreat of the Carolina coastline, the newly islanded light finds itself located the same distance offshore that it once lay inland.[43]

Lighthouses date from the ancient world but became common on the coasts of both Europe and America by the nineteenth century. They were hard to get to except by boat, and keepers could expect few visits except from those who washed up on nearby shores. The great lighthouse engineer Robert Stevenson once noted that "the light-keeper occupies a place apart among men." It was a low-status occupation, thought to induce homicidal rages and suicide. But these same gothic qualities appealed to the first generation of romantics, and in the Victorian period lighthouses attracted growing numbers of day-trippers, forerunners of the contemporary tourists who have made remaining lighthouses the most visited places on most coasts. The same isolation that drove men mad has now made lighthouses ideal escapes from humdrum mainland existence.[44]

In an extraordinary reversal of fortune, that which was slated for abandonment and demolition has become one of the coasts' premier attractions. In Europe, lighthouses remain a public trust, but under America's 2000 National Lighthouse Preservation Act, decommissioned lighthouses are often bought for private use or turned into tourist accommodations. "Lighthousing," visiting as many as possible, has become a competitive sport, suggesting that something deeper is going on, a longing for the security of place in an otherwise placeless world. Coastal communities now identify more with their lighthouses than with any other landscape feature. But so too do inlanders, as whole regions and provinces have adopted beacons as unifying symbols. In New England they have displaced the village church steeple in iconic importance. As villages are swallowed up by suburbanizaton, the isolated lighthouse stands out as a symbol of stability in an otherwise topsy-turvy world.[45]

It was precisely when lights ceased to have a maritime purpose that they took on these new cultural functions. It was as if the beacon that had once swept the sea had swiveled inland, serving as both an attraction and a warning to entire continents. The attachment to coastal heritage is so strong today that proposals to move threatened structures back from the sea can arouse passionate opposition. In part this is due to real-estate interests' fear that any retreat from the shore will reduce property values, but others see withdrawal from the sea as a sign of weakness. Such

FIGURE 43. Move path of the Cape Hatteras Light, 1999. Courtesy of the North Carolina Division of Highways.

an alliance came into play in the 1990s, when Cape Hatteras Lighthouse was threatened by erosion and scheduled for relocation. It was not until 1999 that the beacon was moved, because many people saw any retreat as a surrender to malevolent nature. It was reported that many thought of the lighthouse as a "symbol of strength and stability and as a monument to the cause of coastal heroes, who had. . . . engaged a battle of wits with the sea," and believed that "to turn tail and run by moving the lighthouse would" be a betrayal.[46]

Danger in Paradise

Once valued for their military purposes, coasts have become some of the most peaceful places on earth. There we let down our guard and forget just how dangerous the sea can be. The geography of utopias, which in the nineteenth century was located well inland, has shifted decisively to the shore. Eden has taken up residence on the beach—but is still imagined

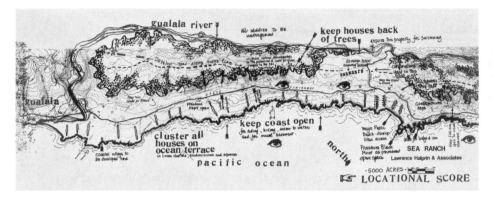

FIGURE 44. Architect Lawrence Halprin's vision of Sea Ranch, from his *The Sea Ranch: Diary of an Idea*. Courtesy of the Architectural Archives of the University of Pennsylvania.

in wholly terrestrial terms. In the United States, two utopian communities that have garnered particular attention—Florida's Seaside and California's Sea Ranch—are both located on the shore but founded on wholly landlocked principles. Neither gives much recognition to the ecotonal qualities of their respective coastal environments.[47]

Of the two, Seaside is the more conventional, rather like a suburb by the sea, but with the faults of suburbia removed. It is a densely built, walkable community, minimizing automobile congestion and pollution, but also set well back from the sea in the manner of the old coastal villages it claims to emulate. Seaside promises the benefits of coastal life without being coastal in anything but location. Sea Ranch, on the other land, is more like a resort, not meant for year-round occupancy, but close enough to the San Francisco Bay Area to be attractive for weekend and extended stays. It offers no shopping or services. Seaside occupies just eighty acres on the Gulf of Mexico, while Sea Ranch is located on a stunning part of the Mendicino coast, spread out over five thousand acres, with each house conforming to a strict environmental code to preserve the nature of the woods and grasslands. Its appeal is its location astride an edge of the San Andreas Fault. Its creators describe it thus: "The experience of being here is thus dominated by the fall of the land toward the sea as well as the constant call of the ocean . . . the eye is constantly drawn toward the shimmering horizon. . . . It is the coast, primarily, that brings people here—the touch of the wild that is so vigorously embodied in the shoreline itself."[48]

Sea Ranch was intended to be neither a resort nor a suburb. "The experience of the coastline was to be shared, not sequestered in separate private ownership," even though the houses are individually owned. The lead architect, Lawrence Halprin, approached the project with an ecological perspective: "I was convinced that we could avoid another suburbia and instead develop a social community for people of like minds, with a love of nature and of this site in particular, for whom 'living lightly on the land' would be a governing principle." He was determined not to build on the cliffs in what he called "Malibu Wall" style. He identified with the Pomo Indians and sheep ranchers who had lived there before him, and his models were early New England farming communities, which he imagined (wrongly) to have been organized around a commons. It was not wilderness that Halprin and his collaborators sought but a place where humans and nature coexist. "I became convinced that the Sea Ranch could become a place where wild nature and human habitation could interact in a kind of intense symbiosis where ecology could allow people to become part of the ecosystem." In contrast to earlier inland utopias based on shared work, what was supposed to bond Sea Ranchers was a shared landscape, or to be more specific, a shared view of a landscape, that "shimmering horizon" Halprin spoke of in the original plan. While every effort was made not to disturb the nature of the place, one exception was permitted: the cutting of trees that blocked a member's sea view.[49]

Once again we encounter the privileging of sight over all the other senses. Sea Ranchers were little interested in access to the sea. No harbors or marinas were built, and the sea was too cold for swimming. The initial plans provided for no public right-of-way to the shore itself, something that violated California coastal codes and held up further development of the property for eight years until public rights were negotiated. In the end, Halprin himself was disappointed by the degree to which private interests prevailed and the sense of a "nature-oriented outdoor recreational community" atrophied. A shared seascape, absent any real collective engagement with the sea itself, is incapable of generating either community or strong sense of place, for, as the English writer Adam Nicolson reminds us, "a landscape is seen: a place is experienced and known."[50]

Indeed, Sea Ranchers' relationship with their shore is not really different from that of residents of any of the other seaside resorts and residential communities that now line coasts around the world. The sign I encountered on my visit there—NEVER TURN YOUR BACK ON THE OCEAN—differs in no way from those posted elsewhere. For a public that has no real experience with the sea, the dangers posed by riptides and rogue waves is very real. Apart from the hundreds of thousands who have been killed by tsunamis, hundreds are drowned every year even on lifeguarded shores. The more attractive the coast, the greater the dangers. People are regularly swept from the rocks at the edge of Maine's Acadia National Park. Just offshore on Great Gott Island, a place where I have summered for a half-century, on August 23, 2009, we witnessed a rogue wave generated by Hurricane Bill hundreds of miles offshore. It arrived on a cloudless afternoon and tore apart two sea-cliff cottages. None of our neighbors was killed, but a few moments later, when the same wave arrived at Acadia, a tragedy occurred. Thousands had gathered at its famous Thunder Hole to view the surf; several people were pulled into the sea and a young girl drowned.[51]

Nova Scotia calls itself Canada's Ocean Playground, but it has few swimmable beaches and many unsafe scenic overlooks. At supposedly idyllic Peggy's Cove, tourist reveries are rudely interrupted by a marker that reads

WARNING

INJURY AND DEATH HAVE REWARDED CARELESS SIGHT-SEERS HERE

THE OCEAN AND ROCKS ARE TREACHEROUS

SAVOUR THE SEA FROM A DISTANCE[52]

Earlier coastal peoples never needed to be reminded of the dangers of the sea. As we have already seen, Prince Edward Islanders were wary of "chasing the shore" in any weather. Fishers and mariners had always assumed the ocean's destructive, death-dealing powers. In the past, beaches were littered with shipwrecks, *memento mori*, from which were fashioned so many cautionary tales. Today's Edenic beaches are, like the cruise ships that lie anchored just offshore, engineered to mask real danger and produce an illusion of security. Yet the threats posed by seas remain undeniable, and with each tsunami, hurricane, or oil spill, consciousness of its power to disrupt even the most powerful civilizations comes to the fore. Today coastal wrecks are rare, but a new nightmare lurks offshore. In the 1990s, reports began to surface of huge container ships and giant oil tankers simply disappearing without a trace. The cause, it seems, is an increase in oceanic storms producing rogue waves measuring over a hundred feet in height. In 1995, the *Queen Elizabeth II* was hit by two ninety-five-foot waves. To its captain, Ronald Warwick, it "looked as if the ship was heading straight for the white cliffs of Dover." Now mariners face their worst fears not at the edge of the sea but in a place they had always regarded as relatively safe: midocean.[53]

CONCLUSION: LEARNING TO LIVE WITH COASTS

Eventually man, too, found his way back to the sea.
RACHEL CARSON, *THE SEA AROUND US*[1]

Over the last half-century there has been a surge to the shore that in speed and volume rivals any of the great migrations in human history. Today half of the world's population resides within 120 miles of the sea. By 2025 it is estimated that this could reach 75 percent. In the United States, 54 percent of the population lives in what are defined as coastal counties, within 50 miles of the sea, and 3,600 people arrive in coastal regions every day. In California, fully 80 percent of state residents live within 30 miles of the shore. Areas defined as coastal make up just 15 percent of the nation's land area, which means they are three times more densely settled than interiors. We are used to oceans crashing against the shore, but now for the first time it is a human wave that is rolling seaward.[2]

In the nineteenth century, millions crossed oceans to inhabit new lands. Facilitated by canal and rail, they passed quickly into the interior, turning their backs on the sea and leaving little mark on the shore, apart from their ports of entry. Today, portals like Ellis and Angel Islands are pilgrimage sites for the descendants of those who entered there. But the new human tsunami that moves from the interior to the coasts does not require a passport or a visa. Most mass migrations throughout history have been involuntary, triggered by want or war, associated more with fate than with freedom. This one is different, for it has been driven as much by desire as by necessity. Until recently it went largely unnoticed, but neither the migration nor its impact on coasts can any longer be ignored.[3]

To be sure, people are coming back to the seaside for a variety of reasons. By far the largest numbers are drawn by megacities like Bangkok, Shanghai, and Lagos. These began as seaports but are no longer maritime in anything but location. They are less centers of production than loci of consumption. Sailor towns have largely disappeared, and waterfronts are now crowded by shopping malls and condominiums. The fishing industry employs fewer and fewer people, and shipping has moved to new ports well away from the city as such. Discoveries of oil and gas just offshore account for some coastal growth, as do military installations, but cities by the sea are more likely to offer employment in the service than in the industrial sector. It is tourism, the largest single employer worldwide, that accounts for much of the growth of smaller seaside communities. It is as if worlds are being turned inside out, with the edges of islands and continents displacing interiors as centers of demographic gravity.

In the Era of Real Estate

This surge to the sea was not anticipated. The late nineteenth and early twentieth centuries saw a depopulation of coasts and inshore islands as fishing and shipping became mechanized. The current human tsunami began as a trickle whose vanguard was wealthy inlanders who first arrived as seasonal tourists and then began to acquire property. We have seen how these elites spent much of the later nineteenth century clearing the shores of lesser folk, building their exclusive enclaves, and keeping the great unwashed at a distance. The railroad and then the automobile ultimately brought the shores within reach of urban middle classes, but until the late twentieth century working-class access was restricted by a lack of money and leisure time.

This class dimension did not go unnoticed. In 1928 J. Spencer Smith, president of the American Shore and Beach Preservation Association, remarked, "There was a time, just a few years ago, when only a relatively few favored ones could visit the shore of Old Neptune." He was pleased to report that "the old order has changed, however, and today the ocean fronts belong to the multitudes." Smith was speaking of the New Jersey and New York shores, which by the 1920s were becoming popular destinations, and not just during the summers and weekends. During the Second World War, when I first saw the sea from the sands of Atlantic City, movement toward the sea stalled as beaches became the first line of defense in every theater of war, off limits to civilians. Some coasts, like the Baltic, remained thinly populated during the Cold War era, but the 1950s and 1960s saw the acceleration of development that Smith had envisioned. His organization represented the interests of coastal developers, resort owners, and entrepreneurs of America's emerging leisure worlds, who now appreciated the value of attracting a mass consumer base. In Smith's view, the beach would promote not only prosperity but also class reconciliation. "Neither communism, socialism, nor any other 'ism' will ever secure a foothold in this country so long as masses of humanity are given the opportunity to enjoy Nature's great gifts within the bounds to which they are entitled."[4]

Those bounds would be strictly delimited, however. Traditionally, the shore below the high tide line had been open to the public. Just where the line between the public domain and private property was drawn varied over time and by place. Before the era of the surveyor, it was determined as much by custom and community consent as by law. Now, in what Ruth Moore calls the era of real estate, boundaries are clearly marked and shore property has become a commodity, a highly desirable investment, a place from which to watch one's wealth increase at the expense of the environment.[5]

The American Shore and Beach Protection Association has always lobbied successfully for this kind of beach restoration but has been careful to confine the masses to the sands. Its populist appeals for universal beach access disguise the fact that it opposes any regulation that would infringe on the rights of the individual and corporate property owners who are its membership base. It defends their right to build seawalls and groins that contribute mightily to the beach erosion that necessitates sand replenishment. The association is only too happy to have taxpayers foot the bill for programs of protection and replenishment that have been both enormously expensive and largely ineffective. And it has consistently opposed the kind of planning that would get to the roots of the real problems of coastal erosion.[6]

This brings us to the crux of today's coastal problems, consequences less of the huge numbers of coast dwellers than of the way they live on the shore. The old coastal population of farmer-fishers and mariners has been reduced to a very small minority. The part of the shore that always served as a working waterfront has been similarly constricted. In Maine, for example, only 25 of the 5,300 miles of coastline any longer serve public purposes. The rest has become private property, much of it prime residential real estate. The protection of this property now takes precedence over all other considerations—above all, over the animate nature of the shore, a place that is itself as alive as any of the creatures who make their home there, including us.

Public awareness of climate change and sea rise is now so intense that it comes as something of a shock to realize that these issues were not even discussed before the 1980s. Reliable knowledge about the history of sea levels is even more recent, and still very incomplete, especially for earlier periods. We can be fairly certain that during the period of the so-called

FIGURE 45. Storm surge during Hurricane Carol, 1969, as it swept away the Rhode Island Yacht Club. Courtesy of the NOAA Photo Library.

Little Ice Age, 1350–1850, sea levels were relatively stable. Then seas began to rise by about 2 millimeters per year for a century or so. Now this rate has accelerated to 3 millimeters per year as glaciers and ice sheets melt, global warming expands the sea's temperature and volume, and ocean basins alter their shapes. The future is notoriously difficult to predict, and estimates of the rise by the year 2100 have varied greatly. Careful scientists think that the rise could be as little as 0.9 meters and as much as 2 meters. This is much lower than many of the more alarming predictions, but when the sea-level rise is combined with an increase in storm activity and changes to both land and sea due to global warming, the impact will be drastic, particularly for the 100 million people who live just a meter above sea level.[7]

The effects of climate change are very real, but coasts were in trouble long before the most recent acceleration in sea-level rise, due to a combination of natural and human factors. Oil drilling arrived at the beach before it went offshore. The draining and filling in of wetlands has been going on for centuries, the greatest part over the past century or so. Today, 70 percent of the world's wetlands are gone. In the United States, the loss is even higher: 80 to 90 percent.

The armoring of coasts, meant to protect coastal dwellers, has produced a false sense of security. In Japan, though 65 percent of its vulnerable coasts are seawalled or otherwise protected, nothing could stop the great tsunami of March 11, 2011. At Taro, people standing atop the town's monster seawall felt they were safe, but all were washed away. In Japanese, *tsunami* means "harbor wave," and in many ways the engineering of modern harbors increased the destructive velocity of this most recent surge. Fishermen had long complained that seawalling limited their ability to see waves coming. Seawalls also reduced the coastal population's awareness of the sea more generally. The public's understanding of environmental history is shallow in any case, and only a few Japanese fishing villages still nourish memories of previous tsunamis. But those that did had a better record of successful evacuations than those who had forgotten the past. There are huge costs to be paid for what Peter Kahn has been called our "generational environmental amnesia," which prevents us

FIGURE 46. Results of Japanese tsunami, 2011, photo by Yomuri Shimbun. Courtesy of Getty Images.

from knowing not only the long-term causes of degradation but also the ways we can adapt to them.[8]

Learning from the Past

Every schoolchild now knows that sea waters are rising, but few know anything about the multiple ways that our species has coped, often successfully, with earlier episodes of inundation. To date, there has been far more public discussion of mitigation of human influences on climate change than serious consideration of adaptation. Clearly, the two must go hand in hand, but it is imperative that we bring the past into a dialogue with the present and future. Over the last two and a half million years, there have been sea-level oscillations of as much as 500 feet. Before the end of the last interglacial era, just ten thousand years ago, oceans were 400 feet lower than they are today. As we have already seen, inundations are capable of inducing massive population movements and radical changes in ways of life. In the region we now call the Netherlands this has happened many times: 1170, 1362, 1703, 1916, 1953. All over the world there are long lists of floods and towns lost to the sea.[9]

But history provides not just a catalog of catastrophes but also instructive lessons in human adaptability. From the earliest times, coastal people have lived amphibiously atop pilings or, like the Marsh Arabs, on floating islands of reeds. As we have seen, our coastal ancestors, both Native American and European, knew not to build too close to the water. European as well as indigenous migratory fishers camped rather than settled on the shore. When they did build shelters, they made them capable of being taken down and removed quickly. The European fishermen of eastern Long Island, who arrived in the late seventeenth century, learned where to camp from Native Americans, with whom they initially had good relations. Known as Bonackers, the whites hunted and fished in ways similar to the Indians, and the two groups sometimes intermarried. Later, when they combined fishing with farming, they built on higher ground, but as late as the 1930s they kept prefab shanties near the shore; they fished from the beach by launching their boats directly into the surf. Old-timers remember that Bonacker shanties would be taken apart in the fall and stored for the next fishing season. They were also removed when storms threatened.[10]

Sandy shores, like those on Long island, are always on the move, fluid and alive. Bonackers like Bill Lester are well aware of the nature of the environment they inhabit. "Nothing but a little sand bar" was the way he de-

FIGURE 47. Fishing huts on the Long Island shore, 1902. Photo of Captain Joshua Fournier by Hal B. Fullerson. Courtesy of the Suffolk County Historical Society.

scribed Long Island. When interviewed in the 1970s, he was already worried about the consequences of beach development: "Still there's plenty of room where people can build in the woods. Instead of that they've gone down on the beach and taken our sand over. Yes, our sandy beach. Now that sand was built up from the ocean over thousands of years. And now they've got big houses all along the beach. There shouldn't be houses where the sea washed up sand there for all these years."[11]

The long sand spit on the southwest corner of Cape Cod known as Monomoy Island tells another story of adaptation, in this case strategic retreat. At times it has been a peninsula, at other times one or more islands. It was the haunt of wreckers before it attracted fishermen in 1710. They avoided Wreck Harbor in favor of Powder Hole, establishing a small village called Whitewash. In the 1850s, when the entrance to Powder Hole was blocked by shifting sands, the residents either abandoned their houses

or barged them to the mainland. Later, summer people converted the remaining dwellings to their own purposes, but after Monomoy became a
national wildlife refuge in 1970, the remaining houses were taken down
when their owners died. Today, only the Old Monomoy Light House Station remains.[12]

Such strategic retreats were in no way surrenders to nature but reasonable accommodations to what the Dutch call the "water wolf." Neth-
erlanders had been building artificial islands since Roman times, but they
also knew the value of dunes as buffers and were careful not to intrude on
them. Thus, when the Dutch came to North America in the seventeenth
century, they turned their backs on Long Island's sandy beaches, preferring instead to settle beside the Hudson River. The Moken of Thailand,
known to their neighbors as "sea people," were sufficiently attuned to the
signs of tsunami in 2004 that they were able to flee inland when 175,000
others drowned. On the coasts of Peru and Colombia, fishing villages
are now purpose-built so that they can be moved back when inundation
threatens. In Alaska, Inuit peoples are considering retreating from the
coast, and the same is true of villages in the Niger Delta of West Africa. In the world's most vulnerable islands, the Maldives, people have
already moved to high ground, and the government is buying land in
India and Sri Lanka in anticipation of massive resettlement. In Venice,
which is beset by both subsidence and rising sea levels, causing St. Mark's
Square to be under water one-third of the year, the population has already
dropped substantially and there is some talk of permanent evacuation. In
the meantime, the British are considering selective abandonment of certain parts of their coastline, though opponents are quick to call this "the
surrender option."[13]

The idea of the houseboat is at least as old as Noah's ark. People and their
animals have long taken to the sea when there was no longer a place for
them on land. The colonization of the Pacific proceeded in this manner,
and it continues in many parts of Asia today. On the nineteenth-century
west coast of North America, temporary dwellings floated on large logs
provided shelter for thousands of timber workers. Floating homes continued to offer cheap housing in Vancouver, Seattle, Portland, and San
Francisco Bay. In the wake of the Second World War, these became popular with bohemians and hippies, "water squatters" in places like Sausalito.
But by the 1970s, their reputation for being polluting and unsightly led
cities including Vancouver to remove them from their waterfronts. Nevertheless, gentrified houseboat communities equipped with their own
sewage systems have not only survived but flourished in places like Seat-

FIGURE 48. Effects of coastal erosion, Dauphin Island, Alabama, November 2005. Courtesy of Center for Land Use Interpretation.

tle's Lake Union and Vancouver's Sea Village Marina. When Stanley and Daphne Burk moved to Sea Village in 1978, they reasoned, "We all came from the water, after all, and it's comforting to be near it."[14]

People are coming back to the sea with dreams both big and small. In New York Harbor, the idea of an ecologically sound housing unit called the Waterpod has been floated, while on the west coast the grandiose Seasteading project has been launched. Founded in 2008 by libertarian Silicon Valley entrepreneurs, the Seasteading Institute offers a vision of an oceanic frontier of floating sovereign nations, freed from the laws of both sea and land, places where new ideas could be tested. Inspired technologically by offshore drilling rigs and cruise ships without home ports, Seasteaders would live at sea without, however, being connected to it any way but location. Seasteaders come back to the sea as libertarian exiles from the mainstream as well as the mainland. They are more inspired by Ayn Rand than by Rachel Carson. They do not enter into the sea mentally or imaginatively, for theirs is not an environmental dream but a political one. In most respects they remain landlubbers.[15]

Muddying the Waters

There is no ark capacious enough to sustain the billions of people who may be displaced by coastal erosion and flooding. What is really needed is a fundamental rethinking of not just how but why we build on coasts. We will not engineer our way out of our current vulnerabilities, but we can reconsider the relationship between land and sea, recognizing that coasts constitute a unique ecotone requiring a wholly different way of life. Coasts are moving, and we must also move to survive. There was a time when only buildings directly related to maritime activity were located at the shore and all other residences were built well inland. It seems time to go back to that very reasonable principle. It is also the moment to abandon the very notion of shoreline defense, whether that be by seawalls, groins, or beach replenishment, accepting the scientific evidence that nature can do the job for us if only we will allow it to do so. The State of Maine moved in 1982 to end all shoreline defense engineering. Now is time for other regions, where erosion is even greater, to follow suit, saving billions of wasted dollars.[16]

From the beginning, Western culture has cast the sea in the role of antagonist. Now that coasts have ceased to be our first line of defense against human invaders, we are confronted with a whole set of new threats—tsunamis, rogue waves, red tides—that would seem to justify drastic interventions on our part. Weather forecasting is rife with military metaphors, and the struggle against beach erosion has everywhere become the moral equivalent of war. In the wake of Hurricane Camille in 1969, Mississippians broke out their American flags as if they had been in battle. It is not that flooding and storm surges are not a real threat, but that to date many of the defenses against them have proven unrealistic.[17]

Engineering will provide no fix. Nothing less than a new mindset, a new cultural paradigm, is needed if we are to live *with* rather than simply *on* our shores. For too long we have thought of sea and land as two different things, when historically they constitute one single dynamic coastal system. We must stop drawing lines so rigidly and begin to practice what Eviatar Zerubavel calls "mental plasticity." We need to remind ourselves that nature itself does not draw lines or make sharp distinctions. It is time to embrace the idea of flow with respect to both time and space, for it is clear that our efforts to pin down coasts, to fix them to maps and timetables, is not working. Maps are very good at some things, but they do not capture human experience.[18]

FIGURE 49. Houseboats at Sausalito, California, 2004. Courtesy of Wikimedia Commons.

We must rethink not only the relationship between land and sea but that between humanity and nature, giving up distinctions that separate us from other creatures. Wallace Kaufman and Orrin Pilkey remind us that "there are no catastrophes or disasters in nature," only processes that are part of nature's way of making its own corrections. We should heed advice given by Francis Bacon some four hundred years ago: "Nature to be commanded must be obeyed."[19]

As we have seen, a great deal more fear than understanding is still focused on the sea and its creatures. We talk of *invasive* species, when we have created the conditions for them to thrive in places where humans like to dwell. Like the wolf and the mountain lion, sharks are seen as invaders, when it is humans who have been encroaching on their territories. On some shores, seaweed has been declared the enemy by those who like their beaches clean and sterile, when in fact for two centuries it is land that has intruded on water, leading to ever greater pollution and

FIGURE 50. *The Evolution of Man*, cartoon by Nicholas Garland, 2009. Courtesy of the artist and the Telegraph Media Group.

erosion. Perhaps it is time to call a truce between land and water, between ourselves and nature.

A first step in this process is to recognize that land and water are not opposites but inseparable parts of an ecological continuum, especially along the shore. We need to abandon the traditional blue-water assumption that oceans are elemental and timeless, and adopt what might be called a brown-water acknowledgment of the dynamic hybrid nature of our coastal water worlds. Only after we have muddied the waters a bit can we begin to acknowledge the fluid nature of what we have mistaken for terra firma. Once we have grasped that wind, earth, and water are all parts of one dynamic system of which humankind is also a member, we will better understand not just our terraqueous planet but also ourselves.

ACKNOWLEDGMENTS

I begin by thanking those who have been companions in my coastal explorations. My parents first brought me to the Jersey shore. It was through my wife, Christina, that I came to Maine and to the island, Great Gott, that has featured prominently in my writings. There I first encountered *Homo littoralis* in the persons of Russell Gott and Lyford Stanley and through the writings of Ruth Moore. My sons, Christopher and Benjamin, lured me to the edge of the sea, as do my grandchildren, Peter and Astrid. The writings of E. B. White encouraged me to take up sailing and inspired the name of my boat, the *Hint of Trouble*. Hours spent on Blue Hill Bay in the company of my mate and mentor Philip Silver allowed me to see the coast and ocean in whole new ways.

There are also the institutions that have facilitated my work. The National Endowment for the Humanities funded two summer institutes at the Library of Congress, where I discovered the riches of its photo collections. As a Fulbright Senior Scholar I enjoyed the hospitality of Godfrey Baldacchino and the Island Studies Program at the University of Prince Edward Island. The University of Victoria, British Columbia, sponsored three lectures on coastal matters when I was a Lansdowne Fellow there. Parts of this book have been presented to the Geography Department at the University of California, Berkeley, the San Francisco Estuary Institute, St. Mary's College of California, California State University Channel Islands, and international environmental meetings in Copenhagen, Denmark, and Turku, Finland. Cal Winslow invited me to speak in Mendicino, while the Art and Islands conference at Guernsey in 2010 provided an opportunity to talk about the origins of modern seascapes. The Age of Sail conference at Vancouver in 2010 and the American Historical Association meeting in San Diego the same year proved equally stimulating. The Rachel Carson Center for Environment and Society in Munich has been supportive in innumerable ways, beginning with the conference on the future of environmental history convened in Washington in spring 2010 in cooperation with the National History Center. My thanks to Christof Mauch and James Banner Jr. for arranging that occasion.

I am in debt to Eric Leed, Orvar E. Lofgren, Michael Pearson, and Ted Koditschek for their close, supportive reading of the manuscript. I can trace back to discussions with David Lowenthal, Al Howard, David Hooson, Donna Merwick, Greg Dening, Carl Guarneri, and Rhys Isaac the origins of this study, but I am no less grateful to Owe Ronstrom, Phil Hayward, Jerry Bentley, Jo Guldi, Rainer Buschman, Godfrey Baldacchino, Robert Grudin, Jennifer Gaynor, Lige Gould, Lowell Moorcroft, Penny Ismay, Danny Vickers, Jack Russell, Gray Brechin, Isaac Land, Karen Wigen, Iain Boal, Margaret Cohen, Richard Walker, Jack Crowley, Felipe Fernandez-Armesto, Peter Pope, Charles Mann, Elizabeth Mancke, and Michael Williams. Special thanks go to Ole Mouritsen, who called my attention to the evolutionary impact of shellfish diets and who, together with Kirsten Drotner, guided me around the coasts of Denmark.

I am particularly indebted to all those who gathered at the Island Institute in Rockland, Maine, in fall 2011 to explore islands, coasts, and oceans. Franziska Torma of the Rachel Carson Center proved a superb coconvenor, while the institute's Philip Conkling and Rob Snyder outdid themselves as hosts. Philip Steinberg, Paul D'Arcy, Steve Mentz, Jeff Bolster, Helen Rozwadowski, and Michael Pearson led a series of stimulating discussions, participated in by Stefan Helmreich, Kimberly Peters, Julia Heunemann, Adam Keul, Stuart Morrison, Chris Pastore, Joe Christensen, Ryan Jones, Alistair Sponsel, Glenn Grasso, Petr Kopecky, Samuel Senanyon, Robert Deal, Matt McKenzie, Alexander Kraus, Christian Fluery, Michael Reidy, and Ingo Heidbrink.

I am indebted to the Folk Life Center archives at the Library of Congress, to the libraries of the University of California at Berkeley, to the very able technical assistance of Mike Jones and Darin Jensen of the Geography Department at Berkeley, and to the editor of *California Coast & Ocean*, Rasa Gustaitus.

Artists and writers have been no less important to the genesis of this book. Eric Hopkins, Peter Ralston, and Tom Killion are the artists who have contributed most to my coastal imaginings. No less important are writers Rebecca Solnit, Rowan Jacobsen, Christina Gillis. and Josh Jelly-Schapiro. But I am no less grateful to my insightful editor, Robert Devens; my copyeditor, Ruth Goring; and my publicists Jeff Waxman and Scott Manning. And, of course, there is Rachel Carson, whose imaginative and scientific gifts have had no parallel.

NOTES

Introduction

1. John A. Murray, introduction to *The Seacoast Reader*, ed. John A. Murray (New York: Lyons, 1999), xvii.
2. Kristin M. Crossett et al., *Population Trends along the Coastal United States, 1980–2009* (Washington, DC: National Oceanic and Atmospheric Administration, 2004); Don Hinrichsen, *Coastal Waters of the World: Trends, Threats, and Strategies* (Washington, DC: Island Press, 1998).
3. John R. Gillis, "Being Coastal," *California Coast and Ocean* 23, no 1 (2007): 10–15.
4. Rachel L. Carson, *The Sea around Us* (New York: Oxford University Press, 1951), 15.
5. Ruth Moore, "The Offshore Islands," in *The Tired Apple Tree: Poems and Ballads* (Nobleboro, ME: Blackberry Books, 1990).
6. John Gillis, "Filling the Blue Hole in Environmental History," in *The Future of Environmental History: Needs and Opportunities*, ed. Kimberly Coulter and Christof Mauch (Munich: Rachel Carson Center for Environment and Society, 2011), 16–18.
7. For the distinction between living in as opposed to living on, see Owe Ronstrom, "In or On? Island Words, Island Worlds, II," *Island Studies Journal* 6, no. 2 (2011): 277–44.
8. James Hamilton-Paterson, *Seven-Tenths: The Sea and Its Thresholds* (New York: Europa Editions, 2009), 23; Rachel L. Carson, *The Edge of the Sea* (Boston: Houghton Mifflin, 1998), 1.

Chapter 1

1. Rebecca Solnit, "Seashell to Ear," in *Unraveling the Ripple*, ed. Helen Douglas (Edinburgh: Pocketbooks, 2001), n.p.
2. Eric Leed, *The Mind of the Traveler: From Gilgamesh to Global Tourism* (New York: Basic Books, 1991), 19; *A Dictionary of Creation Myths*, ed. David Leeming and Margaret Fleming (New York: Oxford University Press, 1995), 99; Max Oelschlaeger, *The Idea of Wilderness: From Prehistory to the Age of Ecology* (New Haven, CT: Yale University Press, 1991), 45–46; Christopher Connery, "There Was No More Sea: The Suppression of the Oceans, from Bible to Cyberspace," *Journal of Geographical History* 32 (2006): 495–505.
3. *Dictionary of Creation Myths*, 93–94, 111.
4. Hugh Brody, *The Other Side of Eden: Hunters, Farmers, and the Shaping of the World* (New York: Free Press, 1994), 86, 13–14.
5. Zygmunt Bauman, *Liquid Times: Living in an Age of Uncertainty* (Cambridge, UK: Polity, 2007), 98–99; Steve Mentz, *At the Bottom of Shakespeare's Ocean* (London: Continuum, 2009), 98.

6. This and subsequent quotations from Robert Alter, *Genesis: Translation and Commentary* (New York: W. W. Norton, 1996).

7. Alain Corbin, *Lure of the Sea: The Discovery of the Seaside in the Western World, 1750–1840* (Berkeley: University of California Press, 1994), 2, 5.

8. Brody, *Other Side of Eden*, 97.

9. Ibid., 118–23; also David Christian, *Maps of Time: An Introduction to Big History* (Berkeley: University of California Press, 2004), 181–91.

10. Alan Dundes, "The Flood as Male Myth of Creation," in *The Flood Myth*, ed. A. Dundes (Berkeley: University of California Press, 1988), 167–82: W. H. Auden, *The Enchafed Sea, or The Romantic Iconography of the Sea* (New York: Random House, 1950), 45.

11. Samuel Eliot Morison, "The Ancients and the Sea," in his *Spring Tides* (Boston: Houghton Mifflin, 1965), 45; Auden, *Enchafed Sea.*

12. John R. Gillis, *Islands of the Mind: How the Human Imagination Created the Atlantic World* (New York: Palgrave/Macmillan, 2004), chaps. 1–5.

13. Helen M. Rozwadowski, *Fathoming the Ocean: The Discovery and Explanation of the Deep Sea* (Cambridge, MA: Harvard University Press, 2005), chap. 1; Gisli Palsson, *Coastal Economics, Cultural Accounts: Human Ecology and Icelandic Discourse* (Manchester: Manchester University Press, 1991), 97–101.

14. Gillis, *Islands of the Mind*, 10–16; Francis Pryor, *Stonehenge: A Quest for Life and Death in Bronze Age Britain* (London: Harper Perennial, 2008), 13.

15. Steven Mithin, *After the Ice: A Global Human History 20,000–5000 BC* (Cambridge, MA: Harvard University Press, 2004), 3; Max Uhle, *The Emeryville Shellmound*, University of California Archaeology and Ethnology 7, no. 1 (Berkeley: University of California Press, 1907), 31.

16. David Yesner, "Maritime Hunter-Gatherers: Ecology and Prehistory," *Current Anthropology* 21, no. 6 (December 1980): 734; Douglas J. Kennett, *The Island Chumash: Behavioral Ecology in a Maritime Society* (Berkeley: University of California Press, 2005); chap. 8; Jon M. Erlandson, "The Archaeology of Aquatic Adaptations: Paradigms for a New Millennium," *Journal of Archaeological Research* 9, no. 4 (December 2001): 738.

17. See David R. Harris, "'The Farther Reaches of Human Time': Retrospect on Carl Sauer as Prehistorian," *Geographical Review* 92 (2002): 526–44; Carl Sauer, *Agricultural Origins and Dispersals* (New York: American Geographical Society, 1952), 23–28, 96; Gisli Palsson, "Hunters and Gatherers," in *History, Evolution and Social Change*, ed. T. Ingold, D. Richer, and J. Woodburne (Oxford: Berg, 1988), 203; Roy Ellen, "Modes of Subsistence: Hunting and Gathering in Agriculture and Pastoralism," in *Companion Encylopedia of Anthropology*, ed. Tim Ingold (London: Routledge, 1994), 206; Yesner, "Maritime Hunter-Gatherers," 727.

18. Tom Koppel, *Lost World: Rewriting Prehistory* (New York: Atria Books, 2003), 121; Erlandson, "Archaeology of Aquatic Adaptions," 287–88, 304–5.

19. Alister Hardy, "Was Man More Aquatic in the Past," *New Scientist* 7 (April 1960): 642–45.

20. When it appeared in 1982, the feminist science writer Elaine Morgan's *The Aquatic Ape* was wildly popular among the public but drew severe criticism from anthropologists for expanding on the Hardy thesis. *The Aquatic Ape* (New York: Stein and Day, 1982), 21; Richard Ellis, introduction to *Aquagenesis: The Origins and Evolution of Life in the Sea* (New York: Viking, 2001).

21. Sauer, *Agricultural Origins and Dispersals*, 3; personal communication with Professor Michael Williams, Sauer's biographer, October 28, 2008.

22. Carl O. Sauer, "Seashore—Primitive Home of Man," in *Land and Life: A Selection from the Writings of Carl Ortwin Sauer* (Berkeley: University of California Press, 1963), 309.

23. Ibid., 311.

24. Rachel Carson, *The Sea around Us* (New York: Oxford University Press, 1951), 14–15.

25. Palsson, *Coastal Economics*, 64–66; Erlandson, "Archaeology of Aquatic Adaptations," 294–305.

26. The fate of the theory can be followed in "Aquatic Ape Hypothesis," http:/en.wikipedia.org/wiki/Aquatic_ape_hypothesis; also Simon Bearder. "Flood Brothers," *BBC Wildlife* 18, no. 6 (June 2000): 64–68; an exception is the work of Philip K. Steinberg, *The Social Construction of the Ocean* (Cambridge, UK: Cambridge University Press, 2001); Palsson, *Coastal Economics*, 64–65; Erlandson, "Archaeology of Aquatic Adaptations," 294–95.

27. Spencer Wells, *The Journey of Man: A Genetic Odyssey* (New York: Random House, 2002).

28. Ian Tattersall, *The World from Beginnings to 4000 BCE* (New York: Oxford University Press, 2008), chaps. 4–5; Wells, *Journey of Man*, 47.

29. Richard Forman and Michael Gordon, *Landscape Ecology* (New York: John Wiley and Sons, 1986), 497: Erlandson, "Archaeology of Aquatic Adaptations," 302.

30. Michael A. Crawford, "A Role for Lips as Determinant of Evolution and Hominid Brain Development," in *Polyunsaturated Fatty Acids: Neural Foundation and Mental Health*, ed. Ole G. Mouritsen and Michael M. Crawford (Copenhagen: Royal Danish Academy of Sciences and Letters, 2007), 7–32; Rowan Jacobsen, *The Living Shore: Rediscovering a Lost World* (New York: Bloomsbury, 2009), 117.

31. Erlandson, "Archaeology of Aquatic Adaptations," 289, 293, 331.

32. Simon Winchester, *Atlantic: Great Sea Battles, Heroic Discoveries, Titanic Storms, and a Vast Ocean with a Million Stories* (New York: HarperCollins, 2010), 56–59.

33. Curtis W. Marean et al., "Early Human Use of Marine Resources and Pigment in South Africa during the Middle Pleistocene," *Nature* 449 (2007): 905–8. Curtis W. Manean, "The African Evidence for the Origins of Modern Human Behavior," Nobel Lecture, Gustavus Augustus College, 2008, https://gustavus.edu/events/nobelconference/2008/marean-lecture.php.

34. Robert Walker et al., "Early Human Occupants of the Red Sea Coast of Eritrea during the Last Interglacial," *Nature* 405 (May 4, 2000): 65–69: Marean, "African Evidence."

35. Wells, *Journey of Man*, 99: recent research discovery of stone tools dating to 127,000 years ago in the Arabian Peninsula suggests that some *Homo sapiens* may have gotten farther than the Levant before dying out. "Findings Hint at Early Exit for Humans from Africa," *New York Times*, January 28, 2011, A4.

36. Walker et al., "Early Human Occupants of the Red Sea Coast," 69: Nicolas Wade, *Before the Dawn: Recovering the Lost History of Our Ancestors* (New York: Penguin, 2009), chap. 5; Wells, *Journey of Man*, 80.

37. Wells, *Journey of Man*, 68–76; Jacobsen, *Living World*, 108; Koppel, *Lost World*, xiii–xiv; Jon M. Erlandson et al., "The Kelp Highway Hypothesis: Marine Ecology, the Coastal Migration Theory, and the Peopling of the Americas," *Journal of Island and Coastal Archaeology* 2 (2007): 161–74.

38. Jacobsen, *Living World*, 113–15.

39. Robert Van de Noort and Aidan O'Sullivan, *Rethinking Wetland Archaeology* (London: Duckworth, 2006), chaps. 2–3; Brian M. Fagan, *Ancient North America: The Archaeology of a Continent* (London: Thames and Hudson, 1991), 72–73; Erlandson et al., "Kelp Highway," 170–71.

40. Jacobsen, *Living World*, 96–97; Erlandson, "Archaeology of Aquatic Adaptations," 296–98.
41. Jacobsen, *Living World*, 96–97: Palsson, *Coastal Economics*, 52–53.
42. William J. Mitsch and James Gosselink, *Wetlands*, 3rd ed. (New York: John Wiley, 2000), 3; Karin Sanders, *Bodies in the Bog and the Archaeological Imagination* (Chicago: University of Chicago Press, 2009).
43. Bryony Coles and John Coles, *People of the Wetlands: Bogs, Bodies, and Lake Dwellers* (London: Thames and Hudson, 1989), chap. 2; Van de Noort and O'Sullivan, introduction to *Rethinking Wetland Archaeology*; V. Gaffney, S. Fitch, and D. Smith, *Europe's Lost World: The Rediscovery of Doggerland* (York, UK: Council for British Archaeology, 2009), 135–38.
44. Gaffney, Fitch, and Smith, *Europe's Lost World*, 66; Erlandson, "Archaeology of Aquatic Adaptations," 304.
45. Grahame Clark, *Starr Carr: A Case Study in Bioarchaeology* (Reading, MA: Addison Wesley, 1972).
46. Yesner, "Maritime Hunter-Gatherers," 728; Kennett, *Island Chumash*, 15.
47. Ibid.
48. Dorothy B. Vitaliano, *Legends of the Earth: Their Geologic Origins* (Bloomington: Indiana University Press, 1973), chap. 7; Nancy J. Turner, Iaian J. Davidson-Hunt, and Michael O'Flaherty, "Living on the Edge: Ecological and Cultural Edges as Sources of Diversity for Social-Ecological Resilience," *Human Ecology* 31, no. 2 (September, 2001): 454–55; Van de Noort and O'Sullivan, *Rethinking Wetland Archaeology*, 70–75; Tony Pollard, "Time and Tide: Coastal Environments, Cosmology and Ritual Practice in Early Prehistoric Scotland," in *The Early Prehistory of Scotland*, ed. Tony Pollard and Alexi Morrison (Edinburgh: Edinburgh University Press, 1996), 198–210.
49. Dieter Gerten, "How Water Transcends Religion and Epochs: Hydrolatry in Early European Religion and Christian Syncretism," in *A History of Water*, ser. 2, vol. 1, ed. Terje Tvedt and Terje Oestigaard (London: I. B. Tauris, 2010), 323–42; Van de Noort and O'Sullivan, *Rethinking Wetland Archaeology*, chap. 2; Sanders, *Bodies in the Bog*.
50. Erlandson, "Archaeology of Aquatic Adaptations," 332.
51. Turner, Davidson-Hunt, and O'Flaherty, "Living on the Edge," 454–55.
52. Erlandson, "Archaeology of Aquatic Adaptations," 323–34; Koppel, *Lost World*, 11, 213, 256; Jacobsen, *Living Shore*, 107–9; Yesner, "Maritime Hunter-Gatherers," 453–57, 727.
53. John Noble Wilford, "On Crete, New Evidence of Very Ancient Mariners," *New York Times*, February 16, 2010, D1; Christian, *Maps of Time*, 181.
54. Yesner, "Maritime Hunter-Gatherers," 730.
55. Mitsch and Gosselink, *Wetlands*, chaps. 1. 3; Van de Noort and O'Sullivan, *Rethinking Wetland Archaeology*, 36: Kennett, *Island Chumash*, chap. 2; Jacobsen, *Living Shore*, 42–47; Yesner, "Maritime Hunter-Gatherers," 734; Barry Cunliffe, *Europe between the Oceans: Themes and Variations, 9000 BC–AD 1000* (New Haven, CT: Yale University Press, 2008), 62–70.
56. Cunliffe, *Europe between the Oceans*, 71, 272–30.
57. Christian, *Maps of Time*, 185–87.
58. Jacobsen, *Living Shore*, 98, 110.
59. Cunliffe, *Europe between the Oceans*, 71; Palsson, "Hunters and Gatherers," 198–202.
60. Kennett, *Island Chumash*, 24, and chap. 5; Ellen, "Modes of Subsistence," 205–6.
61. Cunliffe, *Europe between the Oceans*, 89–139; Van de Noort and O'Sullivan, *Rethinking Wetland Archaeology*, 76, 99.

62. Anna Ritchie, "The First Settlers," in *The Prehistory of Orkney*, ed. Colin Renfrew (Edinburgh: Edinburgh University Press, 1985), 52; Pollard, "Time and Tide," 203–6.

63. V. Gordon Childe, *Skara Brae: A Pictish Village in Orkney* (London: Kegan Paul, French, Trubner, 1931), 2; D. V. Clarke and Niall Sarples, "Settlement of Subsistence in the Third Millenium BC," in *The Prehistory of Orkney*, ed. Colin Renfrew (Edinburgh: Edinburgh University Press, 1985), 81, 184.

64. David Clarke and Patrick Maguire, *Skara Brae: Northern Europe's Best Preserved Neolithic Village* (Edinburgh: Historic Scotland, 2000), 27–29.

65. Robert Tignor et al., *Worlds Together, Worlds Apart: A History of the World* (New York: W. W. Norton, 2008), 1:20; Jacobsen, *Living Shore*, 128.

Chapter 2

1. Plato, *Phaedo*, trans. David Gallop (Oxford: Clarendon, 1975), 108c.

2. Fernand Braudel, *The Mediterranean and the Mediterranean World in the Age of Philip II* (New York: Harper and Row, 1972), 1:103.

3. Rachel L. Carson, *The Sea around Us* (New York: Oxford University Press, 1951), 3.

4. Jonathan Raban, *Coasting: A Private Voyage* (New York: Penguin, 1988), 25.

5. Felipe Fernandez-Armesto, *Civilizations: Culture, Ambition, and the Transformation of Nature* (New York: Free Press, 2001), chap. 7; Peregrine Horden and Nicholas Prucess, "The Mediterranean and 'the New Thalassocracy,'" *American Historical Review* 111, no. 3 (June 2006): 722–40; see also entry for thallasocracy in Wikipedia, http://en.wikipedia.org/wiki/.

6. Fernandez-Armesto, *Civilizations*, 412.

7. Michael Pearson, *The Indian Ocean* (London: Routledge, 2003), 3.

8. Robert Walker et al., "Early Human Occupation of the Red Sea Coast of Eritrea during the Last Interglacial," *Nature* 405 (May 4, 2000): 65–69; Ian Tattersall, *The World from Beginnings to 4000 BCE* (New York: Oxford University Press, 2008), 56, 67, 91; Rainer Buschmann, *Oceans in World History* (Boston: McGraw-Hill, 2007), 12–14.

9. Pearson, *Indian Ocean*, 50–51.

10. Ibid., 47; K. N. Chauduri, *Trade and Civilization in the Indian Ocean: An Economic History from Islam to 1750* (Cambridge: Cambridge University Press, 1985), 14–15; Michael Pearson, "Emulating the Mudskipper [*Periophthalmus kroelreuteri*]: Toward an Amphibious History," paper delivered at the meetings of the American Historical Association, San Diego, January 10, 2010, ms. 11–12.

11. *Pearson, Indian Ocean*, 60.

12. Ibid., 62.

13. Nola Cooke and Lia Tana, eds., *Water Frontier: Commerce and the Chinese in the Lower Mekong Region, 1750–1880* (London: Rowman and Littlefield, 2004), 1–17.

14. Buschmann, *Oceans in World History*, 76–77.

15. Nicholas Wade, *Before the Dawn: Recovering the Lost History of Our Ancestors* (New York: Penguin, 2006), 74–75.

16. Patrick D. Nunn, *Vanished Islands and Hidden Continents of the Pacific* (Honolulu: University of Hawaii Press, 2009), v.

17. Walter Grainge White, *The Sea Gypsies of Malaya* (Philadelphia: Lippincott, 1922), 58–60; Wade, *Before the Dawn*, 74–75.

18. Astrid Lindenlauf, "The Sea as a Place of No Return in Ancient Greece," *World Archaeology* 35, no. 3 (2003): 421; Barry Cunliffe, *Europe between the Oceans: Themes and Varations, 8000 BC–AD 1000* (New Haven, CT: Yale University Press, 2008), 61.

19. David Abulafia, introduction to *The Great Sea: A Human History of the Mediterranean* (Oxford: Oxford University Press, 2011); Peregrine Horden and Nicholas Purcell, *The Corrupting Sea: A Study of Mediterranean History* (Oxford: Blackwell, 2000), 133; Lindenlauf, "Sea as a Place of No Return," 417.

20. H. C. Darby, "The Medieval Sea-State," *Scottish Geographical Magazine* 48, no. 3 (May 16, 1932): 136, 146.

21. Fernandez-Armesto, *Civilizations*, 384; Pedrag Matvejevic, *Mediterranean: A Cultural Landscape* (Berkeley: University of California Press, 1990), 7, 10–11; Jonathan Raban, *Passage to Juneau: A Sea and Its Meanings* (New York: Vintage, 1999), 95, 106.

22. Horden and Purcell, *Corrupting Sea*, 11, 133; Tim Ingold, *Lines: A Brief History* (London: Routledge, 2007), 76–9, 152; John R. Gillis, *Islands of the Mind: How the Human Imagination Created the Atlantic World* (New York: Palgrave Macmillan, 2004), 61–64.

23. Ingold, *Lines*, 76–79, 152.

24. Margaret Deacon, *Scientists and the Sea, 1650–1900: A Study in Marine Science* (London: Academic Press, 1971), 11.

25. Braudel, *The Mediterranean and the Mediterranean World*, 161.

26. Ibid., 109–15.

27. Cunliffe, *Europe between the Oceans*, 89–99; 270–76; Horden and Purcell, *Corrupting Sea*, 134.

28. Herodotus, quoted in Wolfgang Rudolf, *Harbor and Town: A Maritime Cultural History* (Erfurt, Germany: Edition Leipzig, 1980), 9; I owe this insight to Michael Pearson.

29. Quoted from Plato's *Laws*, 4, cited in Steven Mentz, "Toward a Blue Cultural Studies: The Sea, Maritime Culture, and Early Modern English Literature," *Literature Compass* 6, no. 5 (2009): 998; Lindenlauf, "Sea as a Place of No Return," 416–33; Wallace Kaufman and Orrin H. Pilkey, *The Beaches Are Moving: The Drowning of America's Shoreline* (Durham, NC: Duke University Press, 1983), 152; Rudolf, *Harbor and Town*, 23–26.

30. Robert D. Foulke, "Odysseus's Oar: Archetype of Voyaging," in *Maritime History as World History*, ed. Daniel Finamore (Gainesville: University Press of Florida, 2004), 184; Braudel, *The Mediterranean and the Mediterranean World*, 104; Alain Corbin, *The Lure of the Sea: The Discovery of the Seaside in the Western World, 1750–1840* (Berkeley: University of California Press, 1994), 12.

31. Denis Cosgrove, "Island Passages," in *Bridging Islands: The Impact of Fixed Links*. ed. G. Baldacchino (Charlottetown, PEI, Canada: Acorn, 2007), 17–19: on the notion of "inside-out" geography, see Horden and Purcell, *Corrupting Sea*, 133.

32. Braudel, *The Mediterranean and the Mediterranean World*, 115–26: on varieties of Mediterranean peninsulas, see Matvejevic, *Mediterranean*, 20–21.

33. See "archipelago," in *Oxford English Dictionary*.

34. Gillis, *Islands of the Mind*, chaps. 3, 5.

35. Ibid., 9, and chaps. 3, 5; Horden and Purcell, *Corrupting Sea*, 134; Cosgrove, "Island Passages," 20–21.

36. Braudel, *The Mediterranean and the Mediterranean World*, 160–61; Cunliffe, *Europe between the Oceans*, 3–5.

37. Horden and Purcell, *Corrupting Sea*, 11.

38. Cunliffe, *Europe between the Oceans*, chaps. 3–5.

39. Christopher Connery, "There Was No More Sea: The Suppression of the Ocean, from Bible to Cyberspace," *Journal of Geographical History* 32 (2006): 499–506; quote from Hesiod from Samuel Eliot Morison, *The European Discovery of America: The Northern Voyages, A.D. 500–1600* (New York: Oxford University Press, 1992), 4.

40. Matvejevic, *Mediterranean*, 17; Cunliffe, *Europe between the Oceans*, 258–64; Francis Pryor, *Seahenge: A Quest for Life and Death in Bronze Age Britain* (London: Harper Perennial, 2001), 140, 214; Cunliffe, *Facing the Ocean*, 10.

41. Alan Villiers, *The Western Ocean: The Story of the North Atlantic* (London: Museum Press, 1957), 13; Cunliffe, *Europe between the Oceans*, 31, 38; Michal Mollet de Jourdon, *Europe and the Sea* (Oxford: Blackwell, 1993), 4; V. Gaffney, S. Fitch, and D. Smith, *Europe's Lost World: The Rediscovery of Doggerland* (York, UK: Council for British Archaeology, 2009).

42. David Kirby and Merja-Liisa Hinkanen, *The Baltic and the North Sea* (London: Routledge, 2000), 28–30; Cunliffe, *Facing the Ocean*, 31,48; Cunliffe, *Europe between the Oceans*, 72–80.

43. Cunliffe, *Europe between the Oceans*, 138–39; Cunliffe, *Facing the Ocean*, 17, 136–38: Pryor, *Seahenge*, 68–69.

44. Cunliffe, *Facing the* Ocean, 29–31, 138.

45. Kirby and Hinkanen, *The Baltic and the North Sea*, 23.

46. Cunliffe, *Facing the Ocean*, 34–35; Jonathan M. Wooding, *Communications and Commerce along Western Sealanes* (Oxford: Tempvs Repartivm, 1996): Nils Stora, "Landscape, Territory, Autonomy, and Regional Identity: The Aland Islands in Cultural Perspective," in *Nordic Landscapes: Region and Belonging on the Northern edge of Europe*, ed. Michael Jones and Kenneth Olwig (Minneapolis: University of Minnesota Press, 2008), 446; Darby, "Medieval Sea-State," 139.

47. Darby, "Medieval Sea-State," 148–49; Lauren Burton, *A Search for Sovereignty: Law and Geography in European Empires, 1400–1900* (Cambridge: Cambridge University Press, 2010), chaps. 1, 3.

48. Cunliffe, *Europe between the Oceans* 56; Gillis, *Islands of the Mind*, 47–51.

49. Christian Buchet, *The Eternal Sea* (New York: Abrams, 2006), 9: Cunliffe, *Facing the Ocean*, 9.

50. Lindenlauf, "Sea as a Place of No Return," 421; Karin Sanders, *Bodies in the Bog and the Archaeological Imagination* (Chicago: University of Chicago Press, 2009): Robert van de Noorte, "An Ancient Seascape: The Social Context of Seafaring in the Early Bronze Age," *World Archaeology* 35, no. 3 (2003): 404–15; Gillis, *Islands of the Mind*, 40: Paul Rainbird, "Islands of Time: Toward a Critique of Island Archaeology," *Journal of Mediterranean Archaeology* 12, no. 2 (1999): 216–34: Matvejevic, *Mediterranean*, 17.

51. Matvejevic, *Mediterranean*, 17; Cunliffe, *Facing the Ocean*, 30–32; David Thomson, *The People of the Sea: A Journey in Search of the Seal Legend* (London: Barrie and Rockliffe, 1965); also "Selkie," http://en.wikipedia.org/wiki/Selkie.

52. Dorothy Dinnerstein, *The Mermaid and the Minotaur: Sexual Arrangements and Human Malaise* (New York: Harper and Row, 1976), 2; Christer Westerdahl, "Seal on Land, Elk at Sea: The Ritual Landscape at the Seaboard," *International Journal of Nautical Archaeology* 34, no. 1 (2005): 2–23.

53. Richard Ellis, *Monsters of the Sea* (New York: Alfred A. Knopf, 1995), 375; Yi-Fu Tuan, *Landscapes of Fear* (New York: Pantheon, 1979), 10; Corbin, *Lure of the Sea*, chap. 1.

54. Ellis, *Monsters of the Sea*, 77–107, 372–76; Harriet Ritvo, *The Platypus and the Mermaid and Other Figments of Classifying Imagination* (Cambridge, MA: Harvard University Press, 1997), 89, 183.

55. Colin Renfrew, *Prehistory: The Making of the Human Mind* (New York: Modern Library, 2009), 120–33; Paul Rainbird, *The Archaeology of Islands* (Cambridge: Cambridge University Press, 2007), 12–15; Curtis Marean et al., "Early Human Use of Marine Resources and Pigment in South Africa during the Middle Pleistocene," *Nature* 449 (October 18, 2007): 905–8; Cunliffe, *Facing the Ocean*, 31, 362; Gillis, *Islands of the Mind*, 28.

56. Charles Westin, "The Region and Its Landscapes," in *The Baltic Sea Region: Cultures, Politics, Societies*, ed. Eitold Maciejewski (Uppsala, Sweden: Baltic University Press, 2002), 137–34; Zbigniew Kobylinski, "Ships, Society, Symbols, and Archaeologists," in *The Ship: A Symbol of Prehisoric and Medieval Scandinavia*, ed. Ole Crumlin-Pederson and Birgitte Murch Thye (Copenhagen: National Museum, 1995), 9–18; Chris Ballard et al., "The Ship as Symbol in the Prehistory of Scandinavia and Southeast Asia," *World Archaeology* 35, no. 3 (2003): 385–403; Gunilla Larsson, *Ship and Society: Maritime Ideology in Late Iron Age Sweden* (Uppsala, Sweden: Department of Archaeology and Ancient History, 2007), 382.

57. Larsson, *Ship and Society*, 254–57, 296–98.

58. Dan Carlsson, "Harbors and Farms on Gotland," in *Europeans or Not: Local Level Srategies on the Baltic Rim*, ed. Nils Blankrist and Sven-Olaf Lindquist (Visby, Sweden: Centre for Baltic Studies, 1998), 115–21; in *Vikings: The North Atlantic Saga*, ed. William Fitzhugh and Elizabeth Ward (Washington, DC: Smithsonian, 2000), chap. 2.

59. Kirsten Hastrup, "Icelandic Topography and Sense of Identity," in *Nordic Landscapes: Region and Belonging on the Northern Edge of Europe*, ed. Michael Jones and Kenneth Olwig (Minneapolis: Minnesota University Press, 2008), 55; Simon Winchester, *Atlantic: Great Sea Battles, Heroic Discoveries, Titanic Storms, and a Vast Ocean of a Million Stories* (New York: HarperCollins, 2010), 79.

60. Quoted in Magnus Magnusson and Hermann Pälsson, introduction to *The Vinland Sagas: The Norse Discovery of America* (London: Penguin, 1965), 15.

61. Hastrup, "Icelandic Topography and Sense of Identity," 59.

62. Ibid.; on this process, see James Hamilton-Paterson, *The Great Deep: The Sea and Its Thresholds* (New York: Random House, 1992), 67.

Chapter 3

1. T.S. Eliot, "The Dry Salvages," *The Four Quartets* (New York: Harcourt, Brace and Jovanovich, 1943), 36.

2. The concept of "rimland" is Felipe Fernandez-Armesto's. See his *Civilizations: Culture, Ambition, and the Transformation of Nature* (New York: Free Press, 2001), 309–15.

3. Robert J. Hoeksema, *Designed for Dry Feet: Flood Protection and Land Restoration in the Netherlands* (Reston, VA: American Society of Civil Engineers, 2006), chap. 1; Basil B. Cracknell, *Outrageous Waves: Global Warming and Coastal Change in Britain through Two Thousand Years* (Chichester, UK: Phillimore, 2005), preface; David Kirby and Meja-Liisa Hinkkanen, *The Baltic and the North Sea* (New York: Routledge, 2000), 24; Hubert Lamb, *Historic Storms of the North Sea, British Isles, and Northwest Europe* (Cambridge: Cambridge University Press, 1991), 17.

4. V. Gordon Childe, *Ancient dwellings at Skara Brae* (Edinburgh: Her Majesty's Stationery Office, 1950), 6–7; Lamb, *Historic Storms*, 19–20; Kirby and Hinkanen, *The Baltic and the North Sea*, 25.

5. Hans Meyer, *City and Port: Urban Planning as a Cultural Venture in London, Barcelona, New York, and Rotterdam* (Rotterdam: International Books, 1999).

6. Kirby and Hinkanen, *The Baltic and the North Sea*, 24: Hoeksema, *Designed for Dry Feet*, 10–11.

7. From a description of 1610, quoted in H. C. Darby, *The Draining of the Fens* (Cambridge: Cambridge University Press, 1956), 23, 55, 46; also see Robert Van de Noort and Aidan O'Sullivan, *Rethinking Wetland Archaeology* (London: Duckworth, 2006), 77–78.

8. Darby, *Draining of the Fens*, 56, 90.

9. Van de Noort and O'Sullivan, *Rethinking Wetland Archaeology*, 78; Young in 1799, quoted in Darby, *Draining of the Fens*, 154; Patrick Sutherland and Adam Nicolson, *Wetland: Life in the Somerset Levels* (London: Michael Joseph, 1986), 7–8. In the Fenlands, the Isle of Ely offers another example of the same thing.

10. Sutherland and Nicolson, *Wetland*, 23; Wolfgang Rudolph, *Harbor and Town: A Maritime Culural History* (Erfurt, Germany: Edition Leipzig, 1980), 12–14.

11. Barry Cunliffe, *Facing the Ocean: The Atlantic and Its Peoples, 8000 BC–AD 1500* (New York: Oxford University Press, 2001), 553.

12. John Dyson, *Business in Great Waters: The Story of British Fishermen* (London: Angus and Robertson, 1978), 35–41; Bonnie McCay, "The Culture of Commoners: Historical Observation on Old and New World Fisheries," in *The Question of the Commons: The Culture and Ecology of Communal Resources*, ed. B. McCay and James Acheson (Tucson: University of Arizona Press, 1987), 196–201.

13. Cunliffe, *Facing the Ocean*, 543; John R. Gillis, *Islands of the Mind: How the Human Imagination Created the Atlantic World* (New York: Palgrave Macmillan, 2004), 27–28: Kirby and Hinkanen, *The Baltic and the North Sea*, 59.

14. Orvar Loefgren, "From Peasant Fishing to Industrial Trawling: A Comparative Discussion of Modernization Processes in some Northern Atlantic Regions," in *Modernization and Marine Fisheries Policy*, ed. John Maolo and Michael Orband (Ann Arbor, MI: Ann Arbor Science, 1982), 154; Liv Schei and Gunnie Moberg, *The Orkney Story* (London: n.p., 1985), 147; Harold Fox, *The Evolution of the Fishing Village* (Oxford: Leopard's Head Press, 2001), chaps. 2–3.

15. Fox, *Evolution of the Fishing Village*, 35.

16. Ibid.; Loefgren, "From Peasant Fishing to Industrial Trawling," 155–76; M. A. Herubel, *Peches maritimes* (Paris, 1911), quoted in Harold A. Innis, *The Cod Fisheries: The History of an International Economy*, rev. ed. (Toronto: University of Toronto Press, 1978), 494.

17. Steve Higgonson and Tony Wailey, *Edgy Cities* (Liverpool: Northern Lights, 2006), 68; Paul Thompson, Tony Wailey, and Trevor Lummis, *Living the Fishing* (London: Routledge and Kegan Paul, 1983), 12–13.

18. Gisli Palsson, *Coastal Economies, Cultural Accounts: Human Ecology and Icelandic Discourse* (Manchester: Manchester University Press, 1991), 29–31; Kirby and Hinkanen, *The Baltic and the North Sea*, 186–87; John R. Gillis, *Youth and History: Tradition and Change in European Age Relations, 1770–Present* (New York: Academic Press, 1974), chap. 1.

19. Thompson, Wailey, and Lummis, *Living the Fishing*, 4–14; W. Jeffrey Bolster, "Putting the Ocean in Atlantic History: Maritime Communities and Marine Ecology in the Northwest Atlantic, 1500–1800," *American Historical Review* 113, no. 1 (February 2008): 46.

20. Richard C. Hoffmann, "Economic Development and Aquatic Ecosystems in Medieval Europe," *American Historical Review* 101, no. 3 (June 1996): 633; on evidence of recreational fishing, see Richard Hoffmann, *Fisher's Craft and Lettered Art: Tracts on Fishing from the End of the Middle Ages* (Toronto: University of Toronto Press, 1997); quote from Callum Roberts, *The Unnatural History of the Sea* (Washington, DC: Island, 2007), 159.

21. Roberts, *Unnatural History of the Sea*, 636–42.

22. Mark Kurlansky, *Cod: A Biography of the Fish That Changed the World* (New York: Walker, 1997), 24.

23. Bolster, "Putting the Ocean in Atlantic History," 26–29.

24. Roberts, *Unnatural History of the Sea*, chap. 2; quotation from ibid., 33.

25. Bolster, "Putting the Ocean in Atlantic History," 26.

26. Innis, *Cod Fisheries*, chaps. 3–6; Gerald M. Sider, *Culture and Class in Anthropology and History: A New Foundland Illustration* (Cambridge: Cambridge University Press, 1986), 14–15.

27. Lewes Roberts, *Merchants Mappe of Commerce* (London, 1638), quoted in Peter Pope, *Fish into Wine: The Newfoundland Plantation in the Seventeenth Century* (Chapel Hill: University of North Carolina Press, 2004), 234.

28. Elizabeth Mancke, "Spaces of Power in the Early Modern Northeast," in *New England and the Maritime Provinces*, ed. Stephen J. Hornsby and John G. Reid (Montreal: McGill-Queens University Press, 2005), 32–33; D. H. Meinig, *The Shaping of America* (New Haven, CT: Yale University Press, 1986), 1:81.

29. *An Account of the Island of Prince Edward by a Late Resident of that Colony* (London: James Aspeare, 1819), 14; Rosemary E. Ommer, *From Outpost to Outport: A Structural Analysis of the Jersey-Gaspe Cod Fishery, 1767–1886* (Montreal: McGill-Queen's University Press, 1991), chap. 2.

30. Roberts, *Merchants Mappe of Commerce*, 83–87; Bolster, "Putting the Ocean in Atlantic History," 32–35.

31. Roberts, *Merchants Mappe of Commerce*, 99–113, 159.

32. Elizabeth Mancke, "Early Modern Expansion and the Politicization of Oceanic Space," *Geographical Review* 89 (April 1998): 225–34.

33. Lauren Benton, *A Search for Sovereignty: Law and Geography in European Empires, 1400–1900* (Cambridge: Cambridge University Press, 2010), chaps. 1–4; quote from James E. Vance, *Capturing the Horizon: The Historical Geography of Transportation* (New York: Harper and Row, 1986), 102.

34. G. Malcolm Lewis, "Native North Americans' Cosmological and Geographical Awareness: Their Representations and Influence on Early European Exploration and Geographical Knowledge," in *North American Explorations*, ed. John L. Allen (Lincoln: University of Nebraska Press, 1997), 1:81–82; Harold Prins, "Children of Gluskap: Wabanaki Indians on the Eve of European Invasion," in *American Beginnings: Exploration, Culture, and Cartography in the Land of Norumbega*, ed. Emerson W. Baker et al. (Lincoln: University of Nebraska Press, 1994), 75.

35. John Stilgoe, "Archipelago Landscape," in *Visions of America: Landscape as Metaphor in the Late Twentieth Century* (New York: Harry M. Abrams, 1994), 74; Wilcomb E. Washburn, "The Intellectual Assumptions and Consequences of the Geographical Exploration of the Pacific," in *The Pacific Basin*, ed. H. Frits (New York: American Geographical Society, 1967), 327–28.

36. Meinig, *Shaping of America*, 1:58; Benton, *Search for Sovereignty*, 46–50.

37. Washburn, "Intellectual Assumptions and Consequences"; Douglas H. McManis, *European Impressions of the New England Coast, 1497–1620*, Research Paper 139 (Chicago: University of Chicago Department of Geography, 1972), 37–38; James Gibson, "The Exploration of the Pacific Coast," in *North American Exploration*, ed. John L. Allen (Lincoln: University of

Nebraska Press, 1997), 2:328–96; James D. Drake, *The Nation's Nature: How Continental Pre-sumptions Gave Rise to the United States of America* (Charlottesville: University of Virginia Press, 2011).

38. Stephen J. Pyne, *How the Canyon Became Grand: A Short History* (New York: Viking, 1998), 5; Pedrag Matvejevic, *Mediterranean: A Cultural Landscape* (Berkeley: University of California Press, 1990), 16; John F. Roberts, *The Unending Frontier: An Environmental History of the Early Modern World* (Berkeley: University of California Press, 2005), 7.

39. Gillis, *Islands of the Mind*, 87–92; Donna Merwick, *The Shame and the Sorrow: Dutch-American Encounters in New Netherlands* (Philadelphia: University of Pennsylvania Press, 2006), 53, 28, 53, 88–89, 93.

40. Dan G. Kelley, *Edge of a Continent: The Pacific Coast from Alaska to Baja* (Palo Alto, CA: American West, 1971), 272.

41. Meinig, *Shaping of America*, 62, 65, 88.

42. Ibid., 65.

43. The notion of maritime transhumance is Rosemary Ommer's. Rosmary E. Ommer, "Rosie's Cove: Settlement Morphology, History, Economy, and Culture in a Newfoundland Out-port," in *Fishing Places, Fishing People: Tradition and Issues in Canadian Small-Scale Fisher-ies*, ed. Dianne Newall and R. Ommer (Toronto: University of Toronto Press, 1994), 23; Pope, *Fish into Wine*, 251; Mancke, "Spaces of Power," 35.

44. Innis, *Cod Fisheries*, chaps. 1–4; Sider, *Culture and Class in Anthropology and History*, chap. 2; Joseba Zulaika, *Terranova: The Ethos and Luck of Deep-Sea Fishermen* (Philadelphia: Insti-tute for the Study of Human Issues, 1981), 34.

45. Bolster, "Putting the Ocean in Atlantic History," 32–33; Mancke, "Spaces of Power," 36–37.

46. William Cronon, *Changes in the Land: Indians, Colonists, and the Ecology of New England* (New York: Hill and Wang, 1983), 37, 39, 51, 53.

47. Ibid., 37; Charles C. Mann, *1491: New Revelations of the Americas before Columbus* (New York: Alfred A. Knopf, 2005), chap. 2.

48. Robert Swan, *Coast, the Sea, Canadian Art* (Stratford, ON: Gallery, 1978); John Stilgoe, *Alongshore* (New Haven, CT: Yale University Press, 1994), ix; Benjamin Labaree et al., *America and the Sea: A Maritime History* (Mystic, CT: Mystic Seaport Museum, 1998), 4.

49. Walter Prescott Webb, *The Great Frontier* (Austin: University of Texas Press, 1975), 2, 7–21; for a comprehensive survey of extractive frontiers, see John F. Richards, *The Unending Frontier: An Environmental History of the Early Modern World* (Berkeley: University of Cali-fornia Press, 2005).

50. Cronon, *Changes in the Land*, chaps. 1, 3.

51. John Smith, *A Description of New-England, by Captain John Smith*, in *The Complete Works of Captain John Smith, 1550–1631*, ed. Philip L. Barbour (Chapel Hill: University of North Carolina Press, 1986), 1:331, 333, 335, 347; Roberts, *Unending Frontier*, 33; Cronon, *Changes in the Land*, 22; Jonathan Raban, *Passage to Juneau: A Sea and Its Meanings* (New York: Vintage, 1999), 62–63.

52. Roberts, *Unending Frontier*, 33; Cronon, *Changes in the Land*, 22; Raban, *Passage to Juneau*, 62–36.

53. On the many ways that the American environment had been altered long before the arrival of Europeans, see Mann, *1491*. When diseases introduced by Europeans killed 95 percent of the Amerindian population and led to massive reforestation, a cooling period during that is known as the Little Ice Age, 1540–1760, set in. Lecture by Richard Nevle, Geography

Department, University of California at Berkeley, February 16, 2011; Rowan Jacobsen, *The Living Shore: Rediscovering a Lost World* (New York: Bloomsbury, 2009), 3–12.

54. M. J. Bowden, "The Invention of American Tradition," *Journal of Historical Geography* 18, no. 1 (1992): 3–12; Bolster, "Putting the Ocean in Atlantic History," 36; W. Jeffrey Bolster, "Opportunities in Marine Environmental History," *Environmental History* 11 (July 2006): 567–97; Geoff Bailey et al., "Historical Ecology of the North Sea Basin," in *Human Impacts on Ancient Marine Ecosystems*, ed. Torben Rich and Jon Erlandson (Berkeley: University of California Press, 2008), 215–42; J. B. C. Jackson, "What Was Natural in the Coastal Oceans," *Proceedings of the National Academy of Sciences* 98 (2001): 5411–18; J. B. C. Jackson et al., "Historical Overfishing and Recent Collapse in Coastal Ecosystems," *Science* 243 (2001): 629–39; Michael Pauly and Jay MacLean, *In a Pefect Ocean: The State of Fisheries and Ecosystems in the North Atlantic Ocean* (Washington, DC: Island, 2003), 15–16.

55. Joseph E. Taylor, *Making Salmon: An Environmental History of the Northwest Fisheries Crisis* (Seattle: University of Washington Press, 1999), chap. 1. On Icelanders' view that fish determined the fate of humans, see Gisli Palsson, *Coastal Economies, Cultural Accounts: Human Ecology and Icelandic Discourse* (Manchester: Manchester University Press, 1991), 129, 162.

56. Arthur F. McEvoy, *The Fisherman's Problem: Ecology and Law in the California Fisheries, 1850–1980* (Cambridge: Cambridge University Press, 1986), chap. 2.

57. Ommer, "Rosie's Cove," 116; Hugo Grotius, *Mare Librum* (1608), quoted in Philip Steinberg, *The Social Construction of the Ocean* (Cambridge: Cambridge University Press, 2001), 92; Mancke, "Spaces of Power," 32–49.

58. Cronon, *Changes in the Land*, 38, 53; on Maine Indians, see Philip P. Conkling, *Islands in Time: A Natural and Cultural History of the Islands of the Gulf of Maine*, 2nd ed. (Camden, ME: Down East Books, 1999), chap. 1; Bunny McBride and Harold E. L. Prins, *Indians in Eden: Wabanakis and Rusticators on Maine's Mount Desert Islands, 1840s–1920s* (Rockland, ME: Down East Books, 2009), 1–5.

59. Gerald C. Pocious, *A Place to Belong: Community, Order, and Everyday Space in Newfoundland* (Athens: University of Georgia Press, 1991), 200; Robert Mellin, *House Launching, Slide Hauling, Potato Trenching, and other Tales from a Newfoundland Fishing Village* (New York: Princeton Architectural, 2003); Robert Finch, *The Primal Place* (Woodstock, VT: Countryman, 1983), 100.

60. Samuel Eliot Morison, *The Maritime History of Massachusetts, 1783–1860* (Boston: Houghton Mifflin, 1921), 11; Daniel Vickers with Vince Walsh, *Young Men and the Sea: Yankee Seafarers in the Days of Sail* (New Haven, CT: Yale University Press, 2005), 11; Joseph Reynolds, *Peter Gott, the Cape Ann Fisherman* (Boston: Jewett, 1956), 128; W. H. Bunting, *Portrait of a Port: Boston, 1852–1914* (Cambridge, MA: Harvard University Press, 1971), 2–4.

61. David Vickers, *Farmers and Fishermen: Two Centuries of Work in Essex County, Massachusetts, 1630–1850* (Chapel Hill: University of North Carolina Press, 1994), 52–103; Reynolds, *Peter Gott*, 81; Bunting, *Portrait of a Port*, 6–7; Vickers and Walsh, *Young Men and the Sea*, 1–4.

62. Vickers, *Farmers and Fishermen*, 108–41, 252.

63. Alexis de Tocqueville, *Democracy in America* (New York: Alfred A. Knopf, 1945), 1:429.

64. Susan Parman, *Scottish Crofters: A Historical Ethnography of a Celtic Village* (Fort Worth, TX: Holt, Reinhart and Winston, 1990), 73; Pocious, *Place to Belong*, 79; Mellin, *House Launching*, 110; Robert Finch, *The Iambics of Newfoundland: Notes from an Unknown Shore* (Berkeley, CA: Counterpoint, 2007), 59.

65. Finch, *Iambics of Newfoundland*, 258; Eliot, "Dry Salvages," 36.

66. Matvejevic, *Mediterranean*, 16; George Putz, *The Maine Coast* (Secaucus, NJ: Chartwell Books, 1985), 25.

Chapter 4

1. Beryl Markham, *West with the Night* (San Francisco: North Point, 1983), 245.
2. See Paul Carter, introduction to *The Road to Botany Bay: An Exploration of Landscape and History* (New York: Alfred A. Knopf, 1981); for Bostonians in 1800, "the Coast" was the west coast, where they focused their trading operations. Samuel Eliot Morison, *The Maritime History of Massachusetts, 1783–1860* (Boston: Houghton Mifflin, 1961), 53; Paul Carter, "Dark with Excess of Light," in *Mappings*, ed. Denis Cosgrove (London: Reaktion Books, 1999), 125–47.
3. The 1863 account of Nova Scotia coasts is quoted in Ian McKay, "Among the Fisherfolk: J. F. B. Livesay and the Invention of Peggy's Cove," *Journal of Canadian Studies / Revue d'etudes canadiens* 27, nos. 1–2 (Spring 1988), 29–31; Alain Corbin, *The Lure of the Sea: The Discovery of the Seaside in the Western World, 1750–1840* (Berkeley: University of California Press, 1994), chap. 1; John R. Gillis, *Islands of the Mind: How the Human Imagination Created the Atlantic World* (New York: Palgrave Macmillan, 2004), 10–12; Shauna McCabe, *Littoral Documents* (Charlottestown, PEI: Confederation Centre Art Gallery, n.d.), 12.
4. Harold F. Wilson, *The Jersey Shore: A Social and Economic History of the Counties of Atlantic, Cape May, Monmouth and Ocean* (New York: Lewis Historical Publishing, 1953), chaps. 2–3.
5. Karl F. Nordstrom et al., *Living on the New Jersey Shore* (Durham, NC: Duke University Press, 1986), 4; Christopher Camuto, *Time and Tide in Acadia: Seasons on Mount Desert Island* (New York: W. W. Norton, 2009), 1; Henry David Thoreau, *The Maine Woods* (Princeton, NJ: Princeton University Press, 1972), 82; Donald W. Meinig, *The Shaping of America: Atlantic America, 1492–1800* (New Haven, CT: Yale University Press, 1986), 57–65; James E. Vance, *Capturing the Horizon: The Historical Geography of Transportation* (New York: Harper and Row, 1986), 110; James Drake, *The Nation's Nature: How Continental Presumptions Gave Rise to the United States of America* (Charlottesville: University of Virginia Press, 2011).
6. Vance, *Capturing the Horizon*, 102; David Hackett Fischer, *Champlain's Dream* (New York: Simon and Schuster, 2008), 105–226; Meinig, *Shaping of America*, 62.
7. Martin W. Lewis and Karen E. Wigen, *The Myth of Continents: A Critique of Metageography* (Berkeley: University of California Press, 1997), 24–28. On the notion of hinterland, see http://en.wikipedia.org/wiki/Hinterland.
8. Camuto, *Time and Tide in Acadia*, 108; Carter, "Dark with Excess of Light," 125–47; Mark Monmonier, *Coastlines: How Mapmakers Frame the World and Chart Environmental Change* (Chicago: University of Chicago Press, 2008), chap. 11.
9. Paul Shepard, *Man in the Landscape: A Historic View of the Esthetics of Nature* (New York: Alfred A. Knopf, 1967), 43; James Hamilton-Paterson, *Seven Tenths: The Sea and Its Thresholds* (New York: Europa Editions, 2009), 23, 59–60; Martin Lewis, "Dividing the Ocean Sea," *Geographical Review* 89 (1999): 199–200.
10. Horace P. Beck, *The Folklore of Maine* (Philadelphia: Lippincott, 1957), chap. 1.
11. Roger Stein, *Seascape and the American Imagination* (New York: Clarkson N. Potter, 1975), 4–8, 16; John Wilmerding, *A History of American Marine Painting* (Boston: Little, Brown, 1968), chaps. 1–8; David Tatham, "Winslow Homer and the Sea," in *Winslow Homer in the*

1890s: Prout's Neck Observed (New York: Hudson Hills, 1990), 81; John R. Gillis, "Artists on the Edge," paper delivered at "Art, Islands, and Islomania," Small Islands Cultures Research Initiative Conference, Guernsey, June 2010.

12. Carter, "Dark with Excess of Light," 147.

13. Nathaniel Philbrick, *Mayflower: A Story of Courage, Community, and War* (New York: Penguin, 2006), chap. 5.

14. Alice Garner, *A Shifting Shore: Locals, Outsiders, and the Transformation of a French Fishing Town, 1823–2000* (Ithaca, NY: Cornell University Press, 2005), 48–49; Carter, "Dark with Excess of Light," 125–47; Monmonier, *Coastlines*, chap. 11; McCabe, *Littoral Documents*, 18; Jean-Didier Urbain, *At the Beach* (Minneapolis: University of Minnesota Press, 2003), 65.

15. Tim Ingold, *Lines: A Brief History* (London: Routledge, 2007), 152; William H. Bunting, *Portrait of a Port: Boston, 1852–1914* (Cambridge, MA: Harvard University Press, 1971), xvii.

16. Martin Jay, "Scopic Regimes of Modernity," in *Vision and Visuality*, ed. Hal Foster (Seattle: Bay, 1988), 3–28.

17. Allan Sekula, *Fish Story* (Dusseldorf, Germany: Richter Verlag, 1995), 53–54; Paul Theroux, "The True Size of Cape Cod," in *Fresh Air Fiend* (Boston: Houghton Mifflin, 2000), 148.

18. John R. Stilgoe, *Shallow Water Dictionary: A Grounding in Estuary English* (New York: Princeton Architectural, 2004), 54, 56.

19. John Brickerhoff Jackson, *Discovering the Vernacular Landscape* (New Haven, CT: Yale University Press, 1984), 14; Michael Pearson, "Littoral Society: The Concept and the Problem," *Journal of World History* 17, no. 4 (December 2006): 356; David Kirby and Merja-Liisa Hinkamen, *The Baltic and the North Sea* (London: Routledge, 2000), 59.

20. Raymond Lewis, *Sea Coast Fortifications of the United States* (Washington, DC: Smithsonian Press, 1970); Christopher Somerville, *Coast: A Celebration of Britain's Coastal Heritage* (London: BBC Books, 2005), 10; http//en.wikipedia.org/wiki/Martello_tower.

21. Margaret Cohen, "Modernity and the Waterfront: The Case of Hausmann's Paris," in *Urban Imaginations: Locating the Modern City*, ed. Alexis Cinvar and Thomas Bender (Minneapolis: University of Minnesota Press, 2007), 68–69; Dirk Schubert, "Transformation Processes in Waterfronts in Seaport Cities—Causes and Trends between Divergence and Convergence," in *Port Cities as Areas of Transition: Ethnographic Perspectives*, ed. Waltraud Kokot et al. (New Brunswick, NJ: Transaction Books, 2008), 25–46.

22. Kirby and Hinkamen, *The Baltic and the North Sea*, 76–81; see map of dog hole ports at Whaling Station Museum, Point Lobos State Reserve, Carmel, CA.

23. Kirby and Hinkamen, *The Baltic and the North Sea*, 82, 151; Fischer, *Champlain's Dream*, 112.

24. Warren Goeschenstein, *Historic American Towns along the Atlantic Coast* (Baltimore: Johns Hopkins University Press, 1999), 11–12; remark by R. G. F. Candage, master mariner, 1881, quoted in Bunting, *Portrait of a Port*, 56.

25. John Robert McNeill, *Atlantic Empires of France and Spain: Louisbourg and Havana, 1700–1763* (Chapel Hill: University of North Carolina Press, 1983), 17.

26. Donna Merwick, *The Shame and the Sorrow: Dutch-Amerindian Encounters in New Netherlands* (Philadelphia: University of Pennsylvania Press, 2006), chaps. 1–3; Bunting, *Portrait of a Port*, 2.

27. Schubert, "Transformation Processes in Waterfronts," 29; Hans Meyer, *City and Port* (Rotterdam: International Books, 1999), 21; Vance, *Capturing the Horizon*, 102.

28. Michael Reidy, *Tides of History: Ocean Science and Her Majesty's Navy* (Chicago: University of Chicago Press, 2008), 60–74. In Japanese, *tsu* means harbor, *nami* means wave. See "tsunami," in *Wikipedia*. The term began to be used in English in the early twentieth cen-

tury, ultimately becoming a subject of scientific study. See "tsunami" in *English Oxford Dictionary*.

29. Quoted in Gillis, *Islands of the Mind*, 125.

30. Daniel Vickers with Vince Walsh, *Young Men and the Sea: Yankee Seafarers in the Age of Sail* (New Haven, CT: Yale University Press, 2005), 2–4, 28, 248–51.

31. Bunting, *Portrait of a Port*, 5; Schubert, "Transformation Processes in Waterfronts," 29; Cohen, "Modernity and the Waterfront," 63, 67.

32. Phillip Lopate, *Waterfront: A Walk around Manhattan* (New York: Random House, 2004), 15, 61; Meyer, *City and Port*, 33; Vickers and Walsh, *Young Men and the Sea*, 210; Schubert, "Transformation Processes in Waterfronts," 29, 43; Bunting, *Portrait of a Port*, 46, 451; Wolfgang Rudolf, *Harbor and Town: A Maritime Cultural History* (Erfurt, Germany: Edition Leipzig, 1980), chap. 2; Isaac Land, *War, Nationalism, and the British Sailor, 1750–1850* (New York: Palgrave Macmillan, 2009), chaps. 1–4.

33. Mark Kurlansky, *The Big Oyster: History on the Half Shell* (New York: Ballantine Books, 2006), xvii.

34. Cohen, "Modernity and the Waterfront," 65; Herman Melville, *Moby-Dick* (New York: Barnes and Noble Books, 1993), 2.

35. Melville, *Moby-Dick*, 3, 4; T. S. Eliot, "The Dry Salvages," in *The Four Quartets* (New York: Harcourt Brace Jovanovich, 1943), 36.

36. June Nadal-Klein, *Fishing the Heritage: Modernity and Loss along the Scottish Coast* (Oxford: Berg, 2003), 8; Vickers and Walsh, *Young Men and the Sea*, 28.

37. Paul Thompson, Tony Waily, and Trevor Lummis, *Living the Fishing* (London: Routledge and Kegan Paul, 1983), 9–13; Orvar Loefgren, "From Peasant Fishing to Industrial Trawling: A Comparative Discussion of Modernization Processes in Some North Atlantic Regions," in *Modernization and Marine Fisheries Policies*, ed. John Maiolo and Michael Orbach (Ann Arbor, MI: Ann Arbor Science, 1982), 151–55.

38. Lena Lencek and Gideon Bosker, *The Beach: The History of Paradise on Earth* (New York: Penguin, 1999), 82.

39. Harold Fox, *The Evolution of the Fishing Village* (Oxford: Leopold's Head, 2001), chap. 4; James Coull, "The Development of Fishing Communities with Special Reference to Scotland," in *Managing Britain's Marine and Coastal Environments: Towards a Sustainable Future*, ed. Horace D. Smith and Jonathan S. Potts (London: Routledge, 2005); Samuel Eliot Morison, *The Maritime History of Massachusetts, 1783–1860* (Boston: Houghton-Mifflin, 1931), 11–12.

40. Morrison, *Maritime History*; Jean-Didier Urbain, *At the Beach* (Minneapolis: University of Minnesota Press, 2003), 49–51.

41. Thompson, Waily, and Lummis, *Living the Fishing*, 8–15; Daniel Vickers, *Farmers and Fishermen* (Chapel Hill: University of North Carolina Press, 1994), 130–32; Vickers and Walsh, *Young Men and the Sea*, 250; Thompson, Waily, and Lummis, 8–9; Sarah Orne Jewett, *The Country of the Pointed Firs and Other Fiction* (New York: Oxford University Press, 1996), 20–21; Rudolf, *Harbor and Town*, 113–40.

42. Corbin, *Lure of the Sea*, 211–27.

43. Land, *War, Nationalism, and the British Sailor*, 161–64.

44. Ibid., 158; John R. Stilgoe, *Alongshore* (New Haven, CT: Yale University Press, 1994), 310–18.

45. The literature on imagined landscapes is summarized by John Urry, *Sociology beyond Societies: Mobilities for the Twenty-First Century* (London: Routledge, 2000), 137–38; Stilgoe, *Alongshore*, 319–33; Ian McKay, *The Quest for the Folk: Antimodernism and Cultural*

Selection in Twentieth Century Nova Scotia (Montreal: McGill and Queen's University Press, 1994), chap. 4; Dona Brown, *Inventing New England: Regional Tourism and the Nineteenth Century* (Washington, DC: Smithsonian Press, 1995), 120–21; James Overton, *Making a World of Difference: Essays on Tourism, Culture, and Development in Newfoundland* (St. Johns, NL: Institute for Social and Economic Research, 1996), 111–15.

46. Earle Shettleworth and W. H. Bunting, *An Eye on the Coast: The Maritime and Monhegan Island Photographs by Eric Hudson* (Gardiner, ME: Tilbury House, 1998), 94; *Robert Swan, Coasts, the Sea, Canadian Art* (Stratford, ON: Gallery, 1978), unpaginated; Garner, *Shifting Shore*, 94; Brown, *Inventing New England*, 120–33.

47. Garner, *Shifting Shore*, 94, chap. 10; on the appropriation of Native American identities by whites in nineteenth-century America, see Philip DeLoria, *Playing Indian* (New Haven, CT: Yale University Press, 1998).

48. McKay, *Quest for the Folk*, 28; Douglas Pope, *DeGarthe: His Life, Marine Art, and Scupture* (Hartsport, NS: Lancelot, 1989).

49. McKay, *Quest for the Folk*, 39–41.

50. Nadal-Klein, *Fishing the Heritage*, 171; Jan Goss, "Disquiet on the Waterfront: Reflection on Nostalgia and Utopia in Urban Archetypes of Festival Marketplaces," *Urban Geography* 17 (1966): 238.

51. McKay, "Among the Fisherfolk," 29; Urbain, *At the Beach*, 37; George H. Lewis, "The Maine That Never Was: The Construction of Popular Myth in Regional Culture," *Journal of American Culture* 16, no. 2 (Summer 1997): 95; McKay, *Quest for the Folk*, 250.

52. Rachel Carson, *The Sea around Us* (New York: Oxford University Press, 1951), 19; Reidy, *Tides of History*, 75–89.

53. Lord Curzon of Kedleston, *Frontiers: The Romanes Lecture of 1907* (Oxford: Clarendon, 1907), 13.

54. Alexis de Tocqueville, *Democracy in America* (New York: Alfred A. Knopf, 1945), 421–34; Denis Cosgrove, "Worlds of Meaning: Cultural Geography and the Imagination," in *Rereading Cultural Geography*, ed. Kenneth Foote et al. (Austin: University of Texas Press, 1994), 390–91; also Eric Leed, *The Mind of the Traveler: From Gilgamesh to Global Tourism* (New York: Basic Books, 1991), 19; Drake, *Nation's Nature*; John Seelye, *Memory's Nation: The Place of Plymouth Rock* (Chapel Hill: University of North Carolina Press, 1998).

55. John Whitehead, "Hawai'i: The First and Last Far West," *Western Historical Quarterly* 23, no. 2 (May 1992): 153–77; Jonathan Raban, *Coasting: A Private Voyage* (London: Penguin Books, 1987), 300–301.

56. Adrian Room, *Dictionary of Places Names in the British Isles* (London: Bloomsbury, 1988), 206, 216–17. I wish to thank Gray Brechin for allowing me to read his unpublished essay "Sacred Force: Ishi Meets the End of the Trail.."

57. Gillis, *Islands of the Mind*, 13–14, 56; W. H. Hudson, *The Land's End: A Naturalist's Impression of West Cornwall* (London: J. M. Dent and Son, 1923), 52.

58. *Voyage Round Great Britain, undertaken in the summer of the Year 1813 and commending from Land's-End, Cornwall by Richard Ayton and views by William Daniell* (London: Longman, Hurst, Rees, Orme and Brown, 1814), iv–2.

59. Hudson, *Land's End*, iii, 52; Fred Gray, *Designing the Seaside: Architecture, Society and Nature* (London: Reaktion Books, 2006), chap. 1.

60. Hudson, *Land's End*, 45.

61. Ibid., 299.

62. Ibid., 302; David Lowenthal, "Living with and Looking at Landscape," *Landscape Research* 32, no. 5 (October 2007): 643; Loren Baritz, "The Idea of the West," *American Historical Review* 66, no. 2 (April 1961): 637–40; Nathaniel Philbrick, foreword to *American Sea Writing: A Literary Anthology*, ed. Peter Neill (New York: Library of America, 2000), xv.

63. Quoted in John McKinney, *A Walk along Land's End: Discovering California's Unknown Coast* (New York: HarperCollins, 1995), vi; see http://en.wikipedia.org/wiki/Navies_of _landlocked_countries.

64. Paul Theroux, *The Kingdom by the Sea: A Journey around Great Britain* (Boston: Houghton-Mifflin, 1985), 5.

65. John Cheever, *The Wapshot Chronicle* (New York: Harper and Brothers, 1954), 188–89; McKinney, *Walk along Land's End*, 172; on beach glass, see Cornelia Dean, *Against the Tide: The Battle for America's Beaches* (New York: Columbia University Press, 1999), 238–39.

Chapter 5

1. Jonathan Raban, *Oxford Book of the Sea* (Oxford: Oxford University Press, 1992), 3.

2. Helen M. Rozwadowski, *Fathoming the Ocean: The Discovery and Exploration of the Deep Sea* (Cambridge, MA: Harvard University Press, 2005), 4; James Hamilton-Paterson, *Seven Tenths: The Sea and Its Thresholds* (New York: Europa Editions, 2009), 210.

3. W. H. Auden, *The Enchafed Flood, or The Romantic Iconography of the Sea* (London: Faber and Faber, 1951), 19.

4. Donald Wharton, "The Colonial Period," in *America and the Sea: A Literary History*, ed. Haskell Springer (Athens: University of Georgia Press, 1995), 32–38; Nathaniel Philbrick, *The Mayflower: A Story of Community, Courage, and War* (New York: Viking, 2006).

5. Steve Mentz, *At the Bottom of Shakespeare's Sea* (London: Continuum, 2009); Raban, *Oxford Book of the Sea*, 4–7; Margaret Cohen, *The Novel and the Sea* (Princeton, NJ: Princeton University Press, 2010).

6. Carl Schmitt, *Land und Meer: Eine weltgeschichtliche Betrachtung* (Leipzig: Reklam, 1942), 66. The word *hinterland* was derived from German and first used in English in 1888 as the equivalent of "backcountry." See *Wikipedia* article on hinterland: http://en.wikipeida.org/ wiki/Hinterland; the concept of the heartland dates to 1904, when Halford J. Mackinder published his *The Scope and Methods of Geography and the Geographical Pivot of History*, reprinted by London's Royal Geographical Society in 1951.

7. Cohen, *The Novel and the Sea*, 109–19; Hans Blumenberg, *Shipwreck with Spectator: Paradigm of a Metaphor for Existence* (Cambridge, MA: MIT Press, 1997), 8; Margaret Cohen, "The Chronotopes of the Sea," in *The Novel*, ed. Franco Moretti (Princeton, NJ: Princeton University Press, 2006), 1.2:658.

8. Raban, *Oxford Book of the Sea*, 27.

9. Rozwadowski, *Fathoming the Ocean*, 17; Hamilton-Paterson, *Seven Tenths*, 146.

10. Quoted in William Cronon, foreword to Marjorie Hope Nicolson, *Mountain Gloom and Mountain Glory: The Development of the Aesthetics of the Infinite* (Seattle: University of Washington Press, 1997), xviii; Lena Lencek and Gideon Bosker, *The Beach: The History of Paradise on Earth* (New York: Penguin Books, 1998), 54–56; Jules Verne, *Twenty Thousand Leagues under the Sea* (New York: Signet, 2001), 12.

11. Jonathan Raban, *Coasting: A Private Voyage* (New York: Penguin, 1987), 8; Raban, *Oxford Book of the Sea*, 9–10; further discussion, Philip Steinberg, *The Social Construction of the*

Ocean (Cambridge: Cambridge University Press, 2001), 118-21; Cohen, *The Novel and the Sea*, chap. 4.

12. For early modern examples, see John R. Gillis, *Islands of the Mind: How the Human Imagination Created the Atlantic World* (New York: Palgrave Macmillan, 2004), chap. 3; on the modern era, see Raban, *Oxford Book of the Sea*, 28-29.

13. Cynthia F. Behrman, *Victorian Myths of the Sea* (Athens: Ohio University Press, 1977), 12-21; Raban, *Oxford Book of the Sea*, 3.

14. Behrman, *Victorian Myths of the Sea*, 13-14, 21-22; Raban, *Oxford Book of the Sea*, 20-22; Philip Plisson, *The Eternal Sea* (New York: Abrams, 2006).

15. Verne, *Twenty Thousand Leagues under the Sea*, 12.

16. Haskell Springer, *America and the Sea: A Literary History* (Athens: University of Georgia Press, 1995), 17-21.

17. Robert Louis Stevenson, from "The English Admirals," 1881, in Raban, *Oxford Book of the Sea*, 285; Blumenberg, *Shipwreck with Spectator*, 8; Roger Marsters, "Fathoming the Ocean's Perils: Romantic Conceptions of the Sea and British Admiralty Hydrology, 1829-1853," paper presented at the Age of Sail conference, Vancouver, October 7-10, 2010.

18. Quoted in Christiana Payne, "Seaside Visitors: Idlers, Thinkers and Patriots in Mid-19th Century Britain," in *Water, Leisure and Culture: European Historical Perspectives*, ed. Susan C. Anderson and Bruce H. Tabb (Oxford: Berg, 2002), 103; Behrman, *Victorian Myths of the Sea*, chaps. 3-5; Peter Unwin, *The Narrow Sea: Barrier, Bridge, and the Gateway to the World—The History of the English Channel* (London: Headline Books, 2003); Springer, *America and the Sea*, 26.

19. Quoted in Payne, "Seaside Visitors," 99; Behrman, *Victorian Myths of the Sea*, 21; Thomas Cole, *The Journey of Life: A Cultural History of Aging in America* (Cambridge: Cambridge University Press, 1992), 118-27.

20. Auden, *Enchafèd Flood*, 23; Steinberg, *Social Construction of the Ocean*, 191-92; Alain Corbin, *The Lure of the Sea: The Discovery of the Seaside in the Western World, 1750-1840* (Berkeley: University of California Press, 1994), 171; Payne, "Seaside Visitors," 90-93; John R. Gillis, "Birth of the Virtual Child: Origins of Our Contradictory Images of Children," in *Childhood and Its Discontents: The First Seamus Heaney Lectures*, ed. Joseph Dunne and James Kelly (Dublin: Liffey, 2002), 31-50.

21. Helen Rozwadowski, "Ocean: Fusing the History of Science and Technology with Environmental History," in *Blackwell's Companion to American Environmental History*, ed. Douglas Cazaux Sackman (Oxford: Wiley-Blackwell, 2010), 447; Mircea Eliade, *Patterns of Comparative Religion* (New York: Meridian, 1963), 431-34.

22. Hugh Clark, "Frontier Discourse and China's Maritime Frontier: China's Frontiers and the Encounter with the Sea through Early Imperial History," *Journal of World History* 20, no. 1 (March 2009): 20-21; Rozwadowski, *Fathoming the Ocean*, 7.

23. W. Jeffrey Bolster, "Putting the Ocean in Atlantic History: Maritime Communities and Marine Ecology in the Northeast Atlantic, 1500-1800," *American Historical Review* 113, no. 1 (February 2008): 19-47.

24. Steinberg, *Social Construction of the Ocean*, 202.

25. Bunny McBride and Harold E. L. Prins, *Indians in Eden: Wabanakis and Rusticators on Maine's Mount Desert Island, 1840s-1920s* (Rockland, ME: Down East Books, 2009), 84.

26. Henry David Thoreau, *Cape Cod* (Mineola, NY: Dover Books, 2004), 133.

27. Ibid., 2-3, 112.

28. Blumenberg, *Shipwreck with Spectator*, 67; Robert Foulke, *The Sea Voyage Narrative* (New York: Twayne, 1997), 12; Washington Irving, "The Voyage," in *American Sea Writing: A Literary Anthology*, ed. Peter Neill (New York: Library of America, 2000), 61.

29. Raban, *Oxford Book of the Sea*, 15: Jonathan Raban, *Passage to Juneau: A Sea and Its Meanings* (New York: Vintage, 1999), 103–4; quotation from William Cronon, *Changes in the Land* (New York: Hill and Wang, 1983), 4.

30. Steinberg, *Social Construction of the Ocean*, 191.

31. William Cronon, "The Trouble with Wilderness, or Getting Back to the Wrong Nature," in *Uncommon Ground*, ed. William Cronon (New York: W. W. Norton, 1995), 79. Cronon does not explicitly mention the sea, but his discussion of wilderness applies to it as well; Thoreau, *Cape Cod*, 133.

32. Thoreau, "Paradise (to Be) Regained," in *The Works of Thoreau*, ed. Henry Seidel Canby (Boston: Houghton Mifflin, 1937), 779; see Hugh Egan, "Cooper and His Contemporaries," in *America and the Sea: A Literary History*, ed. Springer, 76–77; Whitman quoted in Nathaniel Philbrick, *American Sea Writing*, xvi.

33. "Chasing the shore" is a phrase used on Prince Edward Island. See David Weale, *Chasing the Shore: Little Stories about Spirit and Landscape* (Charlottestown, PEI: Tangle Lane, 2007), 9; Dickinson's "Exultation is the going," found in Raban, *Oxford Book of the Sea*, 256–57.

34. Wells in *Oxford Book of the* Sea, 179–80, 217.

35. Karl F. Nordstrom, *Living with the New Jersey Shore* (Durham, NC: Duke University Press, 1986), xi.

36. On wetlands, see Rod Giblett, *Postmodern Wetlands: Culture, History, Ecology* (Edinburgh: Edinburgh University Press, 1996); for an overview, see Godfrey Baldacchino, "Re-placing Materiality: A Western Anthropology of Sand," *Annals of Tourism Research* 37, no. 3 (2010): 763–78.

37. Michael Taussig, "The Beach (A Fantasy)," *Critical Inquiry* 26, no. 2 (Winter 2000): 256.

38. Orvar Loefgren, *On Holiday: A History of Vacationing* (Berkeley: University of California Press, 1999), 113.

39. Susan C. Anderson, "Cultural Ideas of Water and Swimming in Modern Europe," in *A History of Water*, series 2, ed. Terji Tvedt and Terji Oestigaard (London: I. B. Tauris, 2010), 1:250–54; Jean-Didier Urbain, *At the Beach* (Minneapolis: University of Minnesota Press, 2003), 78–94; Harold F. Wilson, *The Jersey Shore: A Social and Economic History of the Counties of Atlantic, Cape May, Monmouth and Ocean* (New York: Lewis Historical Publishing, 1953), chap. 15.

40. Wilson, *Jersey Shore*, 431; Anderson, "Cultural Ideas of Water and Swimming," 258–62.

41. Payne, "Seaside Visitors," 96; Rozwadowski, *Fathoming the Ocean*, 104–7; John R. Stilgoe, introduction to W. H. Bunting, *The Camera's Coast: Historic Images of Ship and Shore in New England* (Boston: Historic New England, 2006), 11; Bernd Brunner, *The Ocean at Home: An Illustrated History of the Aquarium* (New York: Princeton Architectural Press, 2003); Edmund Gosse, quoted in Paul Theroux, *Kingdom by the Sea: A Journey around Great Britain* (Boston: Houghton Mifflin, 1983), 351.

42. Fred Gray, *Designing the Seaside: Architecture, Society and Nature* (London: Reaktion Books, 2006), 135, 201, 225; Wilson, *Jersey Shore*, 536; Urbain, *At the Beach*, 30–31; Charles E. Funnell, *By the Beautiful Sea: The Rise and High Times of the Great American Resort Atlantic City* (New York: Alfred A. Knopf, 1975), 11–12.

43. Alice Garner, *A Shifting Shore: Locals, Outsiders, and the Transformation of a French Fishing Town* (Ithaca, NY: Cornell University Press, 2005), 174.

44. Urbain, *At the Beach*, 37, 85; Gray, *Designing the Seaside*, 132; Garner, *Shifting Shore*, vii.

45. Urbain, *At the Beach*, 59–60.

46. On the role of emptiness, see Gillis, *Islands of the Mind*, chap. 2.

47. See "Beach" in *Oxford English Dictionary*; Urbain, *At the Beach*, chap. 9.

48. Marc Auge, *Non-places: Introduction of an Anthropology of Supermodernity*, trans. John Howe (London: Verso, 1995); Lofgren, *On Holiday*, 237.

49. Lofgren, *On Holiday*, 212, 227; Theroux, *Kingdom by the Sea*, 166; John Walton, *The British Seaside: Holidays and Resorts in the Twentieth Century* (Manchester: Manchester University Press, 2000), 36–49; Wilson, *Jersey Shore*, 1011.

50. Corbin, *Lure of the Sea*, VI; Taussig, "Beach," 270; Gillis, "Birth of the Virtual Child."

51. Urbain, *At the Beach*, 139; John R. Gillis, *A World of Their Own Making: Myth, Ritual, and the Quest for Family Values* (New York: Basic Books, 1996), 104–8; Gillis, *Islands of the Mind*, 156–65; Payne, "Seaside Visitors," 91–93.

52. Robert B. Edgerton, *Alone Together: Social Order on an Urban Beach* (Berkeley: University of California Press, 1979), 169; on the connection between extreme sports and the coast, see John Brinkerhoff Jackson, "Places for Fun and Games," in *Landscape in Sight*, ed. Helen Horwitz (New Haven, CT: Yale University Press, 1997), 1–18.

53. On the phenomenon of beach photography, see John R. Stilgoe, introduction to W. H. Bunting, *The Camera's Coast: Historic Images of Ship and Shore in New England* (Boston: Historic New England, 2006), 7–9; Cornelia Dean, *Against the Tide: The Battle for America's Beaches* (New York: Columbia University Press, 1999), 3; Jan de Graaf, preface to *Europe: Coast Wise*, ed. Jan de Graaf and D'Laine Camp (Rotterdam: 010 Publishers, 1997); Edgerton, *Alone Together*, 6.

54. Orvar Loefgren and Billy Eng, *The Secret World of Doing Nothing* (Berkeley: University of California Press, 2010), 31–33; David E. Sopher, *Observations on Strand Habitats and Cultures of South Asia* (Berkeley: Center for South Asian Studies, 1959), 24.

55. Gillis, *Islands of the Mind*, 146; Payne, "Seaside Visitors," 92.

56. Loefgren, *On Holiday*, 123; Kate Flint, *The Victorians and the Visual Imagination* (Cambridge: Cambridge University Press, 2000), 285–86; Yi-Fu Tuan, *Topophilia: A Study of Environmental Perception, Attitudes, and Values* (Englewood Cliffs, NJ: Prentice Hall, 1974), 115; Edward Casey. "Borders and Boundaries: Edging into the Environment," in *Merlou-Ponty and Environmental Philosophy: Dwelling on the Landscapes of Thought*, ed. Suzanne Cataldi and William Hemrick (Albany: State University of New York Press, 2007), 69; Vincent Crapanzono, *Imaginative Horizons: An Essay in Literary-Philosophical Anthropology* (Chicago: University of Chicago Press, 2004), 14.

57. Theroux, *Kingdom by the Sea*, 188.

58. W. G. Sebald, *The Rings of Saturn* (New York: New Directions, 1998), 52.

59. Herman Melville, *Moby-Dick* (New York: Barnes and Noble / New Directions, 1998), 52: Mathew Arnold, "Dover Beach," 1867, in *Oxford Book of the Sea*, ed. Raban, 275–76; Loefgren and Eng, *Secret World of Doing Nothing*, 36.

60. Roger F. Stein, *Seascape and the American Imagination* (New York: Clarkson N. Potter, 1975), 16; Steinberg, *Social Construction of the Ocean*, 171; Taussig, "Beach," 258.

61. Loefgren, *On Holiday*, 116.

62. John R. Stilgoe, *Alongshore* (New Haven, CT: Yale University Press, 1994), 407; Urbain, *At the Beach*, 137.

63. Quoted in Theroux, *Kingdom by the Sea*, 351.

64. Quoted in ibid.; Loefgren, *On Holiday*, 236; Margaret Drabble, quoted in *Coastline: Britain's Theatrical Heritage* (London: Kingfisher Books, 1987), 37.

Chapter 6

1. Felipe Fernandez-Armesto, *Civilizations: Culture, Ambition, and the Transformation of Nature* (New York: Free Press, 2001), 408.

2. John A. Murray, introduction to *The Seacoast Reader*, ed. Murray (New York: Lyons, 1999), xvii; Jan de Graff with D'Laime Camp, eds., *Europe: Coast Wise* (Rotterdam: 010, 1997), 93–94.

3. Mollat du Jourdan, *Europe and the Sea* (Oxford: Blackwell, 1993), chap. 1; Fernandez-Armesto, *Civilizations*, 462–63.

4. Orrin H. Pilkey and Rob Young, *The Rising Sea* (Washington, DC: Island, 2009), 171; Mike Davis, *Ecology of Fear: Los Angeles and the Imagination of Disaster* (New York: Metropolitan Books, 1998), chaps. 1–3.

5. "Impact of 'Jaws' Has Anglers and Bathers on Lookout," *New York Times*, July 11, 1975, 20; J. A. Robinson and A. Barnett, "*Jaws* Neurosis," letter, *New England Journal of Medicine* 293, no. 22 (November 27, 1975): 1154–55.

6. Horace D. Smith and Jonathan S. Potts, "People of the Sea," in *Managing Britain's Marine and Coastal Environments: Toward a Sustainable Future*, ed. Smith and Potts (London: Routledge, 2005), 7; s.v. "continental," in *OED*; Daniel Vickers with Vincent Walsh, *Young Men and the Sea: Yankee Seafarers in the Age of Sail* (New Haven, CT: Yale University Press, 2005), 248–49.

7. David Helvarg, *Blue Frontier: Saving America's Living Seas* (New York: W. H. Freeman, 2001), chaps. 1, 4.

8. Nicholas Crane, quoted by Neil Oliver, foreword to *Coast: A Celebration of Britain's Coastal Heritage* by Christopher Somerville (London: BBC Books, 2005), 6.

9. Oliver, foreword to *Coast*.

10. The best discussion of the "lost" in modern cultures is provided by Sumathi Ramaswamy, *The Lost Land of Lemuria: Fabulous Geographies, Catastrophic Histories* (Berkeley: University of California Press, 2004).

11. On looming, see John R. Gillis, *Islands of the Mind: How the Human Imagination Created the Atlantic World* (New York: Palgrave Macmillan, 2004), 143.

12. Alan Sekula, *Fish Story* (Düsseldorf: Richler Verlag, 1999), 134.

13. Sekula, *Fish Story*, 49; Fernandez-Armesto, *Civilizations*, 463.

14. David Kirby and Merja-Liisa Hinkanen, *The Baltic and North Seas* (London: Routledge, 2000), 149.

15. Mark Kurlansky, *The Last Fish Tale* (New York: Ballantine Books, 2008), 136; Callum Roberts, *The Unnatural History of the Sea* (Washington, DC: Island, 2007), 203–4.

16. Gisli Palsson, *Coastal Economies, Cultural Accounts: Human Ecology and Icelandic Discourse* (Manchester: Manchester University Press, 1991), 64–65, 110: Paul Thompson, Tony Wailey, and Trevor Lummis, *Living the Fishing* (London: Routledge and Kegan Paul, 1983), 20–30; Orvar Loefgren, "From Peasant Fishery to Industrial Trawling: A Comparative Discussion of Modernization Processes in Some North Atlantic Regions," in *Modernization and Marine Fishing Policy*, ed. John Mailo and Michael Orbach (Ann Arbor, MI: Ann Arbor Science, 1982), 158–59.

17. Kirby and Hinkanen, *Baltic and North Seas*, 246; Vickers and Walsh, *Young Men and the Sea*, 210; for 1823 quotation, see Roberts, *Unnatural History of the Sea*, 163; Joseph E. Taylor III, *Making Salmon: An Environmental History of the Northwest Fisheries Crisis* (Seattle: University of Washington Press, 1999) chap. 1; Arthur F. McEvoy, *The Fisherman's Problem: Ecology and Law in the California Fisheries, 1850–1980* (Cambridge: Cambridge University Press, 1980); Roberts, *Unnatural History of the Sea*, chap. 20; John F. Richards, *The Unending Frontier: An Environmental History of the Early Modern World* (Berkeley: University of California Press, 2005), 568.

18. Loefgren, "From Peasant Fishery to Industrial Trawling," 151–53; M. Estelle Smith, introduction to *Those Who Live from the Sea: A Study of Maritime Anthropology* (St. Paul, MN: West, 1977), 1–22; W. Jeffrey Bolster, "Putting the Ocean in Atlantic History: Maritime Communities and Marine Ecology in the Northeast Atlantic, 1500–1800," *American Historical Review* 113, no. 1 (February 2008): 47; Kurlansky, *Last Fish Tale*, 246.

19. Gisela Jaaks, ed., *Der Traum von der Stadt am Meer: Hafenstadte aus aller Welt* (Hamburg: Hamburg Museum, 2003); Steve Higginson and Tony Wailey, *Edgy Cities* (Liverpool: Northern Lights, 2006); Phillip Lopate, *Waterfront: A Walk around Manhattan* (New York: Anchor Books, 2005), 15; Margaret Cohen, "Modernity on the Waterfront: The Case of Hausmann's Paris," in *Urban Imaginaries: Locating the Modern City*, ed. Alev Cinar and Thomas Bender (Minneapolis: Minnesota University Press, 2007), 55–75; W. H. Bunting, *Portrait of a Port: Boston, 1852–1914* (Cambridge, MA: Harvard University Press, 1971), xvii; Mark Kurlansky, *The Big Oyster: History on the Halfshell* (New York: Ballantine Books, 2006); Jan de Graaf and D'Laine Camp, eds., *Europe: Coast Wise; An Anthology of Reflections on Architecture and Tourism* (Rotterdam: 010 Publishers, 1997), 114–25; Tormod Kleindal, "Men's Response to Changes in the Coastal Zone of Norway," in *Coastal Zone: Men's Response to Change*, ed. Kenneth Ruddle et al. (London: Harwood, 1988), 185.

20. Peter Hall, "Waterfronts: A New Urban Frontier," *Aquapolis* 1, no. 1 (1991): 6; Alex Roland, W. Jeffrey Bolster, and Alexander Keysaar, *The Way of the Ship: America's Maritime History Reenvisioned, 1600–2000* (New York: John Wiley, 2007), pt. 5; on Europe, see Kirby and Hinkanen, *Baltic and North Seas*, 255–59.

21. Sekula, *Fish Story*, 50, 54, 116; Hall, "Waterfronts," 5–8; Lopate, *Waterfront*, 227–30; Wolfgang Rudolf, *Harbor and Town: A Maritime Cultural History* (Erfurt, Germany: Edition Leipzig, 1980), chap. 2; Kirby and Hinkanen, *Baltic and North Seas*, 261.

22. Lopate, *Waterfront*, 227; Hans Meyer, *City and Port: Urban Planning as a Cultural Venture in London, Barcelona, and Rotterdam* (Rotterdam: International Books, 1999), chap. 1.

23. Hall, "Waterfronts," 6–11.

24. Lopate, *Waterfront*, 286; Josef W. Konvitz, *Cities and the Sea: Port City Planning in Early Modern Europe* (Baltimore: Johns Hopkins University Press, 1978) 186; Meyer, *City and Port*, 189.

25. Ann L. Buttenwieser, *Manhattan Water-Bound: Manhattan's Waterfront from the Seventeenth Century to the Present*, 2nd ed. (Syracuse: Syracuse University Press, 1999), 207–8; Meyer, *City and Port*, 25; Kurlansky, *Big Oyster*, xvi; on Europe, see de Graaf and Camp, *Europe: Coast Wise*, 14.

26. Lopate, *Waterfront*, 232.

27. Somerville, *Coast*, 7; Walter Kaufman and Orrin H. Pilkey, *The Beaches Are Moving: The Drowning of America's Shoreline* (Durham, NC: Duke University Press, 1988), 270; James Hamilton-Paterson, *Seven-Tenths: The Sea and Its Thresholds* (New York: Europa Editions,

2009), chap. 2; Alex Kerr, *Dogs and Demons: The Fall of Modern Japan* (London: Penguin, 2001), 18–19.

28. Paul Carter, "Dark with Excess of Light," in *Mappings*, ed. Denis Cosgrove (London: Reaktion Books, 1999), 147; Adam Nicolson, *On Foot: Guided Walks in England, France, and the United States* (New York: Crown, 1998), 121, 78–79; Kaufman and Pilkey, *Beaches Are Moving*, chaps. 5, 7.

29. Andrew Rise, "A Stake in the Sand," *New York Times Magazine*, March 21, 2010, 79; Kaufman and Pilkey, *Beaches Are Moving*, 35; Samuel Eliot Morison, *The Maritime History of Massachusetts, 1783–1860*, 4th ed. (Boston: Houghton Mifflin, 1961), 3.

30. John Walton, *The British Seaside: Holidays and Resorts in the Twentieth Century* (Manchester: Manchester University Press, 200), 69; Harold F. Wilson, *The Jersey Shore* (New York: Lewis Historical Publishing, 1953), 2:1010; Warren Beamscher, *Historic American Towns along the Atlantic Coast* (Baltimore: Johns Hopkins University Press, 1999), 67; Kaufman and Pilkey, *Beaches Are Moving*, chaps. 7–10.

31. John C. Sawhill, introduction to *The Seacoast Reader*, ed. John A. Murray (New York: Lyons, 1999), xi; Kaufman and Pilkey, *Beaches Are Moving*, 183–84; Frances Ruley Karttunen, "A History of Road and Ways in Nantucket County," unpublished manuscript, 2008; Rise, "Stake in the Sand," 66.

32. Jan Goss, "Disquiet on the Waterfront: Reflection on Nostalgia and Utopia in Urban Archetypes of Festival Marketplaces," *Urban Geography* 17 (1996): 238; June Nadel-Klein, *Fishing for Heritage: Modernity and Loss along the Scottish Coast* (Oxford: Berg, 2003), 184, 188, 206–10.

33. Nadel-Klein, *Fishing for Heritage*, 206, 210.

34. Joshua Moore, "The Last Port," http://www.domeast.com/node/13322.

35. John Fowles, *Islands* (Boston: Little, Brown, 1978), 17; Gillis, *Islands of the Mind*, 81; Peter H. Wood, *Weathering the Storm: Winslow Homer's "Gulf Stream"* (Athens: University of Georgia Press, 2004), 16–17.

36. Wood, *Weathering the Storm*, 72–81.

37. Richard G. Fernicola, *Twelve Days of Terror: A Definitive Investigation of the 1916 New Jersey Shark Attacks* (Guildford, CT: Lyons, 2002).

38. Richard Ellis, *The Book of Sharks* (New York: Harcourt Brace Jovanovich, 1975), 172; an account of its origins is found in Peter Matthiessen's *Blue Meridian: The Search for the Great White Shark* (New York: Random House, 1971).

39. Richard Ellis, *Men and Whales* (New York: Alfred A. Knopf, 1991), 457–60; Helen Rozwadowski, *Fathoming the Ocean: The Discovery and Exploration of the Deep Sea* (Cambridge, MA: Harrvard University Press, 2005), 26.

40. Ellis, *Men and Whales*, 250, 462.

41. Hamilton-Paterson, *Seven-Tenths*, 109.

42. Gillis, *Islands of the Mind*, 145; Tom Killion, *Fortress Marin* (n.p., n.d.).

43. Gered Lennon et al., *Living with the South Carolina Coast* (Durham, NC: Duke University Press, 1996), 4.

44. Patrick Beaver, *A History of Lighthouses* (London: Peter Davis, 1971), 136; Lennon et al., *Living with the South Carolina Coast*, 8.

45. Kevin Blake, "Lighthouse Symbolism in the American Landscape," *Focus on Geography* 50, no. 1 (Summer 2007): 14.

46. Hugh Morton, "Cost, Risk Too Great," *News and Observer* (Raleigh, NC), February 15, 1998,

reprinted at http://ncsu.edu/coast/chl/article2.html; Pilkey and Young, *Rising Sea*, 174–75, Blake, "Lighthouse Symbolism," 4.

47. Two books by Yi-Fu Tuan explore the nature of fear and desire with respect to various topographies. See *Landscapes of Fear* (New York: Pantheon, 1979) and *Topophilia: A Study of Environmental Perceptions, Attitudes, and Values* (Englewood Cliffs, NJ: Prentice Hall, 1974).

48. Richard Sexton, *Parallel Utopias: The Quest for Community, with essays by Ray Oldenburg and William Turnbull* (San Francisco: Chronicle Books, 1995); Donlon Lydon and Jim Alinder, *The Sea Ranch* (New York: Princeton Architectural, 2004), 13–14.

49. Lydon and Alinder, *Sea Ranch*, 287–89; Lawrence Halprin, *The Sea Ranch: Diary of an Idea* (Berkeley, CA: Spacemaker, 2002), 17, 25.

50. Halprin, *Sea Ranch*, 41; Lyndon and Alinder, *Sea Ranch*, 13; Adam Nicolson, *Sissinghurst: An Unfinished History* (London: Harper, 2009), 319.

51. Susan Casey, *The Wave: In Pursuit of the Rogues, Freaks, and Giants of the Ocean* (New York: Doubleday, 2010).

52. Robert Swan, *Coasts, the Sea, and Canadian Art* (Stratford, ON: Gallery, n.d.), no pagination.

53. David Weale, *Chasing the Shore: Little Stories about Spirit and Landscape* (Charlottetown, PEI: Tangle Lane, 2007), 9–12; Casey, *Wave*, 112–13.

Conclusion

1. Rachel Carson, *The Sea around Us* (New York: Oxford University Press, 1951), 15.

2. On variations in the definition of a coastal area, see "How Many People Live in Coastal Areas," *Journal of Coastal Research* 23, no. 5 (September 2007): iii–vi; Don Hinrichsen, "Coasts in Crisis," US Geological Survey, 2008, http://pubs.usgs.gov/circ/c1075/intro.html; also Andrew Goldie, *The Human Impact on the Natural Environment*, 6th ed. (Oxford: Blackwell, 2005), 243; Christian Buchel, *The Eternal Sea* (New York: Abrams, 2006), 329; Gary Griggs and Laurent Savoy, *Living with the California Coast* (Durham, NC: Duke University Press, 1985), 1; American Shore and Beach Preservation Association, "Fact Sheet: Restoring America's Beaches: Myth and Reality," fact sheet, n.d., http://www.asbpa.org /publications/fact_sheets/pubs_fs_myth_reality.htm.

3. Edward Wenk, *The Politics of the Sea* (Seattle: University of Washington Press, 1972), 170.

4. Minutes of a meeting of the American Shore and Beach Preservation Association, Coney Island, NY, 1928, 6.

5. Robert Thompson, "Cultural Models and Shoreline Social Conflict," *Coastal Management* 35 (2007): 227.

6. Orrin H. Pilkey and Rob Young, *The Rising Sea* (Washington, DC: Island, 2009), 162–63.

7. Michael S. Kearney, "Late Holocene Sea Level Variations," in *Sea Level Rise: History and Consequences*, ed. Bruce C. Douglas, Michael S. Kearney, and Stephen P. Leatherman (San Diego: Academic Press, 2001), 13–38; W. Tad Pfeffer et al., "Kinesmatic Constraints on Glacier Contributions to 21st Century Sea Level Rise," *Science* 321 (2008): 1340–43.

8. Kazuyuki Kolke, "The Countermeasures against Coastal Hazards in Japan," *Geojournal* 38, no. 3 (1996): 301–12; Stephen Leatherman, "Social and Economic Costs of Sea Level Rise," in *Sea Level Rise*, ed. Douglas, Kearney, and Leatherman, 182–83; Norimitsu Onishi, "A Japanese Town's 'Great Wall' Provided a False Sense of Security," *New York Times*, April 2, 2011, A4–5; Norimitsu Onishi, "Seawalls Offered Little Protection against Tsunami's Crushing

Waves," *New York Times*, March 14, 2011, A8; Peter Kahn, *The Human Relationship with Nature: Development and Culture* (Cambridge, MA: MIT Press, 1999), 7.

9. Pilkey and Young, *Rising Sea*, xi; Robert J. Hoeksema, *Designed for Dry Feet: Flood Protection and Land Reclamation in the Netherlands* (Reston, VA: American Society of Civil Engineers, 2006), chaps. 1, 7; Simon Winchester, *Atlantic* (New York: HarperCollins, 2010), 415; Karl F. Nordstrom et al., *Living with the New Jersey Shore* (Durham, NC: Duke University Press, 1986), 4–5.

10. Nordstrom et al., *Living with the New Jersey Shore*, 4–5; Peter Matthiessen, *Men's Lives* (New York: Vintage, 1988), 3–63; Bay Men Collection, tape 1052, Folk Life Archives, Library of Congress, Washington, DC.

11. Nordstrom et al., *Living with the New Jersey Shore*, xi; Bay Men Collection, interview with Rich Rofihe, Case Files, Folk Life Archives, Library of Congress.

12. William Sargent, *Just Seconds from the Ocean: Coastal Living in the Wake of Katrina* (Hanover, NH: University Press of New England, 2007), 1–6.

13. Wallace Kaufman and Orrin H. Pilkey Jr., *The Beaches Are Moving: The Drowning of America's Shoreline* (Durham, NC: Duke University Press, 1983), xiii, 3, 21, 160–63, 176.

14. Robert Kronenberg, *Houses in Motion: The Genesis, History, and Development of the Portable Building*, 2nd ed. (Chichester, UK: John Wiley and Sons, 2002), 24–25; Nobuhiro Suzuki, "Floating Houses in Seattle," *Aquapolis* 1 (1996): 36–41; David Wolf, "The Houseboats of Sausalito: From Arks to Anarchy and Recent Re-gentrification," *Aquapolis* 1 (1996): 28–35; Ted Laturnus, *Floating Homes: A Houseboat Handbook* (Vancouver, BC: Harbour, 1986), 17.

15. Steven Kurutz, "A Fluid Definition of Self-Sufficiency," *New York Times*, June 4, 2008, D4; on Seasteading, see http://en.wikipedia.org/wiki/seasteading; Eamonn Fingleton, "Seasteading: The Great Escape," *Prospect* 169 (2010).

16. Griggs and Savoy, *Living with the California Coast*, 372; Joseph Kelley et al., *Living on the Coast of Maine* (Durham, NC: Duke University Press, 1989), 12; Kaufman and Pilkey, *Beaches Are Moving*, 289.

17. Kaufman and Pilkey, *Beaches Are Moving*, 113–14.

18. Eviatar Zerubavel, *The Fine Line: Making Distinctions in Everyday Life* (New York: Free Press, 1991), 115–22.

19. Quote from Hinrichsen, "Coasts in Crisis," 1.

INDEX